4030

INTEGRATED PROGRAMMES FOR HANDICAPPED ADOLESCENTS AND ADULTS

Integrated Programmes for Handicapped Adolescents and Adults

Edited by ROY I. BROWN

Volume 1 in *Rehabilitation Education: A Series in Developmental Handicap*

CROOM HELM
London & Sydney
NICHOLS PUBLISHING COMPANY
New York

©1984 Roy R. Brown
Croom Helm Ltd, Provident House, Burrell Row,
Beckenham, Kent BR3 1AT
Croom Helm Australia Pty Ltd, First Floor,
139 King Street, Sydney, NSW 2001, Australia

British Library Cataloguing in Publication Data

Integrated programmes for handicapped
  adolescents and adults.— (Rehabilitation
  education, v.1)
  1. Mentally handicapped—Rehabilitation
  I. Brown, Roy Irwin   II. Series
  362.3'8   HV3004
  ISBN 0-7099-3223-5

First published in the United States of America 1984
by Nichols Publishing Company, Post Office Box 96,
New York, NY 10024

Library of Congress Cataloging in Publication Data
Main entry under title:

Integrated programs for handicapped adolescents and adults.

   1. Mentally handicapped—Rehabilitation—Addresses,
essays, lectures. 2. Mentally handicapped—Education—
Addresses, essays, lectures. 3. Mentally handicapped
youth—Rehabilitation—Addresses, essays, lectures.
4. Mentally handicapped youth—Education—Addresses,
essays, lectures. I. Brown, Roy I.
HV3004.I545   1984   362.3'83   84-14708
ISBN 0-89397-199-5

Printed and bound in Great Britain

CONTENTS

    John W. Jacobson, Associate Planner, Bureau
    of Program Research and Planning, New York
    State Office of Mental Retardation and
    Developmental Disabilities, Albany, New York
    U.S.A.

    Allen A. Schwartz, Director of Planning and
    Special Projects, New York City County Service
    Group, New York State Office of Mental Retarda-
    tion and Developmental Disabilities, New York,
    New York, U.S.A.

    Matthew P. Janicki, Director, Bureau of Program
    Research and Planning, New York State Office of
    Mental Retardation and Developmental Disabilities,
    Albany, New York, U.S.A.

    E. Anne Hughson, Coordinator, Behaviour Support
    Unit, Department of Educational Psychology, The
    University of Calgary, Calgary, Alberta, Canada

    Peter R. Johnson, Programme Director, Vancouver
    Richmond Association for Mentally Handicapped
    People, Vancouver, British Columbia, Canada

    Robin Jackson, Principal Lecturer, King
    Alfred's College, Winchester, England

    Roy I. Brown

PREFACE

This book represents the first in a series of volumes related to an area that we have chosen to call Rehabilitation Education. The first volume is essentially concerned with problems facing adolescents and adults who are handicapped. The examples are largely from the area of mental retardation, but we believe much of the material is relevant, in terms of its principles, to other handicapping conditions. The book addresses concepts and provides demonstration and research principles and strategies which have led or could lead to innovation within the field. There are many texts which give the specifics, but our hope is to question some of the underlying principles and to draw together an integrated theme of practice from a philosophical and demonstration point of view. We believe the field of handicap needs to be re-evaluated, and that there are now new opportunities and ideas which will help to develop the field of rehabilitation over the next decade.

At the present time we are struggling with economic and political problems which threaten the development of rehabilitation services, yet these very threats will give rise to new ideas and interests which can improve rehabilitation practice and the services offered to clients and to students who wish to practice in this area.

In developing this volume I would like to thank my co-authors who have been very willing to respond to comment and suggestion in order to consolidate particular themes within the book. The reader, no doubt, will judge to what extent this has been effective. Editors should not be free from having their own chapters edited and Dr. Robin Jackson and Dr. Peter Johnson carefully reviewed my particular contributions. Their help and advice is much appreciated.

I would also like to thank Linda Culshaw, who put all the chapters onto wordprocessor, and transferred the many editorial corrections to produce the final version. Her efficient and speedy help has much to do with finishing this project on time. I would also like to thank Mary Brown for proofreading the material during the final edit, though the responsibility for remaining errors or oversight must remain mine alone.

Finally, I would like to thank Tim Hardwick of Croom Helm for his encouragement and helpful comments during the development of the book.

R.I.B.
1984

Chapter One

THE FIELD OF DEVELOPMENTAL HANDICAP -
THE DEVELOPMENT OF REHABILITATION EDUCATION

Roy I. Brown

INTRODUCTION

Rehabilitation Education, for the purposes of this book, is defined as *the treatment and training of individuals through the intervention of a variety of social and psychological strategies to improve the learning and performance of handicapped persons.* It is important that the principles of training be recognised in this education for we are not simply talking about counselling and welfare. We are concerned with the processes and principles which constitute programming and are necessary for the permanent change of behaviour in a positive direction. The aim is to assist individuals to maintain themselves effectively in a quality life-style within society without undue support from the social welfare system, in terms of monetary aid or special conditions. There is also, we believe, a body of knowledge which emanates from psychology, education and social work practice that can provide an effective means of support and help for a wide range of handicapped individuals of all ages.
     It is the detailed application of the findings in these areas to regular practice, which constitutes the field of rehabilitation education. It uses curricula and techniques which are essentially behavioural. It has relevance to occupational- and physio-therapy and to medicine, but it must be regarded as one branch of a multidisciplinary approach which can be effective in terms of the training of handicapped persons. Unlike our traditional ideas of education it does not just apply to children. This particular volume is dedicated to the application of the model and the concepts to adolescents and adults. It can be applied in the formal areas of education such as reading, math and writing. It also applies to social educational skills including home management, budgeting, a recognition of money and the application of time concepts. It is

1

relevant to home-living skills, including the purchasing of clothes, the appropriateness of one's dress, preparation of meals, but also involves the development of positive relationships between members of the family. In the area of leisure time it relates not only to how time is spent at home, but how one receives exercise and activity to enhance human development. It applies to the knowledge one gains of one's community and the use one can make of that community in dealing with quality of life. All these areas relate to self interest, the development of positive self concept, and attitudes that the handicapped person has about the society around him. It improves his motivation and, hopefully, in its broadest sense, changes society around him, to be more tolerant of handicap and assists society to modify its approach towards handicapped persons.

This book examines approaches towards the training and treatment of adolescents and adults who are developmentally handicapped. Specifically, it concentrates on mental handicap and it is particularly concerned with an area which we may now define as rehabilitation education. A thesis of the book is that the principles of education in the field of rehabilitation, including aspects of psychology and social work, apply, in general terms, to all levels of handicap and types of handicapping conditions. The principles seem to relate to very severely retarded persons as well as mildly mentally handicapped individuals. Many of the principles apply to visual impairment and auditory handicap, while some of the problems of social disadvantage and social decline in the elderly may also be remediable through the application of the principles outlined in the specific chapters. The levels of programming may differ, but for too long we have ignored the common ideas and concepts which underline the different areas of rehabilitation.

In some countries, rehabilitation is separated from the area of habilitation. The former represents the re-introduction of individuals into society after training, whereas habilitation is reserved for the initial introduction into society of individuals handicapped from birth. Such differences seem to us to be unnecessary, and in many ways undesirable, for they do not appear to be associated in any marked way with different principles. It is argued that the labelling system, so employed, produces artificial barriers between personnel working in these areas. It restricts communication and collaboration between agencies which should be sharing resources. We believe much is to be gained by regarding the total field as one of rehabilitation. We use the word here for convenience. In order to develop the field clearly and effectively, we believe it is necessary to use the same principles, very often the same techniques, though it is recognised that the level of application may differ. The fractionating of the field, which has occurred between rehabilitation and habilitation, is a disservice to the community of handicapped persons and will continue to do harm until personnel in the field recognize their common aims and loyalties to an area which we have chosen to define as Rehabilitation Education.

Rehabilitation has, in the past, been seen as a province of medicine and allied medical professions, such as physiotherapy and occupational therapy. In recent years psychology has also played an important role in the training and treatment of individuals with handicaps, and the field of special education has developed as a province for teachers with specialist knowledge of learning processes in handicapped youngsters.

In many parts of the world education is provided for individuals who intend to spend their professional lives working with handicapped adults, and dealing with social, vocational and home-living aspects of programmes. Yet these developments are of recent origin and many countries have still not developed adequate training programmes for personnel who work with developmentally handicapped adults and adolescents.

Attention is directed towards the types of services handicapped persons need, as well as the types of personnel training which is required to meet some of those needs. A brief history of rehabilitation services is provided, current philosophical models examined, and the need for new systems of rehabilitation discussed, together with the implications these have for the training of personnel.

REHABILITATION OVER TIME

At the present time we function in a period of training and integration of handicapped persons, and yet already we are beginning to see a movement towards a climate of reinstitutionalisation. This change of atmosphere relates to the political and economic context in which training and integration takes place, but the fact that such change is possible appears to relate to the fact that we have few well-trained personnel available for the development and application of effective training programmes. This means that once handicapped people are placed in the community, they do not receive the types of support and help that are necessary in order to maintain them effectively within the community. For example, it is still believed that once an individual has been through some form of training programme, only rudimentary follow-up services are necessary. It is also relevant that as one form of institutionalisation is dealt with another appears. For example, in Canada there is growing concern over the simplistic and rigid models of care provided for many pre-school children in nursery systems.

3

It appears we have not learned the lessons provided by those concerned with early environmental stimulation and our welfare and educational systems are not providing adequate standards and models for such care.

The thrust of this book is that long-term programmes to help people adapt to ever changing environments are critical to the maintenance of individuals in the community. Sadly, when individuals are misplaced or deteriorate within the community, we are apt to cite the limitations of the individuals themselves rather than the lack of service which exists within the training and educational system that we have provided. It is suggested that only when we look to these shortcomings will we indeed begin to answer some of the longer term implications of rehabilitation.

AN HISTORICAL PERSPECTIVE

The history of services for handicapped people shows the development of a gradual awareness of handicapped persons as individuals within a complex background of behaviour and causation. It is only in the last 20 or so years that we have moved away from a model of institutionalised care for handicapped persons and begun to recognise the importance of integrating such people into the surrounding community. Yet it would be unwise to forget that the development of institutions as places of relief and shelter were developed for benign rather than malevolent reasons. All systems, as they become outmoded and outdated, stagnate and cease to provide the type of treatment and care that is required in contemporary society. We would do well to remember this, since the particular forms of treatment and training that we provide at this point in time will very quickly be seen as inappropriate, in some degree, to the future system of education and treatment that is required.

The idea of heterogeneous performance, with varied baselines of behaviour, is of recent origin and reinforces a view of individualised treatment. That this is not fully grasped is shown in our facile models of integration and normalisation. It is only now that we see that most mentally handicapped people suffer from a variety of contributing causation rather than suffering from a specific condition. This is true of many of the handicapping conditions. Intellectual impairment amongst visually impaired individuals and those with hearing loss is common, and likewise in cerebral palsy it is likely that there will be some loss of intellectual function. Many people with mental handicap have problems of motor and auditory impairment. These conditions, then, are not clear cut, and the intellectual loss that is present arises from a mixture of environmental and inherited causes. Yet it was not so long ago that

4

individuals with so-called specific conditions (e.g., mental retardation, epilepsy, blindness) were categorised separately. The treatment of such individuals is still often seen as a separate function and some administrative systems still insist on the use of test material, such as intelligence measures, to classify and predict performance. Such individuals were segregated and for the most part, placed in institutions for particular diagnostic groups. Poor laws provided other institutional settings where the variety of indigent and socially disadvantaged persons could be maintained. Quite frequently such places, though of poor standard by today's criteria, provided care in country areas, away from the industrial communities with their associated diseases, and in environments where food was available.

The standards of treatment varied. There were progressive ideas concerning treatment in some institutions. During the 19th century the possibility of individuals being provided with some work and earning wages for their labor was not unheard of. Some charitably-disposed agencies were run by less optimistic individuals who believed treatment should include castration for handicapped people, who were bound, in their view, to produce handicapped children, were a drain on the economy of society. It is important to recognise that such negative views were held at a time when others held benign views. It is inappropriate to think that the concepts of integration and normalisation are merely features of today's approach. During the 19th century there were practitioners who, in effect, advocated the normalisation of environments and progressive social and educational treatment for handicapped persons (Sloan and Stevens, 1976). Further, the work of Itard and Seguin (Ball, 1970) examined individually handicapped persons in some detail, thus fore-shadowing the specific programme approaches of today which are linked to baseline assessment.

Immediately following the Second World War, most intervention with mentally handicapped individuals was provided through the medical system by nurses who, after training, received a mental deficiency nursing diploma. They provided care, support and some training to handicapped persons. Special schools were provided, some offering day programmes, others residential programmes. But for most young adults the service provided was either through the parent with the individual living at home, or through institutional involvement provided in private homes or agencies, sheltered workshops, and the institutional hospital system.

In Britain, after World War II, psychological services began to develop and a few experimental and demonstration units were provided to see to what extent handicapped persons were able to learn to work on simple tasks of an industrial or semi-industrial nature. It had become recognised during the war that many mentally handicapped individuals could work very effectively in a wide range of jobs. From our vantage point it is apparent that changes in services were directed, not from any concern to meet the needs of the individual, but by necessity as national economic and political considerations. Demand for labour, and particularly male labour, in Britain opened up the possibility of employing handicapped people to carry out certain jobs. It was only later that it was realised, on a wider basis, that there was a need to change the system in relation to handicapped persons so they could learn and thereby enter society. This perhaps exemplifies a primary requirement of change in this field. Societal needs are prime determinants of change, and although rehabilitation may be seen as desirable by parents and professionals, change is unlikely to occur until parents, professionals and politicians are working together. Yet our trainers of special educators and school and clinical psychologists are rarely taught how to manage political and social variables to the advantage of their clients.

There are, of course, many other relevant factors, not least of which are the growth and motivation which occur with many handicapped youngsters. Many, who are handicapped as young children, have minimal handicaps by the time they become young adults. In some cases the discrepancy resulted from a misuse or misapplication of assessment materials, such as intelligence tests, during childhood. Persons of average or above average ability became diagnosed as mentally retarded. We also know that a large proportion of mentally handicapped people, during their late teens and early 20s, grew towards normality in terms of cognitive ability, thus providing opportunities for learning and work, which might not have been available to them at an earlier age. The advent of better assessment and training devices in the area of vision and hearing handicap meant that individuals became susceptible to teaching methods which were not possible earlier. For example, the use of the optacon for those with visual impairment and the use of the inductive loop system for the hearing impaired have provided significant benefits.

However, it should be noted that the process of change was also through intervention of particular kinds. The development of vocational training in sheltered workshops, in institutions and, more recently, within the school system provided opportunities for some training.

On the other hand, workers such as Gold (1978), have argued that much of what occurred was not training, but merely exposure of individuals to work-like situations. Unfortunately this is still largely the preferred programme method. However, a number of agencies have developed vigorous training programmes, although it is true that the training is often of a primitive nature, being what we shall later describe as *concrete*. Material provided was frequently small part assembly work, where an individual carried out a particular job in a particular way at a particular time. This was found to be inadequate in terms of rehabilitation effectiveness and some workers, like Gunzburg (1968), demonstrated the importance of social education. According to a wide range of writers (e.g. Gunzburg, 1968; Brown & Hughson, 1980; Parmenter, 1983) the major failures in the adult's rehabilitation relate to social areas of learning. Close examination of many modern assessment devices which purport to use vocational areas for assessment, such as the Adaptive Functioning Index (Marlett, 1976), are, to a large degree, measures of social functioning which though designed for use in vocational settings are equally relevant to home or community environments.

CURRENT DEVELOPMENTS IN REHABILITATION

We are now beginning to recognise that social skills require much more in the way of a flexible training regime, involving the generalisation of skills. The reason for this is that the receiving community can change over time, so that what is learned as a specific skill by the client, cannot be applied adequately unless it has a flexible or generalisable component. For example, it is possible to train individuals to use a specific bus system, but if a rapid transit or train system is developed, that knowledge may not apply to the new situation.

Even more recently we have recognised that leisure time skills are important. Many government departments regard these as frills, and unnecessary during hard economic times. The opposite argument can also be made. At a time when vocational opportunities are minimal, the maintenance of handicapped persons within the community depends on the ability to participate in leisure and social community activities. Individuals who can function well in these areas do not present as much of a social burden to their parents and can survive well within the community. But leisure time operations, which at their simplest level are concrete in nature (e.g. observer activities or physical games), nevertheless require at a more advanced level the individual to develop interests and make arrangements for leisure time. The individual is trained to become self activating. If people are successful at this level, a considerable advance in performance has been achieved. Vocational and leisure skills as training continua represent two extremes. The vocational may be described as largely concrete for it is frequently limited in time and space, whereas the most advanced leisure programmes are essentially abstract in character requiring flexible skills involving judgment of both time and space. Of course other continua exist in social and home-living skills. Yet within any one of these areas, vocational, social, home-living or leisure time, there is a continuum from rather more concrete to rather more abstract types of activities.

When people are participating in an activity which they like doing, motivation, self image and physical ability, are improved thus helping to produce more healthy and effective individuals. These aspects of human performance are generalisable and it is this aspect which seems so important in leisure programmes. On the other hand, vocational programmes provide highly structured activity which is often welcomed by handicapped persons. The desire for structure is not unique to handicapped individuals and applies to a range of non-handicapped persons, particularly at very young ages. Since incidental learning and transfer of skills tends to be poor amongst handicapped persons, it is important to structure both areas. But this implies a high level of sophistication in our training programmes. For unless we provide experience, structure and training, effective and rapid learning is unlikely to take place. Learning in our training centres tends to be limited to specific skills. It is necessary to devise training which can be generalised. It is also necessary to ensure that learning is internalised so that it can be used by the learner when required, rather than merely provoked in a standard or institutional situation.

Recent work by researchers like Feuerstein (1979) has indicated that these limitations may be overcome by the development of instrumental enrichment techniques which train the individual to develop his own problem solving strategies. Further, many handicapped persons appear to prefer the visual modality over the auditory channel in problem solving (Landino, 1979), which may have relevance to the development of teaching strategies. Yet one suspects that unless structured programming is carried out at an early stage, there may be gross limitations in the range of development. Time is an extremely limited commodity in the rehabilitation field. Many handicapped people may not be able to rise easily to a level where they can overcome more than basic or simple problems. This implies that support of one kind or another will remain a necessary requirement, particularly as society changes and new problems emerge for the individual as he lives his life in the community.

PRINCIPLES OF REHABILITATION

There are a number of concepts which can be applied as a general model within the field of rehabilitation. Behaviour, and consequently learning, develops from the gross to the specific. In normal development there appears to be a hierarchy of sensory development from tactile through visual to auditory processes. This means tactile processes tend to form the base for visual development which in turn is the underlying construct for auditory patterns. Stress and unfamiliarity are therefore likely to reduce auditory performance more than visual. Learning goes from the concrete to the abstract. Certain areas, such as vocational training, represent the concrete continuum whereas other activities, such as social community activities and leisure time activities, have a higher level of flexible application which must be regarded as abstract.

Not only do handicapped persons show a wide range of variability but their behaviour is subject to considerable regression under stress such as unfamiliar circumstances. This is not unique to one particular type of handicap but represents a principle which must be borne in mind when introducing new rehabilitation techniques to any handicapped person.

RESEARCH TO PRACTICE

Such a model comes out of a wide range of research and practical experience. It is the contention of this book that the integration of research and practice is decisive in bringing about effective rehabilitation. This is not to imply that it is the only means by which this progress occurs. Further, the integration of research and practice will be ineffective if we do not take into account the political climate which prevails. Economic and social factors are important, as well as the levels of parent involvement. Many authors have written about the gap between research and practice, and this is equally true in the field of rehabilitation as it is to psychology and education. Even basic research such as that of Ebbinghaus (1885) has taken about 75 years to apply to the area of rehabilitation. Knowledge in the area of general psychology, including concepts of learning, such as improved performance when tasks are broken down into small units and the spacing of practice over time, were not even attempted as research exercises in the field of mental retardation until the early 1950s. Even then the research was often of a highly experimental nature, and it took some while for the concepts and ideas to be put into formal practice.

The integration and reintegration of ideas as new processes are attempts to help ensure that a number of areas come together to provide a more practical base for training. For example, behaviour modification techniques have been broadened and now make use of some of the findings of vocational research (e.g., Clarke and Hermelin, 1955). The result is highly practical methods of training which are primarily based on the logical and objective appraisal of tasks which are confronting the handicapped person (Martin & Pear, 1982).

It is perhaps natural that, in the field of research, laboratory techniques and design are employed initially, at least prior to comprehensive practical application. But it has taken some time for behavioural scientists to recognise that the similarity of their science to the biological sciences suggests that simple behavioural description is necessary prior to designing relevant and effective experimental procedures. Given a background of learning, perceptual and motivational processes, it is appropriate to ask what is their relevance to the areas of rehabilitation. What sort of behaviours do handicapped adolescents and adults show, and does this vary amongst the range of handicapping conditions or amongst handicapped persons diagnosed with the same condition?

Unfortunately there is in psychology, and also in educational research, a purist approach, which suggests that certain types of research are intrinsically more advanced than other types of research. Not only is this derogatory to people who work within the field at a practical level, it also ignores a vast range of data that is fundamental to the understanding of rehabilitation both from a theoretical and practical point of view. It is only when appropriate assessment techniques are applied and observations carried out within the field that we can begin to frame the type of questions that need to be asked in terms of the application of psychological, educational or social knowledge to behaviour within the rehabilitation environment. To some extent this has been, albeit tortuously, carried out with the result that we have some information in terms of the types of assessment techniques that are employed. We have, for example, discovered that many traditional techniques are inappropriate or, at least, inappropriate in a wide range of cases. Research-wise they may have some relevance, but clinical decisions imply not only asking questions about the reliability and validity of data, but seeking to clarify the type of differential programme needed for each client. Behavioural observation in situ is necessary because only under these circumstances are we likely to see the types of behaviour which are typical for the individual and are related to the programme which is to be developed. Indeed, it is only under these conditions that we can see the types

10

of problems which confront handicapped individuals both in terms of their own behaviour, and more importantly, their own behaviour in relation to their environment. Although it is easier for us to measure within a simple test or experimental room than in a classroom or workshop, and, in turn, these last are easier for observing the individual than in social and community, home or leisure time situations, we must recognise the importance of developing techniques for natural areas. Because of our dependence on a traditional model our results become dependent on artificial situations.

Although there is information from more natural environments, it is severely limited. At present the observation of handicapped individuals within their home environments is minimal and it follows that effective programmes for training within the home are few and far between. Those models that have been developed are largely applications from procedures used in various institutional settings. Much of the material is hearsay data from parents who report the activities of their children. Much of this may be useful and of assistance but is no substitute for first hand observation by the researcher or practitioner. Further, our restriction of handicapped people to formal assessment situations prevents us from observing what happens in natural environments. For example, how many detailed studies have been produced of handicapped adults moving around their local community? Sadly, those who have attempted to do this have often been criticised because their work is viewed as unexperimental. The fact remains that observation of what occurs to clients once exposed to local community conditions, such as the work of Gunzburg, leads to a clearer social understanding of the problems that individuals face. Gradually we are beginning to expand the range of behavioural environments examined and, as a result, begin to develop more comprehensive programmes (Brown and Hughson, 1980; Hutchinson, 1982; Whelan and Speake, 1981). This is leading to more rigorous methods and techniques for both assessment and training within a variety of environments, but it also enables us to recognise the wide range of performance involved. For example, the degree of heterogeneity encountered in terms of behaviour immediately casts doubt on the feasibility of constructing reliable control and experimental groups.

Assessment devices, such as the Marlett Adaptive Functioning Index, and the Gunzburg Progress Assessment Charts, which provide us with some measurement of performance within a variety of environments, assist in the measurement of social and vocational behaviours. Yet these measures are restricted in a number of ways. They are often rating scales and present us with a range of difficulties, including the problem of assessing individuals in a reliable fashion. Training needs to be given to staff and, without

11

such training being maintained, high reliability coeffic-
ients between testers may drop from about .9, as recorded in
the Adaptive Functioning Index, down to about .2 or .3, at
which point such assessments become valueless. Objective
tests are now beginning to be incorporated into assessment
devices, such as the social educational test of the Marlett
scale, but still we have a long way to go. For example,
there are a number of areas which are not measured by such
tests. The areas of leisure time and family life, including
sexual behaviours, are minimally mentioned, although
specialised devices are beginning to be developed in these
areas. One example is the Leisure Functioning Index
designed by Possberg and Ford (1984). Yet as we approach
new areas for programme intervention we are thrown back on
traditional techniques. The Leisure Functioning Index is
primarily a rating scale. Although it provides a means of
collecting data from important aspects of life activity, it
can only be regarded as an initial attempt in this area.
    Other questions relate to the generalisability of data.
Tests have proved beneficial in the field of mental handicap
and use has been made of the scales mentioned above with
multiply-handicapped individuals who show motor and sensory
loss. The assessment devices may also have relevance to
other areas of rehabilitation such as the treatment of
accident victims who have recovered from major physical
damage, but where social problems remain a major block to
further recovery. We have used the Marlett scale with some
success in such cases. The same tests and approaches may
also be of value in treatment of senior citizens who, for a
variety of reasons, show social deterioration. For example,
the work of Engman (1979) on the adaptation of the Progress
Assessment Chart test to handicapped geriatric patients was
an interesting venture in this field.

TRAINING

A number of training techniques have been developed from a
research perspective. It has been amply demonstrated by
Clarke and Clarke (1974); Gold (1978); Martin and Pear
(1983) that a wide range of individual techniques borrowed
from experimental psychology have direct application to the
improvement of performance amongst handicapped adults. Such
work is often effective in individual demonstration units,
but there are difficulties in transferring such results to
the field on a general basis. These strategies and techniques are still not routine procedures in the rehabilitation field. It has been possible to apply rehabilitation
knowledge as demonstration models in places like the Unit
for Rehabilitation Studies at Macquarie University in
Australia, and the Vocational and Rehabilitation Research

Institute in Canada. Whelan and Speake (see Chapter 4) have also worked closely with workshop managers in the United Kingdom and, by mutual cooperation, attempted a more general model. Although the results from such demonstrations are important, they generally have two limitations. First of all the demonstration studies do not apply rigorous standards of research control or measurement. This cannot be done because of the breadth and type of work involved and the ethical implications of withholding treatment from some individuals. Furthermore, some clinical bias in subject selection for the demonstration programme frequently occurs, which serves to skew the sample of individuals selected thus casting doubt on the generalisability of the specific findings. Certainly records showing improvement of performance, increased access to the community and individual success or failure are being recorded for handicapped adults but there are many questions concerning the interpretation of results; a matter taken up by McKerracher in Chapter 2.

A second disadvantage is that demonstration models often rely on *on site* training of personnel, which means that educational skill level and rehabilitation approach do not generalise either across time or agencies. The personnel team that is developed is agency specific. The demonstration projects developed under such a framework function for a number of years in a very effective manner, but have limited impact on other units other than demonstration units. They do not appear to result in the overall acceptance of new standards of practice despite impact on their own clients. Probably also related to this problem is a third factor. This is the personality of the leaders and coordinators of specific demonstration projects. Although we are often impressed by the performance of a particular unit or director of a specific programme, replication seems to be restricted to concrete or project-specific aspects of the programme. Time and again impressive rehabilitation results from a new centre or programme are not replicable by others. This is often put down to unreliability of data, chance occurrences, or such factors as the mild nature of handicap involved in the original study. It may well be that the personalities of the leader and the project group are decisive variables, yet we do not measure these aspects of the rehabilitation process. More importantly it may not be unreasonable to suppose that it is the interaction of the service deliverers and their programme which is decisive in producing results. The question then arises *'Who are the effective rehabilitators?'*

The history of teacher selection and the prediction of superior educators from student performance are uninspiring, but it may be important to attempt measurement of personality factors of staff within specific programmes. Further these aspects may be thought worth encouraging in any replication of a particular study. Such variables as leadership quality, enthusiasm of staff, attitudes of staff to likely success or failure of the project may be important. In research one is taught to have an open mind. Believing someone may or may not be successful is not very helpful for one's client either in surgery or rehabilitation!

REHABILITATION EDUCATION

Demonstration models have been built in a number of countries, and the following chapters give some examples of this type of development, and enable us to compare and contrast what has occurred, and note some similarities and differences that may be important. It is necessary, at this stage, not only to learn how to generalise our results so that they find their way into practice in every country, but to recognise that what is developed in one setting for a particular group of handicapped persons may have validity for a wide range of handicapping conditions. It is partly for this reason that we have coined the phrase rehabilitation education. It is only in recent years that there has been a much broader approach towards client integration in the community and a recognition of the possibility of more dynamically advanced therapy, education and treatment. This is particularly true in the area of rehabilitation education.

Although there have been advances in translating research to practice there are nevertheless many gaps in research knowledge. At the present time there is an urgent need for the development of research in the leisure time area and also in the area of emotional disturbance of handicapped persons. The lack of data on personality and emotional characteristics of mentally handicapped persons, the poor knowledge regarding their susceptibility to mental illness and stress, particularly as viewed by a number of the helping professions, is critical, and therefore it is important that this aspect be pursued diligently. For this reason material on these aspects of functioning is included in this particular volume.

It would be wrong to suggest that research is the most or the only important feature in the developments of services for handicapped persons; it is merely one aspect of the development of sophisticated programmes. Research findings will lie dormant or will be inappropriately applied unless there are strong political and social movements within the community for the development and application of services in realistic environments - hence the importance of the parent lobby, the development of advocacy, and the interest of political government in the development of programmes.

Although certain programme gains may come about because of the involvement of pressure groups, the level and sophistication of programming can develop much further if research strategies are applied to the model. Indeed a major concern is that the normalisation philosophy has developed little in the way of technology. The pressures for integration led by parents and the development of the *People First* movement, a North American association of disabled persons who encourage professional and community groups to recognize the individual first and the handicap second, are important, but unless they are matched by effective rehabilitation strategies and techniques, paralleled by the large scale education of competent staff, failure will occur. Thus such movements, though well intentioned, will result on their own in a backlash to the development of humane conditions and innovative rehabilitation. Such ideas will be attempted but be defeated by community apathy, and the lack of an efficient cadre of personnel to put the ideas into practice in a logical fashion.

ETHICAL CONCERNS

There has grown up in rehabilitation and other fields, a wide range of ethical practices to protect the individual client. Although these are important in their own right, nevertheless the application of them during the last decade has shown signs of a lack of sensitivity to the needs of various programmes. In some instances it is not seen as sufficient to keep data anonymous. Data must be destroyed after the results are obtained. Coded numbers need to be used in substitution for names. However, some of the most exciting work is carried out when the observer can apply Darwinian-like principles by simply noting who said what and did what under which conditions. It is important to recognise that knowledge about specific individuals may be just as important as general data about large numbers of individuals. Much valuable information arises from ethological type of evidence, where people are intimately concerned and knowledgeable about the handicapped people they serve. It is critical that this type of research is not destroyed in our efforts to overcome the ethical problems which arise from time to time.

It is important to make it quite clear to parents and personnel that research workers, on the whole, are not dedicated simply to obtaining data but are passionately concerned, or should be, in the people that they are serving. The idea of the unbiased research worker who does not pursue his studies within the context of human service is a notion from the past. Obviously, confidentiality should be respected, and individuals protected from subjection to unnecessary treatment, whatever form this may take. However the control of this cannot simply be left, as it is so often at present, in the hands of a committee, which may not understand the importance of a particular proposal. It is difficult, not to say presumptuous, to assume that a committee can judge the merits of a particular piece of research in relation to ethical controls. This is not an argument to say that research should not be monitored but rather to argue for competent training in ethics and sensitivity during the training of future research workers.

STAFF EDUCATION

A growing recognition that staff, if they are to train properly, must set about training in a systematic manner, rather than by simply exposing people to opportunities, has done much to enrich rehabilitation programmes. The skills required in developing systematised education in special education (such as the Individual Educational Plan (IEP)) can lead to the comprehensive development of new areas of rehabilitation. It is important to recognise this, because such skills cannot remain simply in the hands of psychologists as experimental devices to be applied sometimes to a particular clinical case, but must become part of the base knowledge of a broader profession which is emerging in the field of rehabilitation education. It is important, not only because of the need to ensure that a wide range of personnel have access to these techniques, but also because economy dictates that such personnel cannot be paid at the high salaries of very specialised psychologists and allied personnel. Indeed some of the vigorous arguments brought forward by teachers unions, maintaining that all education must be carried out by teaching personnel, look foolish if we regard the needs of handicapped people and the routine and sometimes mundane education that must be carried out before they can enter what we formally know as education. The time has arrived to recognise that education is a very broad concept. If we are to rehabilitate we shall require a broad range of personnel, and not all of the education required by clients is the exclusive domain of teacher educators. Teachers should be part of a team which seeks to rehabilitate individuals with different problems at different ages.

The preparation of staff to work in the area of rehabilitation has grown out of experience of institutionalisation and care but it has also been influenced by developments in special education. Only now are we beginning to see the need for a wide range of rehabilitation personnel, including the development of many more and new personnel in areas such as rehabilitation education.

In the adult field the standards of training of personnel vary enormously within developed countries. In some countries there are long-standing programmes which provide diplomas or certificates to students who complete practically-oriented training programmes. In more recent years these programmes have been attached to a range of community or technical colleges. This has elevated education from the private or charitable stages of support to a more formal recognition and, in turn to an acknowledgement of the technical and professional status of those so educated. However, many of those working in the field still have little knowledge about handicap. In many countries, personnel entering the field of adult rehabilitation do so because they have particular and important skills such as carpentry, or other aspects of industrial development, not because they have specific knowledge in the training of handicapped persons. This situation was understandable and acceptable when little knowledge existed on the processes of training for handicapped individuals and when little curriculum development had taken place. Now this is no longer the case, for it is imperative that we develop formalised education programmes at advanced levels of rehabilitation training. But the problem runs far deeper than this because social workers and psychologists for the most part receive little education in this area. If placement officers, such as those suggested by Hutchinson (1982), are to assist handicapped persons in obtaining work and living in the community for their adult life, such personnel must be intensively educated both theoretically and practically in rehabilitation education.

However the development of formalised training programmes, one and two year certificates and even degree programmes, have considerable implications for other areas of practice. In Canada the development of two year training programmes for rehabilitation practitioners has been well established over the last 10 years. Many community colleges now run very practical educational programmes covering a wide range of rehabilitation content in child and adult areas. Vocational and residential or home-living skill training is provided, along with a practical knowledge of learning principles. In the near future it seems likely that students from such programmes will be able to gain entry into university bachelor's courses relating to the rehabilitation area, and receive transfer credit in so doing. We appear to be near the time when the continuum of rehabilitation education training will become available to students and staff from pre-university to post-graduate studies. This should do much to improve the system. The newness of the developments in Canada means that most

agencies do not have a wide range of fully trained personnel. In Australia and New Zealand, such development is
less advanced. Here there are nondegree courses and special
education is normally taken after an initial qualification.
Yet the inclusion of special education and rehabilitation
education within a first degree, in some cases without the
requirement of teacher certification, is important. Special
education and rehabilitation, which can be seen as a subset
of the latter, are not just about children or formal education. The concept of rehabilitation education as a global
concept in terms of both age and area of behaviour has at
last arrived.

In Britain, also, there are courses which provide
detailed education of personnel working in the training
centres. In some universities and allied centres innovative
ventures in rehabilitation education are at the developmental stage (Vickerman and Cronin, 1983), and this augurs
well for the development of the profession within this area.
It is important that such developments link to diploma
programmes in colleges, so that individuals obtain university credit for their efforts and are able to move along a
continuum through a bachelor's degree and, if desired to
master's and doctoral qualifications. It is important that
we develop flexible routes through psychology and social
work as well as education. Students involved in such
programmes should receive not only a practical experience,
and most programmes in Canada include at least 50 per cent
of their time in practical application, but also develop a
sound historical perspective as it relates to
rehabilitation. In addition a detailed knowledge of
curricula is required, as well as the principles of education which are fundamental to this area. The ability to
generalise knowledge to a variety of settings is important,
and it is unlikely this will be done without a sound base in
human development.

At present in several countries we are faced with a
situation where two year diploma students may have more
practical knowledge than people trained to degree level in
psychology, social work, or education who also practice with
handicapped persons. The former may not have such a broad
basis to their education, but they have more applied knowledge in developing rehabilitation programming. This may
well result in a major controversy in the field, for without
rehabilitation skills to a high level of professional
expertise, the psychologist and the social worker will prove
largely ineffective. The very fact that general principles
have to be individualised because of variability amongst
clients or students implies the development of particular
knowledge and specific skills. A psychologist should become
a programme designer and a programme builder for individual
cases, and is directed to particular client behavioural

difficulties. The social worker should be a mediator of social adaption and client efficiency.

In North America the development of rehabilitation counselling as a programme area is important, yet it too may not have the direct relevance to this field that is needed at ground level. Rehabilitation counselling does involve a wide range of different verbal techniques. But with mentally handicapped clients, for example, non-verbal techniques are likely to be more relevant (e.g. visual demonstration, modelling, with an accent on non-verbal communication). Much of our university education involves teaching people to become highly verbal, but in practice they need to apply visual and tactile methods of demonstration when working with particular groups of handicapped persons.

Rehabilitation Education must consist of a number of important aspects. It should, for example be grounded firmly in the area of psychological knowledge, insofar as this relates to human development, perception, motivation and learning. It must also employ knowledge from the area of human biology where human structure, anatomy and physiology, and particularly the malfunctioning of the human system in terms of the nervous and motor systems, is clearly recognised. Interaction between disabilities of a physical nature and their psychological counterparts should be clearly taught.

It is important to recognise the history of rehabilitation, for many workers are not even aware of the changes that have occurred over the past 10 to 15 years. For example, institutions are seen by many young students as a thing of the past and they regard institutionalisation with some alarm and believe that the process cannot occur again. We must recognise that cycles of behaviour tend to occur in society, and it seems highly likely that institutionalisation will occur again, though in a different form from that which has previously been experienced. For example in Alberta, Canada, small institutions are being built for very severely handicapped persons and prison and mental health admissions to institutions seem to be on the rise in some countries. It is only with an understanding of the history of such cycles, and the variations that occur in programmes over the years, that students can anticipate and intervene, and thus change the course of history. The development and interaction of the law and handicapped persons is becoming a very important area in a number of countries where human rights have become a critical issue. Choice over such matters as sterilisation, where one chooses to live, and the rights of parents in relation to the life and death of their children, are becoming important issues within our society. The fact that some Down's Syndrome children are deprived of nutrient after birth or are administered potentially lethal doses of drugs must be the cause of major concern. It is important that students learn why these are concerns, how such issues arise, and the processes that need to be developed for dealing with these issues in a professional and ethical manner.

Finally, the area of rehabilitation education demands the development of effective curricula for handicapped persons that will cover home-living, social, educational, leisure time, vocational, and allied skill areas. Such curricula are being written, but are often of poor quality. They often overlap needlessly with previous programme descriptions and are rarely tested in a rigorous fashion. It is critical that detailed curricula should now be developed, not just for the individual within the classroom, which is occurring in a number of countries, but as a full scale continuum of programming that can be employed throughout the life cycle. This includes leisure time education, home intervention, and follow-up and support processes which are applied as necessary through the individual's life.

Young handicapped adults are frequently placed in the community and are expected to survive without support, despite the fact that our changing society demands the learning of new skills in order to be effective within that society. It is essential therefore that some knowledge about ongoing processes of change are built into curricula, and that new means of support and development are provided. A large number of persons run into problems and difficulties of a social nature after they have been placed in the community. They may have initial success and do well for a number of years only to run into problems at a later stage. Yet our system has not developed in a manner such that continuous monitoring and support can be provided, other than of an emergency nature.

The question of quality of life-style, dealt with in the final chapter of this book, has hardly been broached in the terms of rehabilitation. Our concept of the adult having a job, and this being regarded as adequate placement represents the level at which we function in terms of rehabilitation, not whether the person is receiving a quality life, which is rewarding to him and those around him. It may well be that an examination of such quality life-style will move us away from vocational training to other important rehabilitation structures. If this is the case, it may then solve a number of the allied problems for there is little doubt that within the developed world the availability of employment for handicapped people is going to get less and less as unemployment becomes common. The references earlier to cycles of behaviour recognises that employment levels will vary, but the development of rehabilitation aimed at integration of handicapped people into the regular school system means that there is going to be a large increase in the number of young adults who require effective placement, and are capable of some involvement within the community. It is because of this that we must learn to change our attitudes in terms of quality of life-style.

PROJECTION

Some of the issues that have been raised are discussed in the following chapters. The book is not concerned with detailed curricula but as a treatise on the state of the science and art of rehabilitation as it relates to adults, particularly those who are mentally handicapped.
   The following points summarise the major ideas and recommendations made in this particular chapter.

1. Rehabilitation knowledge at the behavioural level has
    advanced to a point where a model of Rehabilitation and
    Education can be prepared.
2. In the adult field this supports an integrated model
    involving vocational, social, home-living and leisure
    training.
3. Rehabilitation Education requires professional and
    technical staff to develop its application which has
    profound implications for university and college
    programmes.
4. Research is an important aspect in the development of
    the field of Rehabilitation Education but must integrate
    with other political and social forces if it is to be
    applied effectively.
5. Research must be conceived in a broad framework where
    ethological study has both a central and catalytic role.
6. The field of rehabilitation in general and rehab-
    ilitation education in particular can only develop
    effectively when its students and practitioners take
    into account historical developments at a national and
    international level. Only then can rehabilitation
    personnel begin to effectively control the future
    development of rehabilitation strategy.

REFERENCES

Ball, T. S. (1970) 'Training Generalized Limitation:
    Variation on a Historical Theme', *American Journal
    of Mental Deficiency, 75*, 135-141.
Brown, R. I. & Hughson, E. A. (1980) *Training of the
    Developmentally Handicapped Adult*, C. C. Thomas,
    Springfield.

Clarke, A. M. & Clarke, A. D. B. (1974) *Mental Deficiency: The Changing Outlook*, Methuen, London.

Clarke, A. D. B. & Hermelin, B. (1955) 'Adult Imbeciles: Their Abilities and Trainability', *Lancet, ii,* 337-339.

Ebbinghaus, H. (1885) *Uber das Gedachtniss Leipzig*: Drucker and Humblat.

Engman, J. M. (1979) *Psychosocial Functioning of the Elderly,* unpublished master's thesis, The University of Calgary, Calgary, Alberta.

Feuerstein, R. (1979) *The Dynamic Assessment of Retarded Performers*, University Park Press, Baltimore.

Ford, V. B. & Brown, R. I. (1984) *Leisure Time Training and Rehabilitation*, C. C. Thomas, Springfield.

Gold, M. (1978) *Try Another Way*, Training Manual, National Institute on Mental Retardation, Marc Gold & Associates, Inc., Austin.

Gunzburg, H. C. (1968) *Social Competence and Mental Handicap*, Bailliere, Tundall & Cox, London.

Hutchinson, D. (1982) *Work Preparation for the Handicapped*, Croom Helm, London.

Landino, J. E. (1979) *Coding in the Mentally Retarded*, unpublished doctoral thesis, The University of Calgary, Calgary, Alberta.

Marlett, N. (1976) *The Adaptive Functioning Index*, Vocational and Rehabilitation Research Institute, Calgary, Revised 1976.

Martin, G. & Pear, J. (1983) *Behavior Modification: What It Is and How To Do It*, 2nd Ed., Prentice Hall Inc., Englewood Cliffs.

Parmenter, T. (1983) 'Evaluation of Rehabilitation Programs for Mentally Retarded Persons in Australia', *Journal of Practical Approaches to Developmental Handicap, 7,* 2, 3-6.

Possberg, E., Beck-Ford, V., Brown, R. I., & Smith, N. E. (1979) *The Leisure Functioning Assessment*, The Vocational and Rehabilitation Research Institute, Calgary, Alberta.

Sloan, W. & Stevens, H. A. (1976) *A Century of Concern*, A History of the American Association on Mental Deficiency, American Association for Mental Retardation.

Vickerman, B. and Cronin, J. 'The Old and the New - A Radical View: The Certificate in the Further Education and Training of Mentally Handicapped People', *Wessex Studies in Special Education, 3,* 165-174.

Whelan, E. & Speake, B. (1981) *Getting to Work*, Human Horizons Series, Souvenir Press (Educational and Academic) Limited, London.

Chapter Two

PROGRESS IN THE ASSESSMENT AND PREDICTION OF VOCATIONAL COMPETENCE IN THE RETARDED

D. W. McKerracher

INTRODUCTION

The study of assessment procedures utilised to evaluate rehabilitation outcome amongst people who are mentally handicapped provides us with a good example of the enigmatic nature of progress. Change must be assessed and documented, yet documentation depends on what is politically and economically seen to be relevant for assessment at any particular point in time.

It could be argued that the main goal of assessment is, like art '...*to hold the mirror up to nature...*' and reflect, accurately, that general skills, accomplishments, interests, wishes or experiences are recordable. This would limit its function to that of description of what has gone before and what is present now. For many training purposes, this might be quite sufficient, because it allows global detection of weaknesses and strengths and helps direct attention to areas of need.

But assessment information is often used for comparison of one stage of development or achievement with another, to determine whether progress is being made. Here the need is to collect detailed information that is specific to definite training objectives and establish relevant baselines from which improvements can be measured. This too is a limited concept of assessment, because it depends upon making assumptions about what is relevant for measuring.

A further use of assessment information is for prediction purposes, where it is of primary importance to have a clear idea of what is to be predicted. The dependent variables associated with vocational competence, whether of an all-encompassing kind, or of a more circumscribed employment type, or involving adjustments in the social and personal area, must be adequately established, before it is reasonable to analyse the selected independent variables that might be hypothesised to be related to them. The problem is that assessment is merely the function of measuring something, in an attempt to describe it quantitatively, yet what is to be assessed often cannot be measured directly, because it is a concept, a quality, an unidentified algebraic hypothesis. What gets measured are the more tangible activities, behaviours and verbalisations that are assumed or pragmatically demonstrated to be associated with the concepts. Unfortunately this means the independent variables that are selected as descriptors of the dependent quality or concept to be predicted are the only identifiable elements of that quality, so that a certain circularity is involved in the process of prediction, unless the criterion to be predicted is definable by variables other than those used to describe it. For example, if vocational competence is defined as including quickness of comprehension, speed of motor movement, ability to follow instructions, knowledge about timetables, ability to identify colours and count up to ten, then any tests devised to measure these attributes on the assumption that they will differentiate the competent from the incompetent, are essentially attempting to assess themselves. That is to say, the independent variables that describe the dependent variable are also being used as predictors of the dependent variable. Even if the quality or concept to be predicted can be defined by variables other than those to be used for prediction purposes (such as vocational competence being regarded as the ability to stay for an arbitrary length of time in paid employment) the discovery that the *competent* are distinguishable from the *incompetent* in a number of independent descriptor variables (such as speed of performance or reading accuracy) does not automatically mean that those variables will therefore be good predictors. The degree of correlation between variables has no necessary implications for a cause and effect relationship. Being able to distinguish between groups in several items does not mean that the magic quality that causes the differences is any closer to being understood. Conversely variables selected for their capacity to discriminate amongst individuals in terms of correctly predicted group placement do not always lend themselves to logical interpretation at face value (McKerracher et al., 1980).

Changes in Concepts of Vocational Competence (the dependent variable).

Amongst that section of any population that is classified as backward, retarded or developmentally handicapped, there is generally a wide range of learning difficulties, physical or sensori-motor impairments, personal inadequacies, unfavourable environmental circumstances and social incompetencies

(Lerner, 1976; Johnson & Morasky, 1977). Few encounter all these obstacles to normal development, and some may have specific skills much in advance of their general abilities. The likely number of persons in any handicapped population capable of attaining successful placement in an unsheltered vocational situation is likely to vary from culture to culture (Sarason & Gladwin, 1958). Sustaining themselves in such situations is also likely to be a variable achievement. Prediction of those likely to succeed can only occur when clear concepts and definitions of vocational competence have been evolved. As indicated above, the dependent variable to be predicted must be adequately specified before the independent variables which might be used as predictors can be meaningfully explored.

In spite of this, a good deal of work has been carried out, based upon intuitive hunches, with independent variables such as intelligence, on the assumption there must **be** a connection with vocational competence and employability. For some professional workers, the primary candidates for successful employment are those categorised as mildly retarded (Brolin, 1976a). Others maintain that the only major hindrances to placement of more seriously retarded subjects have been the inadequacy of training methods (Clarke & Clarke, 1974) and a general public disinclination to accept their employability outside sheltered workshops (Goldstein, 1964). It is generally agreed that the lower the intellectual ability, the greater the probability of severe central nervous system pathology and physical handicap being an associated part of the condition (Penrose, 1963). As a result, severely mentally handicapped people tend to have multiple handicaps and are often reported to find it more difficult to gain competitive employment (Heber, 1964; Collman & Newlyn, 1956; Fulton, 1975) than those who are mildly retarded. Yet there is some evidence (Bayer & Brown, 1982) that up to two thirds of mild or moderately retarded adults can achieve successful vocational placement and a larger proportion can accomplish semi-independent community living, whether in paid employment or on social welfare benefits.

One basic factor liable to affect the numbers finding employment on the open market, is the economic climate of the country in which jobs have to be found. It might be expected that as the level of general unemployment rises, the availability of jobs for handicapped adults will decline. One study found this not to be so (Halpern, 1973). The main conclusion then was that mildly retarded individuals continued to obtain a constant proportion of the jobs, irrespective of the level of unemployment, a position still supported by the Warnock Report (1978). However, the severe world-wide economic recession that has persisted since the seventies, may very well have changed that situation now, because of the enormity of the unemployment problems in most western countries (Simches, 1975). Employment for handicapped persons is a complex issue. One way to examine this is to look at the components involved. Four principles or themes seem to be in operation in connection with the concept of vocational competence: normalisation, employability, stickability and socialisation or personal adjustment.

Normalisation

The process of assisting developmentally handicapped people who have never worked, or of rehabilitating those who have tried and failed, involves an attempt to integrate them into their chosen community life-style. This means helping them to develop patterns of behaviour that conform with the cultural norms to which they must adjust, in the society and neighbourhood where they intend to live and work. This is the principle of normalisation that was put forward by Wolfensberger (1972). It involves much more than obtaining an unsheltered work position. Indeed, being able to perform the work skills in a job is only one step towards achieving normalisation. The best jobs offer more than a place to work. They function as a base from which to learn to communicate with others, experience normal peer relationships, acquire appropriate attitudes to authority figures, observe acceptable standards of conduct and make contacts for the pursuit of leisure interests and recreation (Nirje, 1970; Brown & Hughson, 1980). The *rhythm of life* aspect of normalisation advocated by Wolfensberger (1972) refers to a person's ability to flow with the surrounding society in order to experience a lifetyle as culturally normal as possible. It includes such things as observing natural breaks during the day, changing the pace of living at weekends as well as the type of activities, living reasonably independently without close supervision and, of course, holding down an unsheltered work placement for reasonable periods of time. For the principle of normalisation to be achieved, it is not sufficient to move handicapped persons from institutions or agencies and simply relocate them in the open community in competitively obtained job situations (Beasley, 1980). Some jobs may be in very isolated rural areas, with residential demands that make it difficult for retarded people to be independent or to learn new social skills. There are some who question whether the discharge of moderately or severely intellectually handicapped subjects from institutional care will necessarily result in a better life-style for them. Apparently independent living style in the community, in hostels or rooming houses, does not automatically guarantee a greater degree of normalisation than accommodation in an institutional villa (Graham, 1976). According to his view, if the elements of everyday living that are regarded as essential for normalisation to occur, exist inside as well as outside an institution, there is no real advantage in community placement. Given appropriate economic circumstances the pursuit of human dignity approach advocated by Brown & Hughson (1980) is a feasible undertaking for many people with mild as well as the moderate retardation. But for severely and profoundly handicapped people, the need for specialist services may alsways have to take precedence. The challenge is to find ways of making institutional environments resemble normal living conditions more closely.

EMPLOYABILITY

Placement in unsheltered job situations is nowadays considered to be the ultimate and logical conclusion to vocational training carried out in institutions and agencies (Sigler & Kokaska, 1971). It has not always been so. In 1912, Fernald declared that feeble-minded subnormals were never capable of supporting themselves independently or of managing their own affairs. By 1919, he admitted there were, after all, some who did succeed. These seemed to have received more support and supervision from family and friends than those who failed. Three years later, Mathews (1922) was able to put a figure of 97 per cent upon those who were capable of making a satisfactory community adjustment which often included employment. Since then, the bulk of the work on employability has focussed upon the less severely handicapped, with the Wechsler or Binet range of approximately IQ 50-75. But it is extraordinarily difficult to reach firm conclusions from a perusal of the many studies carried out by a variety of writers over the past sixty years on the subject of vocational success rates for individuals in this classification group.
    The earlier studies ought to provide some idea of the likely proportion of mildly retarded people who could achieve vocational adjustment when there was minimal training intervention and where mainly simple, follow-up studies have been reported. Much of the perspective is blurred, however, because of differences between the studies in variables such as age of subjects, sexual composition of the groups, job availability and complexity, length of follow-up for each subject, and so on. Educational provisions, employment circumstances, community attitudes and research sophistication have also altered drastically over the years. In Britain, Anderson and Fearing (1923) followed 321 feeble-minded school-leavers for periods varying from one to six years. They estimated that about half of the

sample got a job at some stage and about a quarter remained in employment for a year or longer. The Wood report (1929), in the section dealing with the mildly subnormal (IQ 50-70), relayed its findings that 34 per cent were capable of skilled manual occupations; 31 per cent of semi-skilled; 18 per cent of unskilled jobs and nine per cent could manage simple tasks under supervision, but could not find employment. Only eight per cent were regarded as unemployable. Di Michael and Terwilliger (1953) later confirmed these proportions in their studies of the employability of high grade subnormal persons but until mid-century, educators still considered mildly subnormal children to have very limited vocational aptitudes. In the period up to 1950 in the USA, the proportion of mildly retarded individuals who found employment after school was somewhat lower than in Britain. A wide range of unskilled jobs for about 40 per cent of most samples was the consensus of the findings, but the length of time subnormal workers survived in open employment was limited, ranging from a few weeks to more than a year in any one job (Neherer, 1920; Carpenter, 1921; Biglow, 1921; Woolley & Hornell, 1921; Byrne, 1925; Winifred, 1926; Johnson, 1928; Thomas, 1928; Keys & Nathan, 1932). During the war period, 1939-1946, several authors reported on the employment levels of special class pupils in factories and in the armed forces, where the highest recorded level was 54 per cent, with 13 per cent being considered unemployable (Kellogg, 1941; Holt, 1943; Foster, 1944; McKeon, 1944).

An overview of ten projects by Spellman (1968) revealed that the employability of retarded individuals emerging from vocational training programmes ranged from 46-86 per cent, depending on the locality, socio-economic status, job opportunities and intellectual status of the workers. He was not able to reach any conclusions about the effectiveness of training in increasing the likelihood of employment amongst the retarded. Three years after this, he participated in a report on the Kansas Work Study Project (Chaffin et al., 1971). The children in question had all left school for at least one year. In terms of employment outcomes, the effects of intensive vocational preparation upon a group of mildly retarded, special class children were compared with the effects in a similar group of children of not receiving any intensive training. In the trained group, 73 per cent obtained a job compared with 54 per cent in the contrast group; the gross weekly wage of ex-trainees was $90 compared with $62; and the average length of time employed in present job was 18.7 months compared with 10.6 months. Those results were in substantial agreement with the figures published by Bobroff (1956a, 1956b). Special class children who had received vocational preparation at school showed patterns of greater economic achievement than those without such training when followed up a year after leaving school. The conclusions of the Kansas Work Study Project were that at least half of the educable mentally retarded are capable of some form of employment without intensive vocational preparation. Up to three-quarters can normally find a job when vocational training is included and sometimes more than this. But the report's main emphasis was that the goal of work study programmes should not so much be to aim at making students employable as such. Rather it should be an attempt to enhance the features of employability which already exist in most of them.

Other general reviews of research into the occupational success of educable, mentally retarded workers include those by Kolstoe (1961), Windle (1962), Nelson (1963), Goldstein (1964), Cobb (1966, 1972) and Tizard (1974). Most of them indicate that a majority of mildly retarded adults, representing from 50 to 90 per cent of the sampled groups, are to be found in unskilled or semi-skilled jobs, earning a modest wage. A few are successful in gaining entry to skilled occupations, but there are marked differences amongst countries, localities and even regional education districts. Of interest, is the fact that in New Zealand, which is not a heavily industrialised country, the percentage of people who are regarded as educable retarded, in unskilled jobs, ranges between 50 per cent (Wilden, 1974) and 67 per cent (Thompson, 1968). This is a much heavier concentration on low level jobs than in the USA or Britain, where mildly retarded people have been found able to cope with more complex tasks than had been expected (Jerrold & Fox, 1971). Consequently, there are far smaller percentages in unskilled jobs. The overall figures for employment of mildly handicapped persons in New Zealand quoted by Wilden and Thompson (82 per cent and 88 per cent at the time of sampling) do not suffer by comparison with those in other countries. A recent follow-up study of Canadian trainees found that two-thirds were in full-time employment when traced, the length of exposure to risk varying from one month to six years (Bayer & Brown, 1982). The difference in emphasis upon types of job obtained is likely to be a reflection of the range of jobs generally available in different countries, rather than a comment about employability and training. It is obvious that the ingredients which contribute to the principle of employability are far from being obvious.

Stickability

Much less has been written about this principle than about the previous two. Once again, it is the practical difficulty for researchers of tracking down sufficiently accurate data - this time about the length of time a job is kept by a worker - that obscures the issue. It is possible that a factor of persistence or determination is the crucial one in deciding the stability of vocational adjustment achieved. Whatever this factor may be, it has been asserted that the demonstration of the ability to hold down a job for six months is a better predictor of long term vocational success than the ability to obtain a job initially (Appell et al., 1965). Verification of this claim is still lacking, as the bulk of the work carried out has been of a descriptive kind, examining samples of those in employment for varying lengths of time, to see whether there are any significant discriminators of short-term from longer-term employees.

There have been several weaknesses in the research strategies used. The inclusion of part-time job-holders with short-term ones, as part of the same success group, may have a confounding effect upon attempts at prediction (Kennedy, 1948; Chaffin et al., 1971). Similarly, studies which define successful employment as having a job for only two weeks (Song & Song, 1969) are almost bound to differ in their list of predictor variables from studies like that of Fulton (1975) who applied a success criterion of six months' steady work in a full-time job. But interestingly, this stricter criterion produced only one significant independent variable that discriminated between the longer term job-holders and the shorter term: secondary emotional disturbance that detracted from the performance of shorter-term employees. By contrast, Song and Song (1969) found several predictors were involved in separating those who achieved short-term employment from those who failed to gain employment including intellectual, as well as work habit and work skill variables.

The limitations of simple criteria like, *any form of employment for any period of time versus unemployment*, are well recognised (Kolstoe & Shafter, 1961; Chaffin et al., 1971; Eagle, 1967; Mahoney, 1976b). Failure rates vary widely, depending on the definition of success used. Brolin (1976b) examined the records of 5,000 mildly retarded employees in government services and found that only seven per cent dropped out. Their main reasons for being unable to keep their jobs were failure to adapt in the area of personal adjustment skills and lack of development of appropriate socialisation skills. Their loss of employment was not due to difficulties in mastering the practical job skills. A recent study reflected this finding (Malgady et al., 1979). It was shown that the major reasons for job termination were poor verbal manners and poor communication skills.

There is at least one other possible reason why retarded people may find it difficult to stay in a job once they have found one. A technological revolution has erupted upon the world in the early eighties with the advent of the powerful silicon chip, micro-process computers, the space shuttle and ever improving prosthetic devices and robot functions. The capability of providing greater help and support to many handicapped people in their bid to overcome the technical and mechanical drawbacks of their handicap is growing rapidly. But automation is perceived by some to be very threatening to the actual employment prospects of the retarded. Indeed the silicon chip heralds such sweeping technological changes that the impact upon society as a whole is likely to be totally unpredictable and of unprecedented extent (Large, 1979; Jackson, 1980).

Socialisation and Personal Adjustment

Although the vocational component plays an important part in the training and preparation of retarded people for employment and has been recognised to do so since the sixties, it is only relatively recently that attention has begun to be paid to the culitvating of social skills, personal maturity and personality stability as important contributors to the rehabilitation process. This is not to say that there has not been a concern to collect information in these areas over the years. A large amount of data is available. Unfortunately, the studies often suffered from the same design deficiencies that afflicted so many of the studies of employability: differing criteria, definitions and standards of success; unequal periods of follow-up; dissimilar variable studies. In spite of this, an impressive array of facts has been assembled to argue that the social development of retarded individuals is at least as important as vocational skill level in determining the social survival capabilities of those attempting to adjust to open society in a global fashion.

Amongst the early observations made were those suggesting that pupils in special classes tended to come from poor or unstable families (Woolley & Hornell, 1921; Taylor, 1925), where the delinquency rates were high (Byrne, 1925). Several authors have claimed it is extremely difficult for retarded individuals to acquire appropriate social behaviour and allege a high rate of behavioural disturbances (Sarason & Gladwin, 1958; Beir, 1964; Robinson & Robinson, 1965). Independent living in an open community certainly becomes increasingly more difficult for the mentally handicapped to achieve, because of the growing complexity of modern urban environments (Goldstein, 1964). Clearly the evidence suggests that development of social skills could be a crucial factor in the stabilisation of handicapped persons (Bayer & Brown, 1982). All of the studies carried out in

31

New Zealand on this topic reached the same conclusion, namely that the majority of retarded children who failed in open employment, did so on account of social incompetence. With the exception of the physically handicapped, few failed because of poor academic achievement or lack of job skills alone (Winterbourn, 1944; Nelson, 1963; Thompson, 1968; Wilden, 1974).

Other workers confirmed that work skills were not the only determinants of vocational success. Personal appearance and social acceptability to the work group were equally important (Peckham, 1956; Phelps, 1956; Cassidy & Phelps, 1965). Those studies were in agreement with the findings reported by Collman and Newlyn (1957) who wrote that 52 per cent of retarded persons who lost their jobs were discharged for *character defects*, such as lack of punctuality, inappropriate work attitudes, rudeness, laziness and sexual misdeameanours; 26 per cent because of personal maladjustment and temperamental instability, involving refusal to obey orders, quarrelsome and aggressive behaviour, temper outbursts and unwillingness to listen to advice. Only 22 per cent were due to inadequacy of vocational performance skills.

Heber (1959) phrased a definition of social adjustment as *'...the degree to which the individual is able to maintain himself independently in the community and in gainful employment, as well as by his ability to meet and to conform with other personal and social responsibilities or standards set by the community'* (p. 4). This positive approach is to be contrasted with that of Kennedy (1966) who favoured a negative definition of social adjustment couched as, *'...staying out of trouble, not being involved in criminal or anti-social behaviour or not becoming illegitimately pregnant'* (p. 5). The last item is an amusing example of how definitions can become out-dated in less than twenty years, because of changing standards in western society and growing permissiveness towards solo parenthood. It does underline the point that it is extraordinarily difficult to measure the presence of social and personal skills, and very much easier to attend to factual indicators such as marital status, prison record, type of accommodation, number of children raised, and so on.

Some researchers have followed up groups of mildly retarded special class children for varying lengths of time, to discover what happens to them. In most cases, the majority of subjects found employment, were assimilated into the adult community (McKeon, 1944; Krishef & Hall, 1955) and ceased to be identifiable as retarded (Dinger, 1961; Carson, 1965). The main question to be answered is how best to promote this adjustment process in order to increase the likelihood of integration into the normal adult community. The current emphasis upon rigid mainstreaming as an unquestionable panacea to ensure optimal progress for all retarded pupils, overlooks some of the doubts that remain unanswered. One of the most carefully structured studies to address itself to this dilemma was that carried out by Durojaiye (1971). Three groups of subjects were formed with 60 children in each group. All subjects were aged between thirteen years, nine months and fourteen years, nine months. The sex distribution was equitable in all groups and all parents were classified as being within the lower socio-economic range. The fathers were either in service-skilled or unskilled jobs, or were totally unemployed. Two of the groups were formed of children with WISC scores in the IQ 50-75 range, who were two and a half years retarded on the Burt word recognition test. They were also two years behind their age peers in the Vineland Social Maturity test. The third group was formulated as a normal control group. Its members had WISC scores in the IQ 80-105 range and were selected so as to have Burt scores that were no more than one year retarded and no more than one year ahead of their chronological age. Their Vineland scores were also on a par with their age. One control group of retarded children experienced placement in special classes in regular schools and the other was formed of children sent to special schools. The comparison group of children were all in English secondary modern schools. Physical and medical inadequacies were excluded from all three groups. Cases with manifest personality instability were also omitted. The criteria for omission were based on case history information obtained at interview and performance on the Gibson Spiral Maze test indicative of impulsive, careless, rule-breaking behaviour. After leaving school the groups were followed up to study the details of their occupational success during their first two years at work. There were no significant differences between either of the subnormal groups in any of the variables studied. Both groups over-lapped with the comparison group in their range of career choices when tested in school, although the latter did tend to select more of the better paid and more highly skilled jobs. There were no significant differences amongst the groups in terms of actual job procurement and good agreement was found between the career interests indicated at school and the jobs later acquired. The exception was a small group of the subnormal children who had shown a preference for professional occupations in the test. None of them had succeeded in starting to train for such employment at the time of follow-up. Their career interests and expectations were considered somewhat unrealistic. When all three groups were compared in job experiences, both subnormal groups were found to have changed jobs less frequently than the normal group and to express fewer complaints about their present situation.

It is likely that some retarded people will require more intervention and help than others of a similar intellectual level, simply because they have more personal problems to cope with or are more culturally deprived than others. The remedial principle of supplying each individual with whatever help he is perceived to be in need of, may imply that for some children the challenge and stimulation of adjusting to their normal peer environment are all that is required; whilst for others, special class training or, in some cases, special school training, are a necessity. Nevertheless, the evidence selected in this review shows that the majority of children classified as subnormal while at school, with an IQ above approximately 50 on a standard test such as WISC or Binet, has a greater than chance probability of achieving vocational and social competence as adults, without further intensive training. Where such training is available and when low level employment situations are plentiful the change of success rises to somewhere in the 80-90 per cent range, but there is no clear indication of which characteristics contribute most to this success and no vindication of which aspects of training programmes are responsible for promoting it (Bayer & Brown, 1982).

CHANGING CONCEPTS IN ASSESSMENT & PREDICTION OF VOCATIONAL OUTCOME

As Deno (1965) pointed out, in spite of all obstacles, there is a persistent faith that accurate and early predictions about prognosis can be made, on the basis of present information and test data, if only the relevant variables could be identified.

Much of the work carried out before 1970 was heavily oriented towards two categories: simple descriptions of assessment and training procedures, or comparisons of variously defined success or failure groups in terms of personal and social criteria (Cobb, 1972). Steckel (1934), Carson and Arveson (1963), Muller and Lewis (1966) and Spellman (1968) reviewed about 80 programmes in this manner and were unable to reach any conclusions other than to complain that there had been too much emphasis on administrative and descriptive aspects of the programmes being reviewed. Similar comments had been made in other reviews (Shafter, 1957; Windle, 1962; Voelker, 1963, Goldstein, 1964; Tizard, 1974). It was observed by Sparks and Younie (1969) that educational researchers were still scientifically unable to identify the instructional components, nor specify the kind of training programmes which contributed most to the vocational success of retarded students. Amongst the reasons they cited were: an over-dependence on the utilisation of IQ scores when they seemed to have little predictive value in determining vocational adjustment, except at very low levels (IQ 50); too great a diversity in programmes offered, with a veritable potpourri of facts issuing from them; lack of definition to the personal characteristics of those being researched, with resultant inclusion of severely and mildly retarded subjects in the same groups where the needs were quite different, and lack of extended programme help beyond minimum school leaving age. From this, it would seem safe to conclude with Wilden (1974) that there are, *'...no predictive formulae sufficiently refined and verified which can be relied upon to separate, in advance of employment seeking, those who will succeed from those who will fail'*. But, as Gunzburg (1973) has argued, prediction is basic to making case decisions and can never be dispensed with at a practical level. It seems obvious that the shorter the time interval across which predictions have to be made, the more feasible it is to expect some degree of accuracy. From this view-point, assessment is a continuous process, linked to social education and must go in partnership with training. Prediction therefore becomes a matter of making a decision about the next best step to take in terms of a progressive series of adaptive behviours to be learned, rather than a long-term forecast of vocational outcome, based upon a global concept of employability. The review by Cobb (1972) concluded that, in the field of rehabilitation, prediction is poor because mentally handicapped young adults often do better than expected, intelligence quotients have a low correlation with vocational outcome, whilst specific behaviour data about work competence and social skills have immediate relevance only. The latter have very little predictive validity over long periods of time other than to indicate those most likely to succeed at the very next stage or level of train-ing. This position has been confirmed by recent studies (McKerracher et al., 1980; Sinclair, 1983). There is a distinct contrast between those two views of assessment (description V. prediction), though it would seem unneces-sary to consider them mutually contradictory.

PRACTICAL ASSESSMENT

It is pertinent at this point to make some general comments about the practical functions of assessment, particularly when considerable criticism has been expressed about the general utility of assessment of a psychometric kind and more accent given to criterion-referenced measures as preferable alternatives (Glaser, 1970; Bersoff, 1973; Van Etten & Van Etten, 1976). The establishing of baseline skills for specific behavioural parameters derived from a life situation, and the provision of continuous data as a feedback process to reflect the influences of training intervention, have removed the emphasis from traditional periodic psychometric forms of assessment. Criterion-referenced assessment is concerned with mapping the strengths and weaknesses of individual trainees, in terms of their distance from criterion skill levels, and is a process of repeated evaluations of their progress to provide feedback about the effectiveness of education or training and to predict performance in specific skills over short periods of time. Norm-referenced testing undertakes to sample the strengths and weaknesses of individual trainees, in order to compare them with a peer group of some kind and so establish the probability of success or failure of the whole person in some future situation connected with normal-isation of educational, social and vocational functioning. Another way of expressing this difference (Ebel, 1971) is to regard criterion-referenced tests as working with scales that are of maximum interest at the extremities of their range, where high scores represent mastery of defined abilities and low scores indicate absence of them. Norm-referenced tests work with a scale where the interest is focussed upon the midpoint of the range which represents the average level of performance for particular groups with which the individual subject is to be compared. Needless debate has been engendered by proponents of each viewpoint. In favour of the criterion-referenced approach is the work of researchers such as Glaser (1970), Haring and Phillipps (1972), Bersoff (1973), Bijou (1973), Lovitt (1973), Van Etten and Van Etten (1976). They point out the advantages of precise and specific measurement of skill deficiencies, where the information leads to appropriate remedial pro-grammes. In defence of the norm-referenced orientation and critical of the criterion-referenced position are authors like Stake (1970), Resnick (1973), White (1973) and Smead (1977), who question the validity of the *ad hoc* scales created to measure mastery of a skill and the reliability of observations that are made very often by participants in the activity being monitored (e.g., children themselves, parents, teachers etc).

The argument that one type of measurement should supplant the other has theoretical as well as practical limitations. Each serves a different purpose and has its own uses and advantages:

1. Assessment can be regarded as a monitoring of individual activity with a view to evaluating current growth and development, no matter what degree of success is attained in terms of integration into community life and competitive employment in the future (i.e., a reflection of skill levels attained at the present time).

2. Alternatively, its main purpose can be viewed as making
    a prediction of the degree of success likely to be
    achieved by individuals in integrating with the
    community and in demonstrating usefulness to the society
    of which they are a part (i.e., a forecast of the
    effectiveness with which learned skills can be utilised
    in facilitating vocational and social adjustment).

The former evaluation process is concerned with the
maximum amount of self-fulfilment of which people are
capable. In the vocational sense, this means that their
personal needs are taken into consideration, irrespective of
their competitive productivity, because they are matched
with no-one, other than themselves. Humanitarian emphasis
is placed upon individuals, rather than on the quality of
the products for which they are responsible. The most
appropriate kind of assessment, in this case, is of the
empirical, ongoing variety, where the main concern is to
help clients reach their own ceilings of development,
whatever these may be.

The second form of assessment mentioned above addresses
itself to the problem of the extent to which an individual
can be expected realistically to contribute to the earning
capacity of a training programme or to obtain competitive
employment as a result of training. Here, a trainee is
compared with others in terms of the probability of success
at responding to training procedures. Where training
programmes have to meet industrial standards or contract
deadlines and the products earn real money for the institute
and the trainee, there is a possibility that the primacy of
programme needs may take precedence over the personal needs
of a trainee.

Growth and development in subnormal persons is a highly
individual process and some severely retarded people have
shown remarkable and unexpected increases in skills as the
result of intensive training (Clarke & Clarke, 1974). But
there is still no doubt that a section of the subnormal
population remains in need of a long-term, specially
supportive environment, where trainees may become only
partially productive in a vocational sense, in spite of
being encouraged to expand their personal skills to the
limit. Some clients are unlikely to achieve complete,
social independence and, from the point of view of a
community retraining programme, offer a different degree of
challenge from the trainees whose general skill levels
suggst that total integration with the community is a
feasible undertaking.

In a research-oriented training environment with no
shortage of available places, there is clearly little need
for the psychometric type of assessment from the viewpoint
of selection. Indeed, it is not so much selection that is

involved as an applied exploration of each individual's skills and needs which could extend over some months and, in the case of deeply retarded individuals, over some years. It is essential that there be such centres, as they can serve as models and training facilities for service-oriented agencies. There comes a point, however, when the volume of community demand exceeds the availability of resources (Tizard, 1964), due to an increased awareness by the public of the availability of services. Of necessity, a priority selection system of some kind has to be developed, if only to ensure a continuing turnover of successfully trainable clients, thereby freeing places for others.

INTELLIGENCE AND VOCATIONAL ADJUSTMENT

Definitions of successful vocational adjustment have been variously attempted by operational criteria such as ability to find a job; length of time in employment; job complexity; amount of wages earned and so on. Positive correlations were found between measures of intelligence and variables of this kind by several earlier workers (Baller, 1936; Able, 1940; Phelps, 1956; Reynolds & Stunkard, 1960). Harold (1955) reported a significant correlation between measured intelligence and complexity of work tasks efficiently accomplished. In two studies dealing with mentally retarded persons (Kaufman, 1970; Ward et al., 1981). WAIS Full Scale IQ scores were the best predictors of satisfactory from unsatisfactory vocational attainment. Kolstoe (1961) found a slight superiority of intelligence in employed over unemployed groups. The same author (Kolstoe, 1971), although unable to link IQ clearly with measures of employ-ability, remarked that it was only common sense to assume that, *'...it takes more intelligence to be an atomic physicist than a ditch-digger. Such a relationship cannot be denied, but the range of jobs held by the retarded does not extend much beyond those of a semi-skilled nature'* (p. 30).

    In opposition to these findings, no relationship was found between IQ and various measures of employment success by other workers (McIntosh, 1949; Hartzler, 1951; Shafter, 1957). Further support for this position was provided by Chaffin et al. (1971) who were unable to establish any significant association between IQ and employability or wages earned. In a Canadian study of developmentally handicapped trainees at a vocational training institute (McKerracher & Orritt, 1972), it was noted that intelligence was unrelated to job performance measures. This result reinforced that provided in an Israeli study of the same variables (Sali & Amir, 1971), suggesting the international character of these conclusions. Song and Song (1969) have followed Kolstoe (1961) in suggesting that perhaps IQ becomes relevant only when the intellectual demands of vocational tasks are markedly greater than the intellectual level of the trainees undertaking them. The limited range of semi-skilled or unskilled jobs are available to retarded people means that so long as their IQ is somewhere between 50 and 70, they should be intellectually capable of coping with employment in open society.

BIOGRAPHICAL VARIABLES AND VOCATIONAL ADJUSTMENT

A number of case history items readily ascertained from most subjects (e.g., age, sex, length of schooling) have been employed in many vocational prediction studies with varying degrees of success. In general, it would seem that such items have poor predictive validity (Cobb, 1972) although there are some that warrant closer study.

   1. Age: Positive claims have been made for age as discriminator between successful and unsuccessful trainees in an Austrailian work preparation programme (Ward et al., 1981), but these are balanced by negative findings from a comparable Canadian training programme (McKerracher & Orritt, 1972), where no effects for age alone were found in a factor analysis of predictor and target variables. In a follow-up of this project (McKerracher et al., 1980), age failed to emerge as a significant contributor to a discriminant function prediction formula that achieved 80 per cent correct classification between vocationally successful and unsuccessful trainees. However, in the first of the Canadian studies, it was found that age did have some non-linear influence upon outcome. Trainees older than 23 years at entry to the training programme, required a shorter training period than younger trainees before successfully finding a job. Maturation and growth surges following plateaux of slower development could be a possible explanation that deserves closer examination.

   2. Sex: Not a great deal of information about the predictive capabilities of this variable could be found in connection with vocational adjustment. The range of jobs for retarded persons is usually restricted to unskilled and semi-skilled labour (Brolin & Kokaska,1974; Mahoney, 1976a). For subnormal females there seem to be even greater difficulties in finding employment than for their male counterparts, possibly because the types of jobs made available to the retarded commonly involve strenuous working conditions and physical strength that are traditionally regarded as more appropriate for males (Mahoney, 1976b). It could also be there are a greater number of factors, as yet undetected,

for females to cope with in adjusting to employment (Brolin, 1976a). One study did find that subnormal female trainees apparently improved more quickly than males in vocational performance within the training workshops of a rehabilitation institute (McKerracher & Orritt, 1972). The importance of this finding was unfortunately obscured by the fact that the better workers in both sexes tended to be placed in different work areas, the males being given tasks that demanded more complex mechanical ability. However a more recent study at the same institute (Bayer & Brown, 1982) also found that the range of time spent in training was shorter for female trainees than males.

3. <u>Academic Variables</u>: There is a difference of opinion between those who claim there is no significant relationship between numbers of years spent at school by retarded pupils and later vocational adjustment (Greene, 1945; Shafter, 1957; Cowan & Goldman, 1959), compared with those who advocate delayed graduation from secondary schools or high schools, to allow maturation to occur (Baller et al., 1966). The difference may be that longer schooling and vocational preparation exert greater ifluence upon social adjustment of trainees than directly upon their vocational adjustment (Windle, 1962). But another anomaly exists. Logically, it would be reasonable to assume that an extended period of education leads to higher levels of educational attainment and that the latter is also related to vocational and social adjustment. But Kolstoe (1961) unexpectedly found a negative correlation between academic achievement and employment success. This suggests that pupils with longer schooling or more academic skills actually fared less well vocationally, which would be an unusual conclusion to reach. It is quite possible that this failure was due to emotional maladjustments in children who were offered extended training at school because of those very difficult-ies, and that it is personal maladjustment rather than educational attainment as such that is linked to vocational failure. In some ways, this resembles the puzzling finding by McKerracher et al. (1980) that trainees in a rehabilitation institute with higher levels of work performance skills and better manipulative dexterity were more liable to fail vocationally than those with lower abilities of this sort. Here again, it was found that the failures were largely on account of emotional and behavioural instability. The connection between educational attainment and vocational outcome, social adjustment and personality stability there-fore remains somewhat speculative, in spite of the fact that Young (1958) analysed 118 different job categories in which mental retarded persons found employment and reported that some basic academic skills were required in most of them.

Figure 1 presents a hypothetical set of relationships amongst the four variables discussed in the preceeding paragraph.

FIGURE ONE

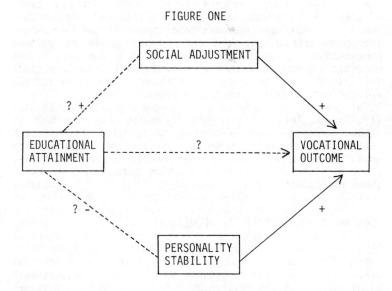

--- putative

—— established

Another area of contention is the respective importance of reading and arithmetical skills in prediction of vocational success. For example, in a survey of retarded workers in employment, Dinger (1971) found that arithmetic skills were more frequently needed than reading skills in their job situations. The importance of arithmetic over reading in the practical sense was reaffirmed by Guralnick (1964). By contrast, as early as 1956, Peckham had listed inability to read as a major problem in placing handicapped people in employment, and Voelker (1963) maintained that illiteracy was one of the major barriers for retarded people to overcome if they were to achieve vocational success. Obviously, basic academic skills in reading, writing and counting are all necessary for practical purposes in employment situations. The fact that there is little consistency in the usefulness of reading and arithmetic accomplishments as predictors of future vocational competence, shows that different jobs require different skills and that what may prove to be useful predictor in one setting, may not be so in another.

4. <u>Home background</u>: Although Shafter (1957) claimed there were no correlations between a number of home background variables and vocational success, other studies have found positive relationships, with subjects from better class homes being favoured (Abel, 1940; Greene, 1945; McKerracher & Orritt, 1972). Most retarded people were found to live in over-crowded conditions and those in better living conditions retained their jobs for longer periods (Ferguson & Kerr, 1960). Disregarding a family's socio-economic status, estimates of the degree of family support for the handicapped member were shown to be significantly related to employment outcome in retarded individuals (Neff, 1959; Cowan & Goldman, 1959). It was suggested by Kolstoe (1961) that the emotional and practical supportiveness of family members was probably independent of a family's place in the socio-economic scale, but it seems more likely there would be an interaction between family status and family solidarity. However, for prediction purposes, the latter seems more useful.

PERSONALITY AND VOCATIONAL ADJUSTMENT

Personality characteristics have consistently been mentioned in the literature throughout the last thirty years or so as being of the greatest importance in the successful vocational adjustment of the retarded. Numerous authors have catalogued the salient features of a favourable or unfavourable nature as described by supervisors, foremen and managers in the various work situations where retarded people have been employed. Some examples will portray the broad spectrum of information available.

The presence of emotional problems in a sample of retarded girls in an institution was found to have adverse effects on their ability to get jobs (Shotwell, 1949) although much also depended upon the sympathy and tolerance of employers. This was corroborated by Collman and Newlyn (1957) and Shafter (1957) who also demonstrated that personality defects can impede vocational adjustment. On the positive side, a number of earlier studies have shown that the presence of certain assets facilitates adaptation: stable temperament and hard-working orientation (Potts, 1952); reliability on the job, persistence, enthusiasm for the job, friendly disposition and other positive features (O'Brien, 1952; Warren, 1961). On the negative side, characteristics such as being unpunctual, rude, aggressive, immature and lazy were linked with job inefficiency and loss of employment (Di Michael & Terwilliger, 1953; O'Connor, 1954; Foale, 1956; Fry, 1956; Hilliard & Kirman, 1957; Dinger, 1961; Kolstoe, 1961; Cobb, 1966; Jerrold & Wright, 1967; Wilden, 1974). Most of these studies were descriptive in nature and were not constituted as actuarial exercises. They presented data about a mixture of postiive and negative attributes and behaviours associated with failure and success in employment.

Chaffin et al. (1971) pointed out that although many personality variables appeared to play an important part in affecting employability, measurement of this factor was difficult, and direct correlations with job success hard to substantiate. Others have gone further than this. Windle (1962) and Mischel (1976), 1979) suggested that explanations of behaviour in terms of personality are often used to disguise a lack of understanding of relationships beteen observable events. The invention of internal motivations and personality configurations that intrude between an antecedent and a reaction, is seen as *noise* within the system, better dampened down or even eliminated.

Attention is drawn to observable behaviours and social skills which are advocated as being more measurable than the subject matter of traditional personality test techniques. Even then, there is disagreement about whether prediction studies should include the broad social skills necessary for independent living, many of which may not be directly connected with work (Marlett, 1971), or concentrate on narrower social skills immediately related to work settings (Walls & Werner, 1977). The problem is to find instrumenta-tion of acceptable validity and reliability. The Walls and Werner study surveyed 39 behaviour checklists that sample vocational behaviour and the social skills associated with them. None was entirely satisfactory. Marlett (1977) described the Adaptive Functioning Index (AFI), as being a successful measure of social as well as vocational skills. This conclusion was supported by Riches (1980) who used the scale to distinguish between subjects who received social skill training and those who did not, with reliabilities ranging from .85 to .99.

Part of the AFI battery consists of a social-educational psychometric test concerned with assessing, writing, reading, number, money and time skills, together with community awareness skills. A factor analysis of these test variables plus measures of verbal intelligence indicat-ed that there was only one factor and the AFI social-educational test was heavily saturated by the intelligence variables (McKerracher, et al., 1980). A further factor analysis involving the vocational checklist of behaviour with the AFI social-educational test variables produced two clear-cut factors without overlap of a significant kind. Factor one was clearly a vocational skills factor with minimal loadings from the variables of the social skills test. Factor two was an intelligence and social-educational factor to which the vocational and social checklist skills did not seem to be related. This suggested that vocational skills training (which in this case was largely social-vocational skills) and social-educational skill training (which involved practical educational skills) would require individual attention with planned overlap, because generalisations from one to the other might not easily be accomplished.

Apart from social skills, there are physical performance skills that are more easily measured and show correlations with personality traits and vocational outcome. Variables such as persistence, dexterity, strength, coordination and self-pacing in work tasks have all been commented on as potentially useful vocational predictors (Peterson & Jones, 1964; Kolstoe & Frey, 1965; Hirst, 1967; Kerr et al., 1973). Motor performances and manipulative dexterity have been emphasised more often than the others as having a substantial effect in determining employability (Warren, 1961; Malpass, 1963; Rarick & Francis, 1960; Stein, 1963; Cratty, 1966; Chaffin, 1969). The Purdue Pegboard emerged as a valid predictor of vocational success in light industrial work (Schulman, 1967; Gorelick, 1968; Overs, 1970). To Kolstoe (1971), it seemed safe to conclude that motor performance had been shown to be a most crucial component of employability and that retarded youngsters were potentially capable of achieving performance levels nearer to normal in this area than in any other.

There has been a move away from heavy reliance upon psychometric tests, in the direction of behavioural sampling, as a result of the growing distrust of normative techniques in the last ten years or so. As a result, manipulative dexterity tasks, such as the Purdue Pegboard or the O'Connor manual dexterity test, are challenged by the appearance of the job sample technique. The crux of this issue is that prediction of whether a person will be able to perform a certain job can only sensibly be made if he is given a practical trial in which the actual skills required of him are sampled (Downs, 1977). The job sample is seen as a close simulation of a real work placement, where the skills, aptitudes and abilities demanded by competitive employment can be assessed by observers (Kaufman, 1970; Stodden et al., 1977). The fact that observations are repeated over a period of time, reduces the likelihood that the estimate of performance ability will be affected by factors such as test anxiety, speech and hearing difficulties as in standard test situations (Hardy & Cull, 1973). Against this, it is argued that many jobs cannot be simulated easily, the subdivision of jobs into constituent parts is not known to provide valid representations of the whole job, and this approach has not been validated in developmentally handicapped populations (Timmerman & Doctor, 1974). This view is shared by Halpern (1973) and Irvin et al. (1981). It is pertinent to note that in the Canadian prediction study described below (McKerracher et al., 1980), the job sample technique contributed nothing to prediction of vocational outcome over a period of a year, although it was relevant in helping to decide the amount of progress made in skill acquisition within workshops.

Extensive use has not been made of personality questionnaires in vocational prediction studies in the field of mental handicap, presumably because of verbal and reading comprehension difficulties or doubts about validity of answers. Yet a simplified version of the Eysenck Personality Inventory has been produced for use with the subnormal (Eysenck, 1966), and applied successfully in the field (McKerracher, 1968). The Jesness Inventory (Jesness, 1966) has been widely used in Britain and the USA (Miller & Neill, 1971) with subnormal delinquents and criminals. Oral presentations of the questions by the examiner, either interpersonally or by means of an audio-cassette, can help overcome much of the reading and comprehension difficulties. One multivariate discrimination analysis study that used tape-recorded presentations (McKerracher et al., 1980) found that the repression subscale of the Jesness was the best single predictor of vocational success and failure in a developmentally handicapped population undergoing employment training in Calgary, Alberta. Other significant predictors were obtained from a test of manual dexterity, vocational interest expressed in computational jobs in the Geist Pictorial test, the value orientation subscale of the Jesness, speed of performance on Raven's Matrices and preference for paranoid faces in the Szondi test (see Table 1). Strangely, the direction of prediction was not entirely what might logically be anticipated. Unsuccessful trainees who were dismissed from the programme, or who dropped out voluntarily, had a low repression score (more cynical); a high value orientation score (more anti-social and rule-violating); a high manual dexterity score (better motor efficiency); were slow in completing Raven's Matrices (more careful approach); and showed high interest in computational occupations (mathematical interests). Conversely the ones who successfully remained within the training programme or were placed in open employment, described themselves as immature, passive and socially conforming, had poorer manual dexterity, were faster at completing an intellectual task (though not more efficient) and had no interest in computational occupations. This is scarcely the popular image of a successfully attuned trainee and might have been considered a questionable finding, were it not for the fact that a recent multivariate study of a similar kind, carried out in New Zealand, produced a similarly unexpected trend in results (Sinclair, 1983). In a successful attempt at discriminating trainees who were successful in obtaining and keeping jobs in the open community for a uniform amount of time, from those who lost their jobs after being successfully placed, Sinclair found that successful subjects were characterised at time of placement by relatively low interpersonal communication ability and less expertise in the use of transport services, finding more difficulties making job-related decisions or taking directions from supervisors, and experiencing more problems in the work skill area than did the employment failures! More credibly, they were rated as being better able to handle personal problems than the vocational failure group and were more punctual. His conclusion was that although it had been technically possible to discriminate between vocationally successful and unsuccessful trainees, using relatively easily administered tests, the discrimination was in a peculiarly negative direction for some scales and it would neither be practically advisable nor theoretically feasible to build them into an instructional programme.

TABLE 1

DISCRIMINANT FUNCTION CLASSIFICATION MATRIX
FORMED BY 6 PSYCHOMETRIC VARIABLES PREDICTING TWO DESIGNATED
GROUPS: TRAINING SUCCESSES (T/S)AND TRAINING FAILURES (T/F)
12 MONTHS AFTER TESTING.   PREDICTORS WERE OBTAINED AT THE 2
WEEK INITIAL ASSESSMENT STAGE

T/S (N=49):   38 trainees still in institute programme (I/P)
               11 trainees placed in community jobs (O/P)

T/F (N=28):   28 trainees who dropped out of the programme
               within the first 12 months after admission
               (D/O)

Predicted Classification

Actual Classification	T/S	T/F	Total
T/S (Successes)	44 (.90)	5 (.10)	49 (1.00)
T/F (Failures)	10 (.36)	18 (.64)	28 (1.00)

Percent of *grouped cases* correctly classified = 80.52%

$Cpro_1$ (proportion classified by chance) : $.64^2 + .36^2 = 54\%$
$Cpro_1$ (proportion classified by chance, corrected for discriminant function classification by error) :
          $(.64 \times .70) + (.30 \times .36) = 56\%$
$Cmax$ (maximum proportion classified by chance, i.e. the larger of the actual proportions) = 64%

Whilst agreeing with this sentiment, it is imperative to take account of the importance of those findings. The situation is that two separate projects, in two different countries, mounting similar vocational training programmes for mildly retarded individuals, both discovered that the trainees who appeared to benefit most from training (having many of the abilities that might rationally be expected in successful workers) did not in fact succeed in employment as well as those with inferior work skills. It could be that individuals with superior vocational and social competence are not satisfied with the kinds of job generally performed by those who eventually prove more successful in a vocational sense. It could also be that the more physically and intellectually able workers are more subject to personal maladjustment. The major reason for their being among the ranks of the subnormal, rather than the dull-normal, may possibly be related to chronic behavioural disturbance and anti-social attitudes that do not change, though their work skills may already be adequate or capable of rapid improvement.

Both of the above studies were based on relatively short-term predictions over the course of a year. It is therefore of interest to report that seven years after the original assessment data collection for the Canadian project, an attempt was made to trace information about the fate of the 77 subjects who had been used in the discrimination analysis which produced a significant (80.5 per cent correct hit rate) two group classification prediction of vocational success and failure across the space of one year. For 65 of them (i.e., 84 per cent of the original sample) some information was found that permitted their being reclassified into *long-term failures* who had not achieved employment status for longer than a few days since leaving the institute and *long-term successes* who, at the least, had frequent short-term job experiences both of a full-time or part-time nature. The actual success group was predicted very accurately (89 per cent) by the psychometric data gathered seven years before, but the actual failure group was evenly split between predicted success and failure (see table 1). In a sense, this retrospective view of the result in terms of Actual Outcome Classification gives an inflated idea of the successful *hit* rate of prediction which was 66 per cent overall. At the moment of prediction, there is no knowledge of whether a trainee will eventually prove to be successful or unsuccessful in actuality. The only information available is what classification is predicted for him. The question for selectors then becomes, what percentage of predicted successes or failures will prove to be correctly classified, rather than what percentage of actual successes or failures was correctly predicted. The same data analysed from this aspect makes it clear that the prediction is prone

to type 1 error of classification. Too many failures are
included amongst predictions of success (see table 3).
However, this over-inclusiveness does mean that 89 per cent
of those who actually prove successful over a seven year
period (see table 1) are indeed predicted correctly. To
base selections upon the actuarial recommendations of likely
success would therefore be fairly safe, in that few good
prospects would be incorrectly spurned and the false posi-
tives would at least be given the opportunity of attempting
training. By contrast, a high percentage of those predicted

TABLE 2

ANALYSIS OF THE PROPORTION OF ACTUAL GROUP OUTCOMES CORRECTLY
PREDICTED SEVEN YEARS EARLIER BY DISDRIMINANT FUNCTION
ANALYSIS BASED ON PSYCHOMETRIC DATA

Initial Predicted Classifications

Actual Classification Seven Years Later	T/S	T/F	Total
Actual TS	25 (.89)	3 (.11)	28 (1.00)
Actual TF	18 (.49)	19 (.51)	37 (1.00)

TS = TRAINING SUCCESS STILL IN EMPLOYMENT SEVEN YEARS LATER

TF = TRAINING FAILURE UNEMPLOYED

TABLE 3

ANALYSIS OF THE CORRECTNESS OF PREDICTED GROUP DESIGNATION
WHEN COMPARED WITH ACTUAL OUTCOME SEVEN YEARS LATER

Initial Predicted Classifications

Actual Classification Seven Years Later	T/S	T/F
Actual TS	25 (.58)	3 (.14)
Actual TF	18 (.42)	19 (.86)
	43 (1.00)	22 (1.00)

TS = TRAINING SUCCESS STILL IN EMPLOYMENT SEVEN YEARS LATER

TF = TRAINING FAILURE UNEMPLOYED

to fail (86 per cent) do in fact fail over a seven year period (see table 3), but reference to Table 2 shows that, of those who actually prove unsuccessful, only 51 per cent are predicted. This means that most of those predicted to fail will indeed fail, but actuarial prediction of vocational failure will detect only half of those who actually do not succeed in getting a job. To reject candidates on the strength of this actuarial advice would not result in many good prospects being wrongly declined (14 per cent). This long-term relative effectiveness of prediction should not be regarded as implying that a blind choice based only on a few test scores is being recommended as a sound policy for training institutions to adopt. It does suggest, however, that actuarial prediction can be more valuable than it is currently fashionable to admit and that, properly used, could be a guide to decision-making where selection of some candidates over others is essential. Even in situations where all candidates can be accepted and no selection is required, an actuarial prediction that signals potential failure for some clients could be viewed as a challenge by trainers. Special attention to the needs of these particular individuals may help prevent their gloomy prognosis being unavoidable.

In terms of relating these findings to personality theory, the acting-out character of the reactions of the unsuccessful trainees and their rule-breaking orientation, suggest they ought to belong in the neurotic extravert quadrant of Eysenck's model, accompanied by a high psychoticism score (Eysenck & Eysenck, 1975). This would render them markedly insensitive to punishing consequences but most susceptible to positive incentives in training (Gray, 1976). Unfortunately, it is not as simple as that. There was no difference between the vocationally successful and unsuccessful samples in the McKerracher study (op. cit.) in any of the scales loaded on extraversion, neuroticism, social maladjustment, anxiety or aggression. The differences lay only in repression and value orientation. Both groups combined yielded a Jesness profile which did not significantly depart from that of the normal population in any variable except immaturity, where there was a general tendency to describe themselves as exhibiting immature behaviour. Moreover, the failure group was slow and deliberate in its handling of Raven's Matrices rather than impulsive and careless as might be expected of subjects in the choleric quadrant. The most that could be said is that this group tended to be extrapunitive rather than intropunitive, following the Quay and Peterson model (1967).

CONCLUSIONS

It is crucial to understand that there can be no rigid formulae that always apply to every rehabilitation situation, no definitive battery of tests nor final focus for behavioural observations that can be routinely operated. Assessment information is time-anchored to the situation in which information is gathered. If the situation alters, the assessment must also change and try to mould itself to each successive new model that it seeks to embody. The type of client applying for rehabilitation, the nature of the resources available, the experience and training of staff members, the economic climate, employment availability or the interest and degree of supportiveness of the local community, must all play an important part in shaping eventual outcome of vocational training. Indeed, it may be increasingly necessary to alter the objectives of rehabilitation programmes deliberately to accommodate to changing circumstances. As Bayer & Brown (1982) point out, if there are no jobs, then why concentrate on vocational rehabilitation? It might be more effective to run other forms of rehabilitation, such as social skill, leisure skill, independence skill programmes that are not dependent upon the trainee finding a job. If this happens, then obviously the assessment measures have to be modified to take account of such changes in emphasis. The need for ongoing assessment of all kinds is vital for rehabilitation programmes. It produces the measurements without which evaluations cannot occur.

Finally, although assessment may take many forms and the techniques or instruments chosen may be legion, it would seem reasonable to conclude from this review that there are several recurring themes associated with normalisation and with vocational or social adjustment. These include manual dexterity, speed of performance, personality, social independence skills and vocational interests. The anomaly that demands further research is that many ostensibly negative personality characteristics are demonstrated by trainees who achieve satisfactory vocational adjustment. Whilst this phenomenon may prove useful for prediction of vocational outcome, it can scarcely be used as the basis for instruction in a training programme.

REFERENCES

Abel, T. M. (1940) 'A Study of a Group of Subnormal Girls Successfully Adjusted in Industry and the Community', *American Journal of Mental Deficiency, 45*, 66-72.

Anderson, V. V. & Fearing, F. M. (1923) 'A Study into the Success of 321 Feeble-Minded Persons', *Mental Hygiene, 7*, 223-225.

Appell, M. J., Williams, C. M. & Fishel, K. H. (1965) 'Factors in the Job-Holding Ability of the Mentally Retarded', *Vocational Guidance Quarterly, 13*, 127-130.

Baller, W. R. (1936) 'A Study of the Present Social Status of a Group of Adults, Who, When They Were in Elementary School, were Classified as Mentally Deficient', *Genetic Psychology Monograph, 18*, 165-244.

Baller, W. R., Charles, D. C. & Miller, E. L. (1966) *Mid-Life Attainment of the Mentally Retarded: A Longitudinal Study*, University of Nebraska, Lincoln.

Bayer, M. B. & Brown, R. I. (1982) *Benefits and Costs of Rehabilitation at the Vocational and Rehabilitation Research Institute*, Final report, Project No. 4558-29-2, Welfare Grants Directorate, Health and Welfare Canada.

Beasley, D. M. G. (1980) *The Integration of Mentally Retarded Persons into Society*, Institute of Mental Retardation, Wellington, New Zealand.

Beir, D. C. (1964) 'Behavioral Disturbances in the Mentally Retarded', in H. A. Stevens & R. Heber (eds.), *Mental Retardation: A Review of Research*, University of Chicago, Chicago.

Bersoff, D. (1973) 'Silk Purses with Sow's Ears: The Decline of Psychological Testing and a Suggestion for Its Redemption', *American Psychologist, 10*, 892-899.

Biglow, E. (1921) 'Experiment to Determine the Possibilities of Subnormal Girls in Factory Work', *Mental Hygiene, 5*, 302-320.

Bijou, S. (1973) 'Behavior Modification in Teaching the Retarded Child', in C. Thoresen (ed.), *Behavior Modification in Education*, University of Chicago Press, Chicago.

Bobroff, A. (1956a) 'Economic Adjustment of 121 Adults Formerly Students in Classes for Mental Retardates', *American Journal of Mental Deficiency, 60*, 525-535.

Bobroff, A. (1956b) 'A Survey of Social and Civic Participation of Adults Formerly in Classes for the Mentally Retarded', *American Journal of Mental Deficiency, 61*, 127-133.

Brolin, D. E. (1976a) 'Value of Rehabilitation Services and Correlates of Vocational Success with the Mentally Retarded', *American Journal of Mental Deficiency, 76*, 644-651.

Brolin, D. E. (1976b) *Vocational Preparation of Retarded Citizens*, Charles-Merrill, Ohio.

Brolin, D. E. & Kokaska, C. (1974) 'Critical Issues in Job Placement of the Educable Mentally Retarded', *Rehabilitation Literature, 35*, 174-177.

Brown, R. I. & Hughson, E. A. (1980) *Training of the Developmentally Handicapped Adult*, C. C. Thomas, Springfield, Illinois.

Byrne, M. E. (1925) 'After School Careers of Children Leaving Special Classes in Minneapolis', *Ungraded, 10*, 75-86.

Carpenter, M. S. (1921) 'A Study of the Occupations of 207 Subnormal Girls after Leaving School', *Special Studies* (University of Michigan, Department of Vocational Education), *2*, 15-26.

Carricker, W. R. (1957) *A Comparison of Post-School Adjustment of Regular and Special Class Retarded Individuals Served in Lincoln and Omaha, Nebraska*, unpublished doctoral dissertation, Nebraska State Department of Education.

Carson, E. O. (1965) 'Jobs Held by Educable Mentally Retarded High School Graduates', *Journal of Social Education, 40*, 19-21.

Carson, E. O. & Arveson, R. G. (1963) 'A Study of Educable Mentally Retarded Students', *Journal of Social Education, 38*, 120-124.

Cassidy, V. M. & Phelps, H. P. (1965) *Post-School Adjustment of Slow-Learning Children: A Study of Persons Previously Enrolled in Special Classes in Ohio*, Bureau of Special and Adult Education, Ohio State University, Columbus, Ohio.

Chaffin, J. D. (1969) 'Production Rate as a Variable in the Job Success or Failure of Educable Mentally Retarded Adolescents', *Exceptional Child, 35*, 533-538.

Chaffin, J. D., Spellman, C. R., Regan, C. E. & Davison, R. (1971) 'Two Follow-Up Studies of Former Educable Mentally Retarded Students from the Kansas Work Study Project', *Exceptional Child, 37*, 733-738.

Clarke, A. M. & Clarke, A. D. B. (1974) *Mental Deficiency: The Changing Outlook* (3rd ed.), Methuen, London.

Cobb, H. V. (1966) *The Predictive Assessment of the Adult Retarded for Social and Vocational Adjustment: A Review of the Literature*, University of South Dakota, Vermillion.

Cobb, H. V. (1972) *The Forecast of Fulfilment*, Teachers College Press, London.

Collman, R. C. & Newlyn, D. (1956) 'Employment Success of Educationally Subnormal Ex-Pupils in England', *American Journal of Mental Deficiency, 60*, 733-743.

Collman, R. C. & Newlyn, D. (1957) 'Employment Success of Mentally Dull and Intellectually Normal Ex-Pupils in England', *American Journal of Mental Deficiency, 61*, 484-490.

Cowan, L. & Goldman, M. (1959) 'The Selection of the Mentally Deficient for Vocational Training and the Effect of the Training on Vocational Success', *Journal of Consulting Psychology, 23*, 78-84.

Cratty, B. J. (1966) *Perceptual Motor Abilities of Mentally Retarded Youth*, University of California, Los Angeles.

Deno, E. (1965) *Retarded Youth: Their School Rehabilitation Needs*, Minneapolis Public Schools, final report of Education project URA-RD-681, Minneapolis.

DiMichael, S. G. & Terwilliger, W. B. (1953) 'Counsellors' Activities in the Vocational Rehabilitation of the Mentally Retarded', *Journal of Clinical Psychology, 9*, 99-106.

Dinger, J. C. (1961) 'Post-School Adjustment of Former Educable Retarded Pupils', *Exceptional Child, 27*, 353-360.

Downs, D. (1977) *Trainability Testing: A Practical Approach to Selection*, H.M.S.O. publishers, London.

Durojaiye, M. O. A. (1971) 'Occupational Choice and Attainments of E.S.M. School-Leavers', *Education Research, 13*, 36-43.

Eagle, E. (1967) 'Prognosis and Outcome of Community Placement of Institutional Retardates', *American Journal of Mental Deficiency, 72*, 232-243.

Ebel, R. (1971) 'Criterion-Referenced Measurements: Limitations', *School Review*, pp. 282-288.

Eysenck, S. B. G. (1966) *The Eysenck-Withers Personality Inventory*, University of London Press, London.

Eysenck, H. J. & Eysenck, S. B. G. (1975) *Manual of the Eysenck Personality Questionnaire*, Hodder & Stoughton, London.

Ferguson, T. & Kerr, A. W. (1960) *Handicapped Youth*, Oxford University Press, London.

Foale, M. (1956) 'The Special Difficulties of the High Grade Mental Defective Adolescent', *American Journal of Mental Deficiency, 60*, 867-877.

Foster, V. H. (1944) 'Employment Status of Subnormal Girls and Boys', *Journal of Exceptional Children, 10*, 189-193.

Fry, L. M. (1956) 'A Predictive Measure for Work Success for High Grade Mental Defectives', *American Journal of Mental Deficiency, 67*, 563-568.

Fulton, R. W. (1975) 'Job Retention of the Mentally Retarded', *Mental Retardation, 13*, 26-29.

Glaser, R. (1970) 'Evaluation of Instruction and Changing Educational Models', in M. C. Wittrock & D. E. Wiley (eds.), *The Evaluation of Instruction*, Holt, Rinehart, New York.

Goldstein, H. (1964) 'Social and Occupational Adjustments', in H. Stevens & R. Heber (eds.), *Mental Retardation*, University of Chicago Press, Chicago.

Gorelick, M. C. (1968) 'Assessment of Vocational Realism of Educable Mentally Retarded Adolescents', *American Journal of Mental Deficiency, 73*, 154-157.

Graham, P. E. (1976) 'The Normalisation of the Mentally Handicapped', *Mental Handicap in New Zealand, 1*, 4-10.

Gray, J. A. (1976) 'The Behavioural Inhibition System: A Possible Substrate for Anxiety', in M. P. Feldman & A. Broadhurst, *Theoretical and Experimental Bases of the Behavioural Therapies*, John Wiley & Sons, London.

Greene, C. L. (1945) 'A Study of Personal Adjustment in Mentally Retarded Girls', *American Journal of Mental Deficiency, 49*, 472-476.

Gunzburg, H. C. (1973) *Social Competence and Mental Handicap* (2nd ed.), Bailiere-Tindall, Baltimore.

Guralnick, D. (1964) 'The Relationship of Personal Characteristics and Educational Experience of Mentally Retarded Persons to Their Successful Utilisation of a Vocational Rehabilitation Programme', *Dissertation Abstracts, 2728*.

Halpern, A. D. (1973) 'General Unemployment and Vocational Opportunities of E.M.R. Individuals', *American Journal of Mental Deficiency, 75*, 123-127.

Hardy, R. E. & Cull, J. G. (1973) *Vocational Evaluation for Rehabilitation Services*, Charles C. Thomas, Illinois.

Haring, N. G. & Phillipps, E. (1972) *Analysis and Modification of Classroom Behavior*, Prentice-Hall, Englewood Cliffs, New Jersey.

Harold, E. C. (1955) 'Employment of Patients Discharged from St. Louis State Training School', *American Journal of Mental Deficiency, 60*, 397-401.

Hartzler, E. (1951) 'A Follow-Up Study of Girls Discharged from the Lauriton State Village', *American Journal of Mental Deficiency, 55*, 612-618.

Heber, R. F. (1959) *A Manual on Terminology and Classification in Mental Retardation*, American Journal of Mental Deficiency publication.

Heber, R. F. (1965) *Vocational Rehabilitation of the Mentally Retarded*, U.S. Government Printing Office, Washington, D.C.

Hilliard, L. I. & Kirkman, B. H. (1957) *Mental Deficiency*, Little & Brown, Boston.

Hirst, W. (1967) 'Occupational Needs of the Socio-Economic Disadvantaged and Other Handicapped Youth of Laramie County School District', *Phase, 1*, 11-27.

Holt, I. (1943) 'Mental Defectives in Industry', *American Journal of Mental Deficiency*, 124-125.

Irvin, L. K., Gersten, R., Taylor, V. E., Close, D. W. & Bellamy, G. T. (1981) 'Vocational Skill Assessment of Severely Retarded Adults', *American Journal of Mental Deficiency, 85*, 631-638.

Jackson, R. (1980) 'Employment Prospects for the Mentally Retarded in a Post Industrial Society', *Journal of Practical Approaches to Developmental Handicap, 3,* 4-9.

Jerrold, M. A. & Fox, R. (1971) 'The Preparation of Immature and Educationally Subnormal School-Leavers for Working Life', *Future Trends, 4,* 15-21.

Jerrold, M. A. & Wright, H. J. (1967) 'Work Preparation for Immature E.S.M. School Leavers', *Bulletin Association Educational Psychology, 22,* 8-12.

Jesness, C. F. (1966) *Manual for the Jesness Inventory,* Consulting Psychology Press, Palo Alto, California.

Johnson, H. A. (1928) *A Summary of the Case Histories of 447 Atypical Pupils Who Have Left School,* Public Schools Bureau Curriculum and Guidance, California.

Johnson, S. W. & Morasky, R. L. (1977) *Learning Disabilit ies,* Allyn & Bacon, London.

Kaufman, H. I. (1970) 'Diagnostic Indices of Employment with the Mentally Retarded', *American Journal of Mental Deficiency, 74,* 777-779.

Kellogg, R. M. (1941) *A Follow-Up Study of 100 Males Who Spent Some Time in the Special Education Class of the Public Schools of Newton, Massachusetts,* unpublished masters thesis, Boston University, Boston.

Kennedy, R. J. (1948) *The Social Adjustment of Morons in a Connecticut City,* Mansfield-Southbury Training School, Hartford.

Kennedy, R. J. (1966) *A Connecticut Community Revisited: A Study of the Social Adjustment of Mentally Deficient Adults in 1948 and 1960,* Connecticut State Department of Health Publishers, Hartford.

Kerr, B. A., McKerracher, D. W. & Neufeld, M. (1973) 'Motor Assessment of the Developmentally Handicapped', *Peceptual & Motor Skills, 36,* 139-146.

Keys, M. & Nathan, J. (1932) 'Occupations for the Mentally Retarded', *Journal of Applied Psychology, 16,* 497-511.

Kolstoe, O. P. (1961) 'An Examination of Some Characteristics which Discriminate between Employed Mentally Retarded Males', *American Journal of Mental Defic iency, 66,* 472-482.

Kolstoe, O. P. (1971) *Teaching Educable Mentally Retarded Children,* Holt, Rinehart & Winston, Colorado.

Kolstoe, O. P. & Frey, R. M. (1965) *A High School Work Study Programme for the Mentally Subnormal Student,* Southern Illinois University Press, Illinois.

Kolstoe, O. P. & Shafter, A. J. (1961) 'Employability Prediction for Mentally Retarded Adults: A Methodological Note', *American Journal of Mental Deficiency, 66,* 287-289.

Krishef, C. & Hall, M. (1955) 'Employment of the Mentally Retarded in Hennepin County, Minnesota', *American Journal of Mental Deficiency, 60,* 182-189.

Large, P. (1979) *Wrong Lines*, The Guardian, Manchester.
Lerner, J. W. (1976) *Children with Learning Disabilities*
    (2nd ed.), Houghton Mifflin Co., Boston.
Lovitt, T. (1973) 'Self-Management Projects with Children
    with Behavioural Disabilities', *Journal of Learning
    Disabilities, 6*, 138-147.
Mahoney, D. J. (1976a) 'A Review of Jobs Undertaken by the
    Mentally Retarded', *Australia Journal of Mental
    Retardation, 4*, 24-27.
Mahoney, D. J. (1976b) 'Factors Affecting the Success of
    the Mentally Retarded in Employment', *Australian
    Journal of Mental Retardation, 4*, 38-51.
Malgady, R. G., Earcher, P. R., Towner, G. & Davis, J.
    (1979) 'Language Factors in Vocational Evaluation of
    Mentally Retarded Workers', *American Journal of Mental
    Deficiency, 83*, 432-438.
Malpass, L. F. (1963) 'Motor Skills in Mental Deficiency',
    in N. R. Ellis (ed.), *Handbook of Mental Deficiency*,
    McGraw-Hill, New York.
Marlett, N. (1971) *The Adaptive Functioning Index*,
    Vocational and Rehabilitation Research Institute,
    Calgary.
Marlett, N. (1977) *The Adaptive Functioning Index Standard-
    isation Manual*, Vocational and Rehabilitation Research
    Institute, Calgary.
Mathews, M. (1922) 'One Hundred Institutionally Trained
    Male Defectives in the Community Under Supervision',
    Mental Hygiene, 6, 332-342.
McKeon, R. M. (1944) *A Follow-Up Study of Special Class
    Boys Who Attended Lodge Street School at Worcester,
    Massachusetts 1932-42*, unpublished masters thesis,
    Boston University.
McIntosh, W. J. (1949) 'Follow Up Study of 1000 Non-
    Academic Boys', *Exceptional Child, 15*, 166-170.
McKerracher, D. W. & Watson, R. A. (1968) 'The Eysenck
    Personality Inventory in Male and Female Subnormal
    Psychopaths', *British Journal of Social and Clinical
    Psychology, 7*, 295-302.
McKerracher, D. W. & Orritt, C. P. (1972) 'Prediction of
    Vocational and Social Skill Acquisition in a Develop-
    mentally Handicapped Population: A Pilot Study',
    American Journal of Mental Deficiency, 76, 574-580.
McKerracher, D. W., Brown, R. I., Ryba, K. A., Marlett, N. &
    Zwirner, W. (1980) *A Study of the Utility of Assess
    ment and Prediction Procedures in the Selection of
    Handicapped Persons for Industrial and Social Rehabil
    itation Programmes*, Final report for project grant No.
    566-34-8, Health & Welfare, Canada, Vocational and
    Rehabilitation Research Institute, Calgary.

Miller, A. A. D. & Neill, M. P. (1971) *The Jesness Invent
    ory: Application to Male Patients at Two Special
    Hospitals*, Special Hospitals Board Unit, Research
    Report No. 4., London.
Mischel, W. (1976) *Introduction to Personality* (2nd ed.),
    Holt, Rinehart & Winston, New York.
Mischel, W. (1979) 'On the Interface of Cognition and
    Personality: Beyond the Person-Situation Debate',
    American Psychologist, 34, 740-754.
Muller, V. & Lewis, M. (1966) 'Work Programme for the
    Mentally Retarded Students', *Journal of Social
    Education, 41*, 75-80.
Neff, W. S. (1959) *The Success of a Rehabilitation Pro
    gramme: A Follow-Up Study of the Vocational Adjustment
    Centre*, Jewish Vocational Centre, Monograph 3,
    Illinois.
Neherer, I. (1920) 'Follow-Up Study of Special Class
    Pupils', *Ungraded, 5*, 116-118 & 150-154.
Nelson, B. G. (1963) *Vocational Training and Employment of
    the Mentally Retarded*, unpublished masters thesis,
    University of Auckland, Auckland, New Zealand.
Nirje, B. (1970) 'The Normalisation Principle: Implica-
    tions and Comments', *Journal of Mental Subnormality,
    16*, 62-70.
O'Brien, M. A. (1952) 'A Vocational Study of Institutional-
    ized Persons', *American Journal of Mental Deficiency,
    57*, 56-62.
O'Connor, N. (1954) 'Defectives Working in the Community',
    American Journal of Mental Deficiency, 57, 56-62.
Overs, R. (1970) 'Vocational Evaluation: Research and
    Implications', *Journal of Rehabilitation, 36*, 18-21.
Peckham, R. (1956) 'Problems in Job Adjustment of the
    Mentally Retarded Children in Selected Ohio Cities',
    Exceptional Child, 23, 58-62.
Penrose, L. S. (1963) *The Biology of Mental Defect*,
    Sidgwick & Jackson, London.
Peterson, D. R., Quay, H. C., Cameron, G. R. (1959)
    'Personality and Background Factors in Juvenile
    Delinquency as Inferred from Questionnaire Responses',
    Journal of Consulting Psychology, 23, 395-398.
Peterson, R. C. & Jones, E. M. (1964) *Guide to Jobs for the
    Mentally Retarded* (Rev. ed.), American Institute for
    Research, Pittsburgh.
Phelps, H. R. (1956) 'Post School Adjustment of Mentally
    Retarded Children in Selected Ohio Cities', *Exceptional
    Child, 23*, 58-62.
Potts, J. H. (1952) 'Vocational Rehabilitation of the
    Mentally Retarded in Michigan', *American Journal of
    Mental Deficiency, 57*, 297-320.
Public Law 93-380 (1974) *Education Amendments Act*,
    Washington.

Public Law 94-142 (1975) *Education of All Handicapped Children Act*, Washington.
Quay, H. & Peterson, D. (1967) *Manual for the Behaviour Problem Checklist*, University of Illinois Press, Urbana.
Rarick, L. G. & Francis, R. J. (1960) *Motor Characteristics of the Mentally Retarded*, U.S. Department of Health, Education & Welfare, Co-op, Research Monograph No. 1. Washington, D.C.
Resnick, L. (1973) 'Hierarchies in Children's Learning: A Symposium', *Instructional Science*, *2*, 311-349.
Reynolds, M. C. & Stunkard, C. L. (1960) *A Comparative Study of Day Classes versus Institutionalised Educable Retardates*, University of Minnesota, Project 192, College of Education, Minnesota.
Riches, V. (1980) 'The Efficiency of Social Interventions of the Personal Adjustment of Mildly Handicapped Adolescents', *Australian Journal of Developmental Disabilities*, *6*, 119-129.
Robinson, H. B. & Robinson, N. M. (1965) *The Mentally Retarded Child - A Psychological Approach*, McGraw-Hill, New York.
Sali, J. & Amir, M. (1971) 'Personal Factors Influencing the Retarded Person's Success at Work: A Report from Israel', *American Journal of Mental Deficiency*, *76*, 42-44.
Sarason, S. B. & Gladwin, T. (1958) 'Psychological and Cultural Problems in Mental Subnormality: A Review of Research', *American Journal of Mental Deficiency*, *62*, 1113-1307.
Schulman, L. S. (1967) *The Vocational Development of Mentally Handicapped Adolescents: An Experimental and Longitudinal Study*, Educational Publication Services, Michigan.
Shafter, A. J. (1957) 'Criteria for Selecting Institutionalised Mental Defectives for Vocational Placement', *American Journal of Mental Deficiency*, *61*, 599-616.
Shotwell, A. (1949) 'Effectiveness of Institutional Training of High Grade Mentally Defective Girls', *American Journal of Mental Deficiency*, *53*, 432-440.
Sigler, G. R. & Kokaska, C. J. (1971) 'A Job Placement Procedure for the Mentally Retarded', *Education and Training of Mentally Retarded*, *6*, 161-166.
Simches, R. (1974) 'Economic Inflation: Hazards for the Handicapped', *Exceptional Children*, *41*, 229-242.
Sinclair, G. (1983) 'Evaluation of training outcomes in an intellectually handicapped population after vocational placement', Massey University, unpublished master's thesis, Palmerston, New Zealand.

Sinclair, G. H. (1983) *Factors Effecting the Success of Intellectually Handicapped People Placed in Unsheltered Employment*, unpublished master's thesis, Massey University, Palmerston, New Zealand.

Smead, V. S. (1977) 'Ability Training and Task Analysis in Diagnostic/Perspective Teaching', *Journal of Special Education*, *11*, 113-125.

Song, A. Y. & Song, R. H. (1969) 'Prediction of Job Efficiency of Institutionalised Retardates in the Community', *American Journal of Mental Deficiency*, *73*, 567-571.

Sparks, H. L. & Younie, W. J. (1969) 'Adjustment of the Mentally Retarded: Implications for Teacher Education', *Exceptional Child*, *4*, 13-18.

Spellman, C. R. (1968) *A Follow-Up Study of 30 Educable Mentally Retarded Students from the Kansas Vocational Rehabilitation and Special Education Co-operative Project*, unpublished masters thesis, Kansas University, Kansas.

Stake, R. (1970) 'Comments on Professor Glaser's Paper', in M. C. Witbrock & D. E. Wiley (eds.), *The Evaluation of Instruction*, Holt, Rinehart, New York.

Steckel, M. L. (1934) 'A Follow-Up of Mentally Defective Girls', *Journal of Social Psychology*, *5*, 112-115.

Stein, J. V. (1963) 'Motor Functions and Physical Fitness for the Mentally Retarded: A Critical Review', *Rehabilitation Literature*, *24*, 230-242.

Stodden, R. A., Casale, J. & Scwartz, S. E. (1977) 'Work Evaluation and the Retarded. Review and Recommendations', *Mental Retardation*, *15*, 25-27.

Taylor, M. (1925) 'After Care Study', *Ungraded*, *11*, 25-34.

Thomas, H. P. (1928) 'The Employment History of Auxiliary Pupils between 16 and 21 Years of Age in Springfield, Massachusetts', *Journal of Psychology Asthen*, *33*, 132-148.

Thompson, G. H. (1968) *Social and Vocational Adjustment of Leavers from Special Classes*, Canterbury University, unpublished masters thesis, Christchurch, New Zealand.

Timmerman, W. J. & Doctor, A. C. (1974) *Special Applications of Work Evaluation Techniques for Prediction of Employability of the Trainable Mentally Retarded*, Quadio Rehabilitation Centre, Ohio.

Tizard, J. (1974) 'Longitudinal and Follow-Up Studies', in A. M. Clarke & A. D. B. Clarke (eds.), *Mental Deficiency: The Changing Outlook* (3rd ed.), Methuen, London.

Van Etten, C. & Van Etten, G. (1976) 'The Measurement of Pupil Progress and Selecting Instructional Materials', *Journal of Learning Disabilities*, *9*, 469-480.

Voelker, P. H. (1963) *The Value of Certain Selected Factors in Predicting Early Post-School Employment for White Educable Mentally Retarded Males,* unpublished doctoral dissertation, Michigan University, Michigan.

Walls, R. T. & Werner, T. J. (1977) 'Vocational Behaviour Checklists', *Mental Retardation, 15,* 30-35.

Ward, J., Parmenter, T. J., Riches, V. & Hauritz, M. (1981) 'Predicting the Outcomes of a Work Preparation Program', *Australian Journal of Developmental Disabilities, 7,* 137-145.

Warnock, M. (1978) *Report of the Committee of Enquiry into the Education of Handicapped Children and Young People,* H.M.S.O., London.

Warren, F. G. (1961) 'Ratings of Employed and Unemployed Mentally Handicapped Males on Personality and Work Factors', *American Journal of Mental Deficiency, 65,* 629-633.

White, R. (1973) 'Learning Hierarchies', *Review of Education Research, 43,* 361-375.

Wilden, C. J. (1974) *The Occupational and Social Adjustment of Experience Class Leavers in Otago,* unpublished masters thesis, Otago University, Dunedin, New Zealand.

Windle, C. (1962) 'Prognosis of Mental Subnormals', *American Journal of Mental Deficiency.*

Winnifred, C. A. (1926) 'Follow-Up Survey of Children in the Developmental Schools of Los Angeles', Los Angeles City Schools, *Education Research Bulletin, 6,* 2-10.

Winterbourn, R. (1944) *Educating Backward Children in New Zealand,* New Zealand Council for Educational Research, Wellington.

Wolfensberger, W. (1967) 'Vocational Preparation and Occupation', in A. A. Baumeister (ed.), *Mental Retardation,* Aldine, Chicago.

Wolfensberger, W. (1972) *The Principle of Normalization in Human Service,* National Institute on Mental Retardation, Toronto.

Wood Report. (1929) *Report of the Mental Deficiency Committee,* H.M.S.O., London.

Woolley, H. T. & Hornell, H. (1921) *Feeble-Minded Ex-School Children: A Study of Children who have been Students in Cincinnati Special Schools,* Studies from the Helen S. Trounstine Foundation, Cincinnati.

Young, M. A. (1958) 'Academic Requirements of Jobs Held by the Educable Mentally Retarded in the State of Connecticut', *American Journal of Mental Deficiency, 62,* 792-802.

Chapter Three

PREPARING THE MILDLY INTELLECTUALLY HANDICAPPED ADOLESCENT
FOR EMPLOYMENT AND INDEPENDENT LIVING: A RESEARCH REVIEW

Stewart Sykes and Helen Smith

INTRODUCTION

The purpose of this paper is to describe aspects of research
undertaken at a Centre which provides vocational and
independent living training for mildly intellectual handicapped adolescents and slow learners.   The Centre which
represents a new and innovative concept in services for the
handicapped in Australia, was established in 1973 as part of
the Commonwealth Rehabilitation Service administered by the
Department of Social Security.
    From 1976 to 1982 an independent team of researchers
from the Faculty of Education, Monash University, Melbourne,
Victoria conducted research at the Centre in the following
areas:

    1) Alternative pathways to employment and independence
    2) Factors associated with mild intellectual handicap
        (sensory, perceptual and motor abilities, learning
        abilities and attitudes).
    3) Parental and socio-cultural influences.
    4) Program development and implementation (work skills
        and social skills).

    Research findings in each of these areas together with
a brief description of the Centre's objectives and structure
follows.

ALTERNATIVE PATHWAYS TO EMPLOYMENT AND INDEPENDENCE

Within the state of Victoria there are a number of avenues
available for mildly intellectually handicapped (MIH)
adolescents and adults to receive pre-vocational and
vocational training and instruction in independent living
skills.   These alternative pathways are outlined below.

61

Victorian Education Department

a) Special Schools: There are 19 Day Special schools and 6 Institutional Special Schools catering for MIH students (IQ 50-70 approximately) between the ages of 4½ years to 16 years and above. At the senior levels increased attention is given to the following areas - pre-vocational, vocational and independent living skills. On the completion of their schooling many students are placed directly in either sheltered or open employment (Ward and Sykes, 1981).

b) Special Development Schools: While most of the MIH students attend Special Schools, some are accommodated in 25 Special Developmental Schools which provide programmes mainly for moderately to profoundly handicapped persons. The senior students (up to 21 years of age) receive some training in pre-vocational skills and independent living skills.

c) Work Education Centres: Three Centres provide addition- al opportunities for MIH adolescents who require further training in work habits and skills (Linardos and Sykes, 1982).

d) Technical and Further Education (TAFE) Programs: Approximately 36 programmes are offered by TAFE for 16 year old and above MIH students and slow learners. While a range of programmes are provided, most focus on the development of vocational and independent living skills.

Health Commission (Mental Retardation Division)

Over 60 facilities provide training for moderately to profoundly intellectually handicapped persons in social competence and, where appropriate, pre-vocational and vocational skills.

Voluntary Organisations

The activities of voluntary organisations are highly significant in the provision of services for handicapped persons. Day Training Centres, catering for mixed dis- ability groups including MIH persons, offer programmes to develop social and work related skills.

Department of Social Security (Commonwealth Rehabilitation Service)

a) Work Adjustment Centre: Disabled persons, including those with MIH receive industrial training as preparation for employment in a variety of semi-skilled occupations.

b) Work Preparation Centres: Two centres provide a comprehensive work preparation training programme for MIH adolescents and slow learners. A brief description of the role and structure of one of the Centres follows.

WORK PREPARATION CENTRE - ROLE AND STRUCTURE

As mentioned the Centre prepares MIH adolescents and young adults and slow learners for open and sheltered employment and independent living (Atkinson and Sykes, 1980).

Who Attends the Centre?

To be eligible, the trainee must:

1) be aged between 15½ and 19 years on referral,
2) be MIH or a slow learner (IQ range approximately 65-85),
3) need vocational and social skills training,
4) have no major psychiatric or behavioural problems,
5) have major medical problems stablised,
6) be able to travel to the Centre on public transport independently (after training if necessary),
7) be motivated towards work in open employment in one or more of the following areas,
          factory process work
          packing
          machine operations
          cleaning
          kitchen hand
8) have the potential for open employment and independent living after a training period of 12-18 months.

Referrals to the Centre

Referrals are usually made from the following sources:

a) Parents, friends or relatives
b) School counsellors, principals, teachers
c) Employment agencies

d) Doctors, psychologists, hospital staff
e) Social workers, welfare officers
f) Community service agencies
g) Department of Social Security

Selection of Trainees

Each potential trainee is assessed in areas including cognitive, language and perceptual-motor abilities, motivation and social skills. The Centre staff also interviews the parents. Some applicants will have an individual interview and a work trial. If the person meets the selection criteria, he or she is admitted for training which includes an initial two month trial period. Approximately 50 trainees attend the Centre at any one time.

Training Program

The Centre's programme is divided into three levels.

1. Introduction and Orientation
2. Pre-vocational, Social and Educational Training
3. Vocational Training

In levels 1 and 2, the emphasis is on the development of educational, personal and social skills and basic work habits and skills. Following a successful trial period the trainee enters level 2 and progresses through the various work skills programmes at their own rate - depending on ability and motivation. During level 3 the major emphasis is on the development and extension of work habits and skills in a factory environment.

Training is structured to meet individual needs and is provided in the following areas:

1) Community Living Skills: Reading, calculating, measurement, time-telling, banking, money handling, budgeting, shopping, travelling and community awareness.
2) Personal and Social Skills: Self-expression and communication, forming relationships, citizenship, sex education, assertiveness, using leisure time, personal care skills including hygiene and grooming, choice and care of clothes, preparation of meals.
3) Work Habits and Skills: Appropriate work habits, general and specific work skills, job choice skills, job-seeking skills and job-maintaining skills.

Staff at the Centre

The following staff are employed at the Centre

Full Time
- Program Director
- Social Worker
- Occupational Therapist
- Welfare Officer
- Vocational Counsellor
- Workshop Manager
- Storeman

Trade Staff
- 6 Instructors
- 2 Foremen

Office Staff
- 3 Clerical/Administrative Staff
- 1 Receptionist

Sessional Staff
- 2 Teachers
- 1 Psychologist
- 1 Speech Therapist
- 1 Dietician

Placement Following Training

After reaching the standard considered appropriate for open employment, trainees are assisted in finding suitable work. The vocational counsellor assists trainees to register at the Commonwealth Employment Service and seeks appropriate employment, but trainees and their families are also encouraged to find their own work if possible. Some subsidies are available to encourage employers to assist trainees find employment.

Trainees who find difficulty in attaining the standard necessary for competitive open employment may be referred to a sheltered workshop or other rehabilitation centres. Some will prefer part-time or voluntary work. All trainees are followed up for at least six months after leaving the Centre.

SELECTED CHARACTERISTICS OF TRAINEES ATTENDING THE WORK PREPARATION CENTRE: A SUMMARY OF RESEARCH

A series of studies investigating selected characteristics of trainees attending the Centre between November 1978 and June 1979 was undertaken. It was envisaged that the information gained would be useful in planning educational, social and work skills programmes.

WORK PREPARATION CENTRE: AN OVERVIEW OF ACTIVITIES

REFERRALS	TRAINING PROGRAMS		PLACEMENT
	LEVELS 1 AND 2 MAJOR EMPHASIS	LEVEL 3 MAJOR EMPHASIS	
EDUCATION DEPARTMENT - SPECIAL SCHOOLS - SECONDARY SCHOOLS - PRIVATE SCHOOLS	1. SELECTION AND TRIAL PLACEMENT 2. EDUCATIONAL PERSONAL AND SOCIAL SKILLS 3. BASIC WORK HABITS AND SKILLS	1. WORK HABITS AND SKILLS - ASSEMBLING AND PACKAGING - DRILLING AND TURNING - WIRING AND SOLDERING - WELDING AND PAINTING - STAMPING AND PRESSING ETC. 2. WORK THERAPY IN OUTSIDE EMPLOYMENT	OPEN EMPLOYMENT MACHINE OPERATION PACKING, ASSEMBLING, FACTORY HAND, CLEANING, KITCHEN HAND, CHILD MINDING, ETC.
DEPARTMENT OF EMPLOYMENT AND INDUSTRIAL RELATIONS			SHELTERED WORKSHOPS
DEPARTMENT OF SOCIAL SECURITY			REHABILITATION CENTRES
OTHER GOVERNMENT DEPARTMENTS			TRAINING CANCELLED
COMMUNITY SERVICE AGENCIES			VOLUNTARY WORK
MEDICAL PRACTITIONERS			
PARENTS AND OTHERS	GENERAL SOCIAL PROGRAMME, INCLUDING OUTINGS, CAMPING, DANCING DURATION: BETWEEN 2-12 MONTHS AVERAGE: 5 MONTHS	BETWEEN 2-12 MONTHS 6 MONTHS	

The total number of trainees attending the Centre in November 1978 was 51 (males = 26, females = 25) with an average chronological age of 17 years 8 months (Range 15-6 to 20-4) and a mean IQ of 72 (Range 61-89). Although there was some movement of trainees through the Centre during this series of studies, the total number in attendance stayed close to 50 and the sample characteristics of age and IQ varied only marginally. A brief summary of the findings of these studies follows.

Auditory Abilities

The following tests were administered to 51 trainees.

1. Pure Tone Audiometry
2. Tympanometry   Audiometric Assessment
3. Acoustic Reflex Threshold Test
4. Speech Reception Threshold Test
5. Speech Discrimination Test (Goldman, Fristoe and
    Woodcock, 1974)
6. Selective Attention Test (Goldman, Fristoe and
    Woodcock, 1974)
7. Visual Aural Digit Span Test (Koppitz, 1977).

Thirty-nine per cent of the population had significant hearing loss (three or more thresholds at or above 25 decibels (ISO) in one or both ears). Difficulties processing aurally presented information involving short-term memory were experienced by 62 per cent. Of the 23 trainees who showed poor short-term memory ability 19 had unsatisfactory attentional skills. The incidence of aural hygiene problems emerged as a matter of particular concern during the survey (Mooney and Best, 1981).

Visual Perceptual Abilities

Fifty trainees were assessed by the following tests.

1) The Motor-Free Visual Perception Test (MVPT,
    Colarusso and Hammill, 1972).
2) Revised Visual Retention Test (RVRT, Benton, 1974).
3) The Weber Advanced Spatial Perception Test (WASP,
    Weber, 1968).
4) Farnsworth Dichotomous Test of Colour Blindness
    (Farnsworth, 1947).

Results indicated that many trainees had visual perceptual difficulties. On the MVPT only 24 trainees reached

the test ceiling of a perceptual age of 9.0 years. Performance on the RVRT suggested that the trainees were working at
a level comparable to 11 and 12 year olds with an IQ of
70-79. The WASP results confirmed that the trainees were
functioning well below age level, with the mean results for
the group not attaining the 13 year old level in any of the
four sub-tests. Only one trainee was identified as being
colour blind. The range of scores obtained made generalisation difficult but specific weaknesses were indicated in
visual attention to detail, visual memory and visual closure
(Duerdoth and Nettleton, 1982).

Motor Abilities

Four tests were administered to 48 traines to assess motor
and perceptual-motor abilities.

1. Right-Left Orientation Test (Benton and Spreen, 1969)
2. Crawford Small Parts Dexterity Test (Crawford and
   Crawford, 1956)
3. The Minnesota Rate of Manipulation Tests
4. The Purdue Pegboard (Tiffin, 1968).

Results of testing and direct observations suggested
that the trainees were generally proficient in fine-motor
dexterity, manipulation and co-ordination. While some
performed the tasks at a relatively slow rate, due basically
to a lack of fine motor fluency, all trainees were considered to have sufficient fine-motor skills to enable them to
commence the work skills training programme.
Where specific deficiencies were identified, for
instance, lack of left-right orientation on confrontation,
these were discussed with the instructors who were then able
to plan and implement appropriate activities in the work
skills training programme (Akerstein and Sykes, 1982).

Academic Abilities

The following tests were administered to 50 trainees.

1. Neale Analysis of Reading Ability - Form A (Neale,
   1958)
2. Word Identification Test (ACER, 1972)
3. Slosson Oral Reading Test (Slosson, 1963)
4. Graded Spelling Test (Daniels and Diack, 1958)
5. Keymath Diagnostic Arithmetic Test (Connolly, Nachtman
   and Pritchett, 1971).

Results of testing can be summarised in the following way. In most areas performances varied considerably among the trainees with a range of between 5 to 7 years being common. The mean reading ages of the trainees were - rate (9 years 9 months), accuracy (9 years 7 months), comprehension (8 years 7 months), word recognition (10 years 5 months) and the average spelling age was 9 years 5 months. In mathematics, a mean numeracy age of 8 years 11 months was obtained with the greatest difficulty being experienced in the following areas - fractions, mathematical reasoning and measurement. The extent of development in language and numeracy during the trainees' stay at the Centre was also measured. Twenty-six trainees were selected to determine progress over approximately six months. The following average gains were recorded - reading accuracy and rate (1 month), reading comprehension (5 months), spelling (4 months), numeracy (6 months) (Turner and Sykes, 1982).

Self- and Work-Ratings and Attitudes

The trainees opinions and attitudes concerning their interests, training and work skills and habits were obtained using a modified version of Speake and Whelan's (1977) *'Me at Work'* rating scale (Turner and Sykes, 1982). The scale has two sections - Section A - Attitudes about work, contains 30 questions and Section B - Attitudes about myself, consists of 17 questions.

An analysis of the responses of the 50 trainees revealed a number of interesting findings. Prominent among these were the following:

1. A very positive attitude to
   a) The Centre (which was seen to develop work skills and habits, social and personal skills),
   b) work and related behaviours,
   c) instructors and supervisors.
2. Generally high positive feelings towards self, peers and fellow workers.
3. An awareness of the need to get on well with fellow workers.
4. A generally confident outlook concerning future work and success.

Trainees in their final stages of training expressed a more positive attitude to light industrial-type work and were more confident about themselves and their future than trainees in the earlier stages of training.

Despite the strong emphasis on light industrial-type training, a substantial proportion of trainees indicated a preference to work in other areas such as gardening, service and clerical work, cleaning, child minding, once they leave the Centre. This finding highlights the following actions or needs. It is necessary:

1. to determine trainees vocational interests and aspirations, during the initial selection process,
2. to broaden the scope of training to include other types of work training (for example, gardening, service and clerical work, child minding, printing and sewing),
3. to carefully monitor the trainees' progress and, where necessary, refer them to other more appropriate training centres,
4. to establish other work preparation centres which could specialise in particular types of training.

PARENTAL AND SOCIO-CULTURAL INFLUENCES

A growing body of literature in the late 1970s stressed the importance of parental involvement in the context of vocational guidance and training for intellectually handicapped adolescents (Brolin, 1976; Mittler, 1976; Whelan and Speake, 1977; Centre for Educational Research and Innovation, OECD, 1978). The important conclusion was that failure to involve parents led to unrealistic expectations about the future. A research study was therefore undertaken to provide insights into the home background influences of all trainees attending the Centre at a particular time. A home interview schedule was developed to provide data on parents' perceptions and expectations, which could then determine the need for parental involvement and support in future programming. The basic aims were to:

a) assess how parents perceived and accepted their mildly intellectually handicapped son or daughter,
b) determine whether they did in reality want and expect him or her to behave as a young adult, and be a member of the adult workforce,
c) to discover whether parents understood and agreed with the Centre's training philosophy which encouraged trainees to aim for maximum independence, and
d) to assess any reinforcement at home which encouraged the practice of new social skills and work skills acquired at the Centre.

The trainee population for this study totalled 43, 21 males and 22 females, with an age range from 16-21 years. The results of the study showed that many trainees were still home-based and family dependent (Smith, 1980; Smith and Sykes, 1980). Some parents were even prolonging the dependence of their young people, rather than reinforcing the training in independent living skills at the Centre. Independent banking illustrates this point. Despite detailed training and practice in independent banking at the Centre, a third of the trainees still had their money supervised and banked by family members. Six trainees had their daily clothes laid out by their mothers and the same number rarely travelled alone on public transport, except to and from the Centre which was a daily requirement. Parents preferred to drive rather than allow the practice of independent travel skills. From comments it was clear that many of these parents did not fully understand or agree with the training goals of independence.

The social relationships and activities of the trainees were few and limited. Nearly half the group spent most of their free time with their families at home; in fact 58 per cent were never or rarely visited in their own homes by friends, and 49 per cent never or rarely went to visit friends. The weekend activity mentioned most frequently was *home chores*, and even then the chores rarely icluded basic survival skills such as supermarket shopping independently. The Centre aims to help trainees extend their social contacts and parents were aware of a lack of friends and leisure time interests. But they seemed unable to channel their concern in a constructive way, and needed guidance to reinforce interests being developed at the Centre.

Most parents expected trainees to be placed in work, directly following their training at the Centre, without much difficulty. But more than half the trainees (58 per cent) were expected by parents to have difficulty keeping a job, that is, sustaining and consolidating an employment role. They suggested such reasons as lack of self confidence, poor social interaction, and behaviour problems, thus confirming the relevance of social and interpersonal factors reported by Peterson and Foss (1980). Parents were clearly anxious about these critical first weeks in trial employment and needed supportive contact themselves.

SOCIO-CULTURAL INFLUENCES: A FOLLOW-UP STUDY

A follow-up study (Smith, 1981) was made to examine the life situations of a selected group of ex-trainees two years or more after they had completed vocational and social training at the Centre. Although Cobb's 1972 review of earlier follow-up studies emphasised competitive employment as the main criteria of a successful life situation, Edgerton and Bercovici (1976) noted a change of emphasis to personal satisfaction with quality of life. Therefore this study focussed on the total life situation, not merely vocational

71

success, and the ex-trainees' assessment of their social and interpersonal adjustment.

Interview discussions were held with 34 ex-trainees, 16 males and 18 females, all of whom were aged 22 or over. At that time 29 per cent had jobs in open employment and 18 per cent were unemployed but had been employed and were actively looking for work, so about half the subjects had some experience of competitive employment. Slightly less than half (41 per cent) attended sheltered workshops or activity centres and 12 per cent were at home.

Most of the subjects currently employed, or attending workshops or Centres, reported satisfaction with the quality of their lives. The latter often referred to their daily occupation as *going to work* and considered their life-style superior to that of young adults unable to find a job. The subjects looking for work seemed depressed and even those with other interests in their lives were pre-occupied by their lack of work. Greatest life satisfaction was noted by subjects with friends and interests and a definite weekday occupation.

None of the subjects lived independently: three stayed in residential hostels, the others were still with their parents. Despite their training in independent living skills at the Centre, only five females and one male seemed competent or even to practise domestic skills. In fact independent living was not seen as a relevant goal, by ex-trainees or their families.

Only 3 of the 34 subjects - all males - had driving licences. Some of the subjects no longer travelled independently, although they had all done so as trainees. Independent money handling was no longer practised by some. The parents of a few trainees had retired and as a result did more rather than less for their sons and daughters. It must be concluded from this follow-up study that many parents represent disabling rather than enabling transition agents (Mercer, 1978), when they restrict attempts to increase and practise independence.

These studies highlighted the overall level of functioning in the trainees over a range of relevant areas, provided important guidelines for general programme development (in reading, numeracy, social skills and work skills) and identified the special needs of individual trainees. The following sections provide information about the development and implementation of two programmes - work skills and social skills.

WORK SKILLS TRAINING PROGRAMME

Results of the comprehensive assessment of trainees at the Centre suggested that they possessed the necessary prerequisite skills and attitudes to commence training in the area of light industrial engineering.

During the planning stage of the training programmes one member of the research team joined with the foreman and instructors of Level 2 at the Centre.

While a variety of training approaches are referred to in the literature (Gold, 1973; Brolin, 1976; Whelan, 1977) it was decided that *learning modules* or *learning packages* would be appropriate in teaching the trainees to use selected tools and machines.

General Principles of the Program

In developing the learning modules the following principles were incorporated.

1) structured, systematic presentation of aims and procedures
2) tasks broken down into sequential steps
3) individualisation of instruction
4) use of verbal and visual instructions
5) reinforced practice
6) tangible signs of progress.

Purposes of the Program

While the basic purpose of the programme was to develop appropriate work skills and habits through the use of selected tools and machinery, additional outcomes were also planned. These included

a) the development of relevant basic abilities (perceptual-motor skills, fine-motor co-ordination and manipulation), social academic skills (reading, writing, numeracy) and social skills (group interaction, forming relationships)
b) the acquisition of self-instructional strategies
c) the transfer of training to a variety of other tasks and settings
d) increased motivation for light industrial work
e) positive encouragement and experience of success.

Five work skill training programmes were developed using the following machines or tools: Bench drill, power press, soldering iron, spot welder, turret lathe. For the purposes of this paper the bench drill programme format is presented, however each of the five programmes has the same basic plan and contains several components which are described below.

1.   Instructors' Aims and Checklist
A list of the basic instructional aims and procedures is
provided and includes the following sections:
     Parts of the machine
     Operations - Safety Factors (clothing and machine)
     Operations - Production of Work
     Operations - Quality of Work.

2.   Trainee's Assessment Checklist and Guidelines
A detailed assessment checklist is provided together with
instructional   guidelines   to   be   used   in   assessing   the
trainee's knowledge and performance in the following areas.
     Parts of the Machine (18 point checklist of knowledge)
     Operations - Safety (14 point checklist of knowledge)
     Operations - Production of Work
               using a jig and clamp (18 point checklist
               of performance)
               using a vice and bolt (12 point checklist
               of performance)
               changing a drill (11 point checklist of
               performance)
     Operations - Quality of Work (11 point checklist of
               performance)
The guidelines were included to:
     - achieve consistency in assessment
     - ease the work load of instructors and assessors
     - pinpoint any areas of uncertainty or difficulty
     - give the trainee the opportunity to experience
       success and satisfaction
     - aid in assessing the efficacy of training.

3.   Trainee's Practice Exercise and Guidelines
A list of exercises and activities is provided for each
trainee including reading and writing words, labelling
diagrams,   answering   questions   and   matching   cards   to
supplement the practical work and reinforce learning in the
following areas.
     Parts of the Machine
     Operations - Safety
     Operations - Production of Work
     Operations - Quality of Work.
The specific objectives of these exercises were to
     - extend vocabulary
     - reinforce language, reading and numeracy skills
     - give practice in following a series of simple
       instructions
     - develop logical thought processes
     - assist in using judgement
     - develop self-confidence and work satisfaction

- encourage self-assessment and correction
- develop the ability to organise written material
- develop independence in learning.

4. Trainee's Manual

Trainees receive a manual to use while they are learning about the particular machine or tool and to keep for later revision and use within and outside the Centre. The manuals are written in a clear and simple style and provide a summary of relevant parts and operations and a list of key words.

SOCIAL SKILLS TRAINING PROGRAMME

The importance of social skills training for this population is repeatedly cited in the literature, particularly as an important factor in vocational success (Brown, 1972; Brolin, 1976; Whelan and Speake, 1977). From the wide range of behaviour described as social skills, certain dimensions have special importance. Malgady, Barcher, Towner and Davis (1979) noted verbal manners and communication skills as the most significant, from their comprehensive factor analysis. Matson and Earnhart (1981) noted that transfer of social learning is optimised when part of the training takes place in the natural community environment. Kehle and Barclay (1979) pointed out that attempts to integrate intellectually handicapped persons without successful social skills training, led to further feelings of inadequacy and isolation. Adkins and Matson (1980) cited research to show that increased experience of socially appropriate behaviour led to reduced time in inappropriate behaviour. Matson and Andrasik (1982) concluded that individuals were much more likely to be well accepted by the community in general when they are trained to refrain from making inappropriate requests and negative statements about others. It was also noted by Matson and Earnhart (1981) that transfer of social learning is optimised when part of the training takes place in the natural community environment.

At the Centre, trainees with social skills deficits are given training in small groups. The programme, devised by Centre staff, aims to develop trainee's confidence and competence in common social situations. Training takes place at the Centre and also in the community. As part of this project, a Social Skills Handbook was developed as resource material, for the instructor to select exercises relevant to each group's particular needs.

The handbook is in four sections:

1. Self-concept building skills
2. Inter-personal communication skills
3. Skills for behaviour in public
4. Social skills in work training.

An individual assessment record lists the skills in each section and provides for ratings to be made by the instructor, using a 5-point scale. The form is simple and allows for ratings made at different times to be entered on one sheet so that performance changes are clear in feedback discussion with each trainee. Training methods include discussion, role play, demonstration, use of video and tape recorder, co-operative tasks, use of written and oral materials, memory testing and practical homework assignments.

Examples from the four sections of the handbook are given below:

Section 1. <u>Self-concept building skills</u>
　　　　　　　3. <u>Success is...</u>
　　　Have the group think of anything each enjoys doing and *can do well*.
　　　Some prompts may help:
　　　e.g. Mastery of current, or a previous job skill.
　　　　　Leisure time activities (who has tried any of the new ones at the Centre?)
　　　　　Cooking.
　　　　　Playing with young brothers/sisters/-neighbours.
　　　　　Cutting the lawn.
　　　Some groups might enjoy drawing a picture to illustrate what they do, and then explain it to the others.
　　　Then ask the group to think about something they cannot do well just now but would like to do well. Have a discussion about these wished-for skills; encourage group members to suggest and consider for each other possible ways to improve their present level of performance. Aim to extend thinking to a range of skills which may not seem possible yet; use example of blind person skiing.

Section 2. Inter-personal communication skills
　　　Skill 5: To Make Appropriate Facial Expressions and Gestures with Attentive Appearance
　　　Exercise 2
　　　Use tape recorded items for the following:
　　　(a) Joke being told.
　　　(b) Account of distressing incident.

76

(c) Frightening story.
(d) Confusing/puzzling account of some happening.
Play these and video tape group's reaction:
(leader may react with appropriate expression and
gestures slightly exaggerated). Re-play video
tape and praise appropriate responses from group
members. If necessary, indicate leader's
responses as models.

Section 3. Skills for behaviour in public
    Skill 6: To Approach Strangers Politely
    Exercise 1
        Ask group members to suggest different situations
        where it is appropriate to approach strangers -
        list these on board.
        (a) Ask directions to the National Gallery.
        (b) In the bank, ask for an interview with the
            manager.
        (c) At the post office, ask for a parcel being
            kept for you.
        (d) At the dentist, make an appointment for
            treatment.
        (e) Explain to receptionist at a factory that you
            have come for an interview.
        (f) In a restaurant, explain to waiter that you
            are to join friends already there.
        (g) In a bowling centre, ask receptionist's
            advice as to what to do.
        (h) In a shop, ask sales assistant for help in
            choosing a fishing rod.
        Have each person take turns to role-play their
        card, asking for volunteers to be the stranger
        approached. After each role-play encourage group
        to discuss alternative things to say and do in
        that particular situation.

Section 4. Social skills in work training
    Skill 4: To Greet and Talk With Workmates
             Appropriately
    Exercise 2
        Have discussion about tea-breaks and lunch breaks
        at the Centre and how these help to get to know
        people.
        Divide group into pairs, making sure that the
        trainees paired do not normally spend breaks
        together. Send pairs to different parts of room
        to chat together for five minutes, and find out
        something new about each other, even if just a
        recent outing the other made. Then form groups of
        three or four people and repeat the exercise.

Emphasise the opportunity of making friends at the
Centre at meal-break times.
Ask group members about reasons for limiting talk
with workmates during work-time, not distracting
others from their job, and sometimes even the
dangers of distraction.

EVALUATION AND DISSEMINATION OF RESEARCH

Following the development and implementation of the work
skills training programme and the social skills programme,
staff at the Centre and other interested persons were
invited to evaluate the appropriateness and efficacy of
these programmes. This on-going evaluation and modification
are seen as crucial aspects of programmatic research.
An integral part of the Centre's activities is the
dissemination of research reports and programmes through
workshops, in-service sessions, lectures, seminars and
visits for teachers, psychologists, social workers and other
human service providers. In these ways the Centre has acted
as an important resource centre, a vital catalyst for
further research and development and a significant stimulus
to heighten the interest and increase the activities of
other government agencies and services provided in the
vocational training of MIH adolescents and slow learners.

SUMMARY

This report has focused attention on two broad factors
considered important in the successful vocational and social
habilitation of MIH persons, namely, the competences of the
individual seeking employment and parental support and
encouragement. Other prominent factors, which were beyond
the scope of our research project and which obviously demand
detailed investigation include the attitude of employers to
handicapped workers, the type of work available and the
prevailing economic and labour market conditions.
As a result of our studies and the recommendations of
other writers and reports (Brolin, 1976; Warnock, 1978;
Mittler, 1979; Mann and Gregory, 1981) the following needs
emerge as warranting careful attention and investigation.

1. The development of more work and life preparation
   centres or units.
2. Closer co-operation between special education and those
   agencies providing vocational habilitation services.
3. The provision of continuing or recurrent educational
   programmes to reinforce learned skills and behaviours
   and to develop new skills.

4. The provision of parent education programmes.
5. The exploration of alternative areas of employment for instance, service and clerical work, horticulture, printing, sewing and cleaning.
6. The development of *significant living without work* activities (Warnock, 1978). Activities that are productive (for instance, crafts, domestic skills, horticultural skills) and leisure or recreational (for instance, games, sports, hobbies).
7. The promotion of MIH persons' special competencies.
8. Greater incentives for employers to employ MIH persons.
9. The establishment of sheltered work stations or enclaves within open industry.
10. Legislative action extended to protect MIH persons against forms of vocational discrimination.

Handicapped persons should receive every possible opportunity to lead satisfying and fulfilling lives. Carefully prepared rehabilitation programmes, which focus on the development of independent living skills and vocational skills, play a crucial role in assisting these persons display their true potentials, cope with either open or sheltered employment, and assimilate successfully into society.

This chapter has focused on aspects of programmatic research. The planning, development, production and implementation of these programmes have involved the close, collaborative efforts of Centre staff and a Monash University research team.

Obviously it is necessary for these programmes to be evaluated, both within the Centre, in schools and other training centres to assess their appropriateness and efficacy.

The Centre needs to continue its crucial role as a resource centre in vocational education for handicapped persons, encouraging new practices and research, disseminating programmes and information and assisting in further programme development, modification and evaluation.

REFERENCES

Adkins, J. and Matson, J. L. (1980) 'Teaching Institutionalized Mentally Retarded Adults Socially Appropriate Leisure Skills', *Mental Retardation, Vol. 18*, pp. 249-252.

Akerstein, G. and Sykes, S. (1982) *A Survey of the Motor Abilities of EMR Adolescents at a Victorian Work Preparation Centre,* MAT Report 16, December.

Atkinson, E. and Sykes, S. (1980) *A Description of the Work Preparation Centre at South Yarra,* MAT Report 5, May.

Australian Council for Educational Research (1971) *Word Identification Test*, Melbourne.

Benton, A. (1974) *Revised Visual Retention Test*, The Psychological Corporation, New York.

Benton, A. and Spreen, O. (1969) *Benton Right-Left Orientation Test*, University of Victoria, Victoria, B.C.

Brolin, D. (1976) *Vocational Preparation of Retarded Citizens*, Charles E. Merrill Publishing Company, Ohio.

Brown, R. I. (1972) 'Research to Practice', International Research Seminar on Vocational Rehabilitation of the Mentally Retarded (Special Publications Series), *American Association for Mental Deficiency, Vol. 1*, pp. 263-268.

Centre for Educational Research and Innovation (1978) *The Education of the Handicapped Adolescent*, OECD.

Colarusso, R. and Hammill, D. (1972) *Motor Free Visual Perception Test*, Academic Therapy, California.

Cobb, H. V. (1972) *The Forecast of Fulfillment*, Teachers College Press.

Connolly, A., Nachtman, W. and Pritchett, E. (1971) *Keymath Diagnostic Arithmetic Test*, AGS, Minnesota.

Crawford, J. and Crawford, D. (1956) *Crawford Small Parts Dexterity Test*, The Psychological Corporation, New York.

Daniels, J. and Diack, H. (1958) *The Standard Reading Tests*, Chatto and Windus, London.

Duerdoth, P. and Nettleton, N (1982) *A Survey of the Visual Perceptual Abilities of EMR Adolescents at a Victorian Work Preparation Centre*, MAT Report 14, December.

Edgerton, R. B., and Bercovici, S. M. (1976) 'The Cloak of Competence: Years Later', *American Journal of Mental Deficiency, 80*, No. 5, pp. 485-497.

Farnsworth, D. (1947) *The Farnsworth Dichotomous Test for Colour Blindness*, The Psychological Corporation, New York.

Gold, M. (1973) 'Research on the Vocational Habilitation of the Retarded: The Present, the Future', in N. R. Ellis (ed.), *International Review of Research in Mental Retardation, 6*, Academic Press, New York.

Goldman, R., Fristoe, M. and Woodcock, R. (1974) *Goldman-Fristoe Woodcock Auditory Skills Battery*, AGS Inc., Minnesota.

Kehle, T. J. and Barclay, J. R. (1979) 'Social and Behavioural Characteristics of Mentally Handicapped Students', *Journal of Research and Development in Education, 12*, No. 4, pp.45-56.

Koppitz, E. (1977) *The Visual Aural Digit Span Test*, Grune and Stratton, New York.

Linardos, G. and Sykes, S. (1982) *A Program for Teaching Mildly Intellectually Handicapped Adolescents to use an Industrial Sewing Machine*, MAT Report 15, December.

Malgady, R. G., Barcher, P. R., Towner, G. and Davis, J. (1979) 'Language Factors in Vocational Evaluation of Mentally Retarded Workers', *American Journal of Mental Deficiency, 83*, No.5, pp. 432-438.

Matson, J. L. and Andrasik, F. (1982) 'Training Leisure Time Social Interpretation Skills to Mentally Retarded Adults', *American Journal of Mental Deficiency, 86*, No.5, pp.533-542.

Matson, J. L. and Earnhart, T. (1981) 'Programming Treatment Effects to the Natural Environment. A Procedure for Training Institutionalized Retarded Adults', *Behavior Modification, 5*, pp. 27-38.

Mann, W. and Gregory, A. (1981) *The Employment Environment for Mildly Intellectually Handicapped Young People*, Education Faculty, Monash University, Melbourne, Australia.

Mercer, J. R. (1978) 'Theoretical Constructs of Adaptive Behaviour: Movement from a Medical to a Social-Ecological Perspective', in W. A. Coulter and H. W. Morrow (eds.), *Adaptive Behaviour: Concepts and Measurement*, Grune and Stratton, New York.

Minnesota Rate of Manipulation Tests, (1969) University of Minnesota, AGS, Minnesota.

Mittler, P. (1976) 'Planning for the Future', In R. J. Kedney and E. Whelan (eds.), *The Education of Mentally Handicapped Young Adults*, Bolton College of Education.

Mittler, P. (1979) *People Not Patients*, Methuen and Co. Ltd., London.

Mooney, J. and Best, G. (1981) *A Survey of the Auditory Abilities of EMR Adolescents at a Victorian Work Preparation Centre*, MAT Report 9, February.

Neale, M. (1958) *Neale Analysis of Reading Ability*, MacMillan Education Ltd., London.

Peterson, S. and Foss, G. (1980) *An Identification of Social/Inter personal Skills Relevant to Job Tenure for Mentally Retarded Adults*, Centre Paper No. 115, Rehabilitation Research and Training Centre in Mental Retardation, University of Oregon, Eugene, Oregon.

Slosson, R. (1963) *Slosson Oral Reading Test*, Slosson Educational Publications Inc., New York.

Smith, H. (1980) *Assessment of Home Background Influences on Selected Trainees Attending the South Yarra Work Preparation Centre*, MAT Report 3, May.

Smith, H. (1981) *The Life Situations of Some Mildly Intellectually Handicapped Young Adults: A Follow-up Study*, MAT Report 11, August.

81

Smith, H. and Sykes, S. (1980) *Assessment of Home Background Influences on Selected Trainees Attending the South Yarra Work Preparation Centre (A Summary of Results)*, MAT Report 4, March.

Speake, B. and Whelan, E. (1977) *Young Persons' Work Preparation Courses - A Systematic Evaluation*, Hester Adrian Research Centre, The University of Manchester, England.

Tiffin, J. (1968) *Purdue Pegboard*, Purdue Research Foundation, SRA.

Turner, M. and Sykes, S. (1982) *A Study of the Self Concept Motivations and Work Attitudes of Trainees Attending the South Yarra Work Preparation Centre*, MAT Report 16, December.

Ward, B. and Sykes, S. (1981) *A Study of the Post School Placement of Leavers from a Victorian Education Department Day Special School*, MAT Report 10, August.

Warnock, M. (1978) *Special Education Needs*, Report of the Committee of Enquiry into the Education of Handicapped Children and Young People, HMSO, London.

Weber, P. (1968) *Weber Advanced Spatial Perception Test*, ACER, Melbourne.

Whelan, E. (1977) 'Basic Work-Skills Training and Vocational Counselling of the Mentally Handicapped', in P. Mittler (ed.), *Research to Practice in Mental Retardation. II*, Education and Training, London: University Park Press, 377-386.

Whelan, E. and Speake, B. (1977) *Adult Training Centres in England and Wales*, National Association of Teachers of the Mentally Handicapped.

Chapter Four

ACTION RESEARCH - WORKING WITH ADULT TRAINING CENTRES IN
BRITAIN

Edward Whelan, Barbara Speake, and Thomas Strickland

INTRODUCTION

This Chapter describes the *Habilitation Technology Project*,
a programme of research funded by the Department of Health
and Social Security England, from 1977 to 1983. The project
was primarily concerned with developing and evaluating
habilitation technology for use with mentally handicapped
and developmentally delayed adolescents and adults. Working
intensively with Adult Training Centres, the goal of the
project has been to produce teaching materials for use by
them and by a wider field.
    The project has operated within an *action research*
framework, having considered the advantages of this as a
strategy for applying research to practice. The importance
of selecting the most effective means of achieving this is
argued in the first section of the Chapter. The authors
hope that two features of the project will contribute to
progress in this field: that its methodology will prove of
interest to other researchers, and that its practical
outcomes (known as the *Copewell System*, described later)
will prove of value to practitioners.

THE IMPORTANCE OF APPLYING RESEARCH TO PRACTICE

Considerable advances have been made in the field of mental
handicap since the early 1970's. Not only has there been
international agreement on a classification and major
statements of rights within the United Nations, but we have
begun to witness the growth of a self-advocacy movement.
Philosophies have shifted, legislation has followed, and
increasing numbers of mentally handicapped people are living
and working in the community.
    The acceleration towards the achievement of normalisa-
tion, however, often supported by legislation, must not be
made at the expense of proper preparation and training of

individuals. Although a great deal is now known, and demonstration projects have shown what is feasible, the advances of the last decade have done little to close the gap between research and practice. Indeed, research findings have so far been of benefit to only a small minority of individuals. Two factors appear to contribute to this: -

1) the proportion of national budgets spent on supporting research in mental handicap continues to be very small when expressed as a percentage of the amount expended on actually providing services for mentally handicapped people and their families.
2) research has often been funded with inadequate resources to permit dissemination and without any clear policy concerning the implementation of findings.

If the value of research in this field is to be recognised and investment continued, then it must be seen to contribute to the solution of real problems. Clarke (1977) placed much of the onus of this on the researcher. In concluding his presidential address to the IASSMD Congress, in Washington, he urged that:

> '...more of us must be involved in seeing that our discoveries are field tested and applied. If we do not, who will? I urge a greater involvement of us all in the corridors of power, and in the sometimes tedious dialogue with governmental agencies.'

We believe Clarke's exhortation to be timely. Free from the day-to-day responsibilities of providing a service, researchers are in a good position to show how many of the good ideas encountered on visits to field settings may be related to research findings and brought together within an overall framework of good practice. Many previous attempts, however, to influence the work of practitioners have produced only short-term effects. A number of papers have been written about these problems (for example: Brown, 1972; Mittler, 1976), and these supported our determination to seek the most effective means possible of overcoming them.

In order to do this it was necessary to learn as much as possible about the ethos and day-to-day problems experienced by practitioners. A unique opportunity for this was afforded by the invitation to conduct the First National Survey of Adult Training Centres in England and Wales (1972-1977). Through this a dialogue was established which enabled practice to influence research, not only vice-versa, as is so often attempted.

FINDINGS OF THE NATIONAL SURVEY OF ADULT TRAINING CENTRES

Adult Training Centres are the main form of community provision for mentally handicapped people over school-leaving age. There are approximately 500 in England and Wales, catering for some 41,000 trainees. Most of the adults are under the age of 35 and 80 per cent still live in the family home, attending the ATC on a daily basis. The survey embraced all ATCs and a representative sample of 36 were selected for more detailed study visits.

One of the major findings of the National Survey and its associated research programme was the small extent to which the findings of educational research were being applied within the ATCs. Between 67 per cent and 78 per cent of programmes relied mostly on unstructured methods of teaching many skills even though these had been rated as *important*, or *very important* on a 5-point scale. This was particularly true in the area of social skills which were mainly taught in an informal way and only when the opportunity arose. Staff were usually unaware of any special techniques for teaching such skills.

Staff had very little contact with researchers, were unaware of research findings, and usually even lacked opportunities to share their experience with colleagues involved in similar work. Although most claimed to carry out some form of assessment, many trainees were unassessed on those skills which research has shown to be most related to successful functioning in the community. The forms and checklists used for assessment were usually self-devised and were often poorly designed. Many Centres provided only a limited choice of activities and in most this consisted mainly of sub-contract work of a simple and repetitive nature. Although usually showing high levels of dedication and enthusiasm, most staff had received no specific training to work with handicapped people. They frequently worked in isolation, though expressing curiosity about the nature of programmes provided in Centres elsewhere. Few Centres had libraries with even basic texts on mental handicap and most staff admitted that they had little time to read even practitioner journals.

A common concern expressed by staff during the Survey related to the lack of national guidelines and an uncertainty about priorities in the provision of individual programmes of education and training. Whilst generally most courteous to the researchers, many staff were clearly despondent about the many pressures which they faced, particularly in respect of inadequate staffing and resources. Nevertheless, there was strong evidence of a growing professional awareness amongst staff, and a wish to consolidate and extend the specialist skills needed to teach mentally handicapped people.

Our main conclusion was that there was an urgent need for a follow-up programme of *research* and *development*. This should be designed so as to take account of the problems and priorities expressed by practitioners and of the various difficulties they faced. Further light was shed on these problems by our other studies carried out about this time. One was of staff responsible for Young Persons' Work Preparation Courses, run by the Manpower Services Commission (Speake and Whelan, 1977), and a second concerned staff in Work Centres for the Physically Handicapped (Schlesinger and Whelan, 1979). In addition to learning about the problems of practitioners, these early studies enabled the researchers to gain a broader understanding of the reasons why many earlier attempts at applying research to practice had proved to be unsuccessful, or short-lived. In brief, although encompassing a variety of strategies, most had provided only a *partial* solution to the problem.

EARLIER STRATEGIES FOR APPLYING RESEARCH TO PRACTICE

In attempting to communicate the results of research to practitioners, recent years have seen the appearance of new practitioner orientated journals, such as *REAP*, and the *'Journal of Practical Approaches to Developmental Handicap'*. These were a response to the complaints by practitioners that research articles were written in unintelligible jargon and that their content was probably irrelevant anyway. It is true that much research is generated in the pursuit of higher degrees or by academics whose promotion is conditional upon having large numbers of publications with *scientific* journals. Although such new journals provide an outlet for those who can spare the time to prepare reports suitable for practitioner consumption, they go only part-way towards solving the problem.

One problem of producing suitable reading material is that many practitioners prefer not to *read* about concepts such as behaviour modification, but to learn about them during practical *demonstrations*, preferably within their own working environment. Hall (1974), working with mental health nurses, used improved typeface and layout in an attempt to make reading material more attractive to them, but to no avail. Among other attempts to communicate these concepts effectively, particular mention may be made of the book by Martin and Pear (1983) entitled, *'Behaviour Modification, What It Is and How to Do It'* which is both practical and very easy to read.

Other measures to improve communication have included the organisation of joint conferences by scientific and practitioner organisations and also the formation of new associations which may span many disciplines (for example, the *Association of Professions for the Mentally Handicapped*). These efforts have certainly helped to create an improved climate for encouraging communication and consultation. Within such a forum, some have seen the similarity between research methodology, involving the set and testing of hypotheses, and the principles underlying the management and review of service delivery systems in which objectives must be set and outcomes measured. The various movements towards the accreditation of services have no doubt been helped in this way.

Unfortunately, however, by the nature of their duties, many practitioners and also researchers are unable to attend such meetings or play an active part in bridging organisations. Experience has shown that a small *conference-going* elite often emerges, though, in support of Hall's findings, the organisation of short *workshops* on specialist issues continues to be more widely popular.

Direct working links between researchers and practitioners have taken a number of forms, in particular short-term demonstration projects within field settings. These have often been well documented and shown what is feasible. Unfortunately, many apparently successful collaborative partnerships evaporate without trace once the *circus has left town* (that is, when the researchers depart). The interest and enthusiasm which staff appear to experience whilst the project is ongoing cannot be sustained under the pressure of normal daily routines, unless the collaborative effort has been aimed at reducing some of these.

Perhaps the best known attempts at bringing researchers and practitioners together have been the *mental retardation centres* (usually university affiliated facilities) in the USA. These have been designed to effect the maximum interaction between research and staff training activities under one roof and in a setting where an ongoing service (for example, vocational rehabilitation) is being provided to the local community. Once again, these have provided a powerful demonstration of what may be achieved and many such centres have achieved an international reputation as show places and leaders in the raising of professional and technical standards.

Once again, however, there are special difficulties associated with the translation of the work of such centres, usually enjoying higher than average resource levels, into the work of more typical local agencies. Staff are ready to point out that similar results would not have been possible within *their* agency, due to several adverse conditions. In some cases staff express resentment, or even hostility, at the implication that some facility, usually geographically distant from their own, could really understand their problems or should significantly affect the way they operate.

Some have advocated a massive programme of staff training as a means of bringing appropriate attitudes and more effective technology into practice. However, at present staff training programmes in themselves have proved disappointing in this respect. Klaber (1971), for example, on the basis of observations of nurse behaviour in a number of residential institutions for retarded people, found little correlation between the grades achieved by nurses upon completion of their training, either in theoretical or practical subjects, and their pattern of nursing activity some time after returning to their ward. Apparently, the prevailing attitudes and practices of the institution were too powerful to be modified by the assertions of a newly qualified member of staff, with low status in the organisation.

In conclusion, it appears that the previous attempts at a solution have only been partially successful. A radical new approach is needed if future attempts to apply research to practice are to benefit from the experiences of the past. Five basic conditions emerge as critical for future success:

1. Research carried out should be relevant to practice. One way of ensuring this is to explore areas wherein practitioners report problems.
2. The research findings should be communicated to practitioners in clear, unambiguous language. There should be joint consideration of the possible applications of the findings.
3. The researchers should demonstrate the applications within the actual (field) setting. The applications should be evaluated in respect of their relevance, acceptability to practitioners, validity and reliability, feasibility, cost effectiveness, and suitability for staff to use even with little training.
4. Practitioners should be given a chance to try out the applications for themselves, under guidance where necessary.
5. The researchers should collaborate with the practitioners concerned, and those with administrative responsibility for the service, in devising ways of ensuring that valuable applications (either products or procedures) are built into long-term practice. One method of achieving this is to include them in the job descriptions prepared for new members of staff.

A NEW SYNTHESIS - THE HABILITATION TECHNOLOGY PROJECT

The research strategy adopted by the *Habilitation Technology Project* was designed with the previous five conditions in mind, and in the light of discussions with colleagues from a variety of disciplines and included visits to innovative schemes in many parts of the world. The research strategy is itself currently the subject of evaluation, but it is presented here in the hope that other research and practitioner colleagues may consider adopting it. We hope that they will communicate their experiences to us and that together we may continue to evolve a strategy with increasing effectiveness.

Essentially, the strategy involves a *partnership* between the researcher and practitioner which addresses itself particularly to the problems of ensuring that the various outcomes of collaboration are built into long-term practice. It will be seen that the design of the project involves a combination of the concepts of *action research* with *lattice theory*. These two theoretical influences will now be briefly described:

<u>*Action Research*</u> (Cunningham, 1976) first requires the establishment of an action research group. Drawn from a particular organisation, this group must be trained, where necessary, to articulate the problems facing the organisation concerned, i.e. they may need help in expressing difficulties in a way which can result in the formulation of specific operational objectives, that can be tackled in turn. Cunningham describes how this may be done. This leads to the setting of agreed objectives, followed by the production of pilot solutions. These must be field tested, and modified where necessary, before final approval and adoption takes place. This form of research is becoming more widely used, especially in relation to organisational development. It is particularly suited to the achievement of practical and useful results within a field-setting. It is not always easy, however, to coordinate such a group's activities, retain sight of priorities, and optimise the contributions of members (drawn from the fields of research and practice). For this reason we set our action research project within the organisational framework provided by Lattice Theory.

<u>*Lattice Theory*</u> was first applied to the field of mental retardation by Budde and Menolascino (1971). They define a lattice as:

> '...*a network of interrelated and interdependent elements or components which are graphically illustrated by cells, containing verbal description. These cells are ranged sequentially left to right and bottom to top, so that they provide a flow and hierarchical structure leading to the attainment of a major objective.*'

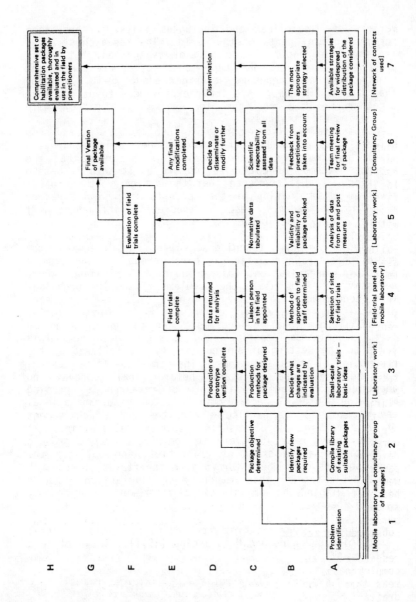

As can be seen from our *programme methodology lattice* (Figure 1), the goal of our action research project is a:

> Comprehensive set of habilitation packages available, thoroughly evaluated, and in use in the field by practitioners.

We believe that the outcome of the partnership between researcher and practitioner must be something more durable than the enthusiasm and ideas which may result. There must be a tangible end product, and we use the general term *habilitation packages* to represent this. We define the term to include new tools or techniques for staff to use. Our first task was to set up the *action research group*. In our case, this consisted of managers of Adult Training Centres, within a 50 mile radius of our research centre, at the University of Manchester, where there were over 100 ATCs. Following a visit to each of the eight key local authorities within these areas, and the appointment of a liaison officer to our project at senior administrative level in each, we met with all the ATC managers of each authority in a series of separate meetings. The managers from each authority selected from among themselves one manager who would represent them at the subsequent meetings of the *Management Consultancy Group*. Two authorities, on account of their size, were allowed to have two representatives each. The first meeting of the Group was held in December 1977, and a total of 59 meetings have been held during the course of the project. During early meetings, the role of the group was clarified and agreement was reached concerning the wording of the goal statement of the project. Common concerns expressed by the managers, on behalf of their colleagues, were tabulated and grouped into areas of priority for the development of teaching packages. Agendas and related papers were sent out in advance of meetings, and agendas were also sent to the liaison officers at Social Services headquarters. New items could be added to the agenda prior to each meeting and detailed minutes were kept, including an *action* column which was always reviewed during the subsequent meeting.

Attendance and enthusiasm was consistently high and the researchers and managers operated as a team, with complementary areas of expertise. Managers were asked to read through and approve, and sometimes contribute to, the drafts of task analyses and exercises to be used in packages. They also were required to report to their fellow managers in their respective authorities on the progress of the project (during their local mangers' meetings).

It can be seen from the lattice that the Consultancy Group of Managers is involved both in identifying the problems of the field and in assisting the research team to develop appropriate solutions to them. The Consultancy Group also plays an important part in deciding when the final version of a *package* is ready for widespread distribution.

THE COPEWELL SYSTEM

During the early meetings of the Management Consultancy Group, considerable discussion took place about the main difficulties experienced by mentally handicapped individuals attending Adult Training Centres and those faced by the staff working with them. Several areas of knowledge and skill needing to be taught were identified. A common concern was also expressed about assessment methods and record keeping. How could individual teaching priorities be determined and in what sequence should different skills be taught?

After many meetings and consultation with their colleagues, the Group and the Project Team decided that the best strategy for developing the series of teaching packages specified as the ultimate goal of the research would be, first of all, to generate a comprehensive curriculum. Each curriculum item would then, in turn, become a package topic itself. The curriculum would become the first essential component of a new teaching system which would also incorporate assessment and recording components and embody sound teaching principles derived from both research and practice.

It was agreed that the overall system should be known as the *Copewell System*, described as follows:

> *'The Copewell System is designed as a basic tool for teacher-instructors working with mentally handicapped adolescents and adults. Its basis is a complete curriculum, divided into four sections: Self Help, Social Academic, Interpersonal, and Vocational. The system consists of three elements; a file box (containing the complete set of 174 numbered curriculum cards, grouped into subject areas within each of the four sections), 174 corresponding teaching packages (teaching plans plus visual aids), and a recording system for individual trainees.'*

This is the statement which appears at the front of every teaching package, enabling the user to retain sight of the whole concept of the system.

The three parts of the Copewell System are described below. They are the:

(a) curriculum,
(b) teaching packages, and
(c) assessment and recording materials.

(a) THE CURRICULUM

In designing the curriculum, account was taken of work currently taking place in Special Schools and in Further and Adult Education Colleges. This together with a study of the literature influenced the content and terminology used in the curriculum. The curriculum is divided into four main sections. Each of these is defined as follows:

Self-help
- The basic skills that an individual must acquire in order to care for and maintain himself both at home and in the community.
These also include skills which allow a person to seek out and use community resources.

Social academic
- Aspects of the more traditional educational or academic skills, geared to functioning in the community.

Interpersonal
- Those skills which enable a person to enter into meaningful and fulfilling relationships with individuals or groups in the community.

Vocational
- The work-related skills, habits and attitudes which are critical to successful adjustment to work.

The Self-help section contains seven major curriculum areas (numbered 1 to 7): Hygiene, Dress, Appearance, First Aid/Health, Domestic Skills, Community Skills and Leisure. Within these seven areas, there are 73 individual curriculum objectives. Eight major areas (numbered 8 to 15): Communication, Numeracy, Literacy, Writing, Money, Time, Telephone and Colour, and 47 specific teaching objectives comprise the Social academic section.
The Interpersonal section contains four major areas (numbered 16 to 19): Bodily awareness, Personal knowledge, Social interaction and Social responsibility and these contain 22 teaching objectives.

93

Finally the <u>Vocational</u> section consists of six major areas: Work skills, Work habits, Work relationships, Work attitudes, Work independence and Job seeking. These areas are numbered 20 to 25 and contain 32 objectives.

The individual objectives which comprise the system will now be presented in Table 1. As can be seen, each objective is preceded by a decimal number linking objectives together within the different areas, as described above.

TABLE 1

<u>COPEWELL CURRICULUM OBJECTIVES</u>

1. HYGIENE
   1.1 Washing hands
   1.2 Washing face, neck and ears
   1.3 Bathing
   1.4 Taking a shower
   1.5 Washing feet
   1.6 Washing and drying hair
   1.7 Cleaning teeth
   1.8 Use of toilet (domestic)
   1.9 Use of toilet (public)
   1.10 Menstrual hygiene
   1.11 Washing clothes (by hand)
   1.12 Washing clothes (by machine)
   1.13 Using a landerette

2. DRESS
   2.1 Selection of clothing
   2.2 Dressing (male)
   2.3 Dressing (female)
   2.4 Undressing (male)
   2.5 Undressing (female)

3. APPEARANCE
   3.1 Hair grooming
   3.2 Shaving (males) using a dry razor
   3.3 Shaving (males) using a wet razor
   3.4 Shaving (famales)
   3.5 Care of nails - hands and feet
   3.6 Use of make-up
   3.7 Posture
   3.8 Use of iron
   3.9 Repair of clothing
   3.10 Awareness of fashion and accessories

4. FIRST AID/HEALTH
   4.1 Handling emergencies
   4.2 Dealing with simple injuries

4.3 Dealing with minor ailments
4.4 Use of, and co-operation with, medical services
4.5 Recognition of health hazards
4.6 Recognition of physical danger
4.7 Correct use and storage of noxious substances
4.8 Attention to balanced diet and weight
4.9 Sensible use of intoxicants

5. DOMESTIC SKILLS
5.1 Preparation of shopping list
5.2 Storage of food and drink
5.3 Use of utensils/gadgets for food preparation
5.4 Preparation of cold drinks
5.5 Preparation of hot drinks
5.6 Preparation of simple snacks (no cooking required)
5.7 Using a cooker
5.8 Preparation of simple snacks (involving cooking)
5.9 Preparing a typical meal (not requiring recipe)
5.10 Setting a table
5.11 Use of correct cutlery
5.12 Acceptable table habits
5.13 Clearing table
5.14 Washing up
5.15 Changing and making the bed
5.16 Simple housework
5.17 Use of electrical equipment in the home
5.18 Maintenance of home environment

6. COMMUNITY SKILLS
6.1 Road safety
6.2 Knowledge of nieghbourhood
6.3 Recognition of function of different types of shop
6.4 Shopping
6.5 Use of bus
6.6 Use of rail services
6.7 Use of hire services for transport
6.8 Recognition of function of different types of community services and amenities
6.9 Use of post office
6.10 Use of bank
6.11 Use of community amenities
6.12 Use of care or restaurant (self service)
6.13 Use of care or restaurant (waiter service)
6.14 Seeking help or advice

7. LEISURE
7.1 Use of leisure in the home
7.2 Knowledge of local leisure facilities
7.3 Use of local leisure facilities
7.4 Club membership

SOCIAL ACADEMIC

8. COMMUNICATION
    8.1 Communication by signs or symbols
    8.2 Speech production
    8.3 Linguistic ability
    8.4 Conversational ability
    8.5 Expression of feelings
    8.6 Expression of opinions
    8.7 Discussion of current affairs

9. NUMERACY
    9.1 Pre-numeracy skills
    9.2 Number recognition and printing
    9.3 Counting
    9.4 Measuring
    9.5 Weighing
    9.6 Addition
    9.7 Subtraction
    9.8 Multiplication
    9.9 Division

10. LITERACY
    10.1 Pre-literacy skills
    10.2 Recognition of alphabet
    10.3 Recognition of useful words
    10.4 Functional reading
    10.5 Reading for pleasure and interest

11. WRITING
    11.1 Pre-writing skills
    11.2 Printing own name
    11.3 Printing address
    11.4 Printing the alphabet
    11.5 Signature
    11.6 Completing simple forms
    11.7 Writing from dictation
    11.8 Writing messages
    11.9 Creative writing

12. MONEY
    12.1 Recognition of coins
    12.2 Recognition of notes
    12.3 Knowledge of monetary values
    12.4 Knowledge of coin and note equivalence
    12.5 Money (spending, and checking change)
    12.6 Understanding pay packet
    12.7 Following a budget
    12.8 Saving

13. TIME
    13.1 Telling the time
    13.2 Association of time with events
    13.3 Estimation of time intervals
    13.4 Knowledge of calendar

14. TELEPHONE
    14.1 Using domestic telephone
    14.2 Using public telephone

15. COLOUR
    15.1 Colour discrimination and matching
    15.2 Colour identification
    15.3 Use of colour

INTERPERSONAL

16. BODILY AWARENESS
    16.1 Knowledge of body parts (male)
    16.2 Knowledge of body parts (female)
    16.3 Knowledge of body measurements and clothing sizes
         (male)
    16.4 Knowledge of body measurements and clothing sizes
         (female)
    16.5 Sexual knowledge

17. PERSONAL KNOWLEDGE
    17.1 Knowledge of personal details
    17.2 Role awareness
    17.3 Self-esteem and aspirations

18. SOCIAL INTERACTION SKILLS
    18.1 Greeting behaviour
    18.2 Good manners
    18.3 Spatial behaviour
    18.4 Visual contact
    18.5 Bodily contact
    18.6 Facial expression
    18.7 Awareness of, and response to, feelings of others
    18.8 Friendship

19. SOCIAL RESPONSIBILITY
    19.1 Knowledge of socially acceptable behaviour
    19.2 Knowledge of sexual behaviour
    19.3 Helping others
    19.4 Knowledge of law-abiding behaviour
    19.5 Moral judgment
    19.6 Discrimination between situations

VOCATIONAL

20. WORK SKILLS
    20.1 Work terms
    20.2 Knowledge of tools
    20.3 Understanding instructions
    20.4 Discrimination skills
    20.5 Quality and accuracy
    20.6 Memory
    20.7 Co-ordination
    20.8 Dexterity
    20.9 Speed
    20.10 Use of basic tools and machinery

21. WORK HABITS
    21.1 Time keeping
    21.2 Safety
    21.3 Clothing at work
    21.4 Adherance to rules and regulations
    21.5 Care of tools
    21.6 Consistency of performance

22. WORK RELATIONSHIPS
    22.1 Response to authority
    22.2 Response to criticism
    22.3 Relations with co-workers

23. WORK ATTITUDES
    23.1 Job satisfaction
    23.2 Adaptability
    23.3 Response to pressure

24. WORK INDEPENDENCE
    24.1 Concentration
    24.2 Work
    24.3 Decision-making
    24.4 Exercise of foresight and initiative
    24.5 Problem solving and originality
    24.6 Leadership

25. JOB SEEKING
    25.1 Vocational exploration
    25.2 Job seeking procedures
    25.3 Completion of job application forms
    25.4 Behaviour at interview

(b) TEACHING PACKAGES

Each package conforms to a standard format and contains visual materials. The major headings in all packages are:

Objective
Pre-requisite knowledge and skills
Preparation
Task analysis and/or exercises provided
Application of the teaching package (suggested
teaching sessions)
Reviewing and recording students' progress
Creating opportunities for knowledge and skills to
be applied
Each of these headings are described briefly:

OBJECTIVE - This restates the objective which appears on the curriculum card; it states what the student will be able to do upon successful completion of the package.

PRE-REQUISITE KNOWLEDGE AND SKILLS - In this section there is a two-column format: the left hand column lists the pre-requisite knowledge and skills and the right hand column, headed *relevant packages*, lists the packages by number and name which cover these knowledge and skills. This heading is particularly important as it links packages with each other, reaffirming how individual packages may be seen as part of the whole system.

PREPARATION - This section provides notes of guidance to enable the user to make the necessary preparations before applying a package. Consisting of three parts, it lists the resources which will be required, the language to be used, and it includes the task analysis and/or suggested exercises which are provided, with which the user should become familiar during the preparatory stage.

1. Resources Required - This section informs the user of the visual aids which are provided within the package together with a list of materials and/or equipment which the user must provide.
2. Adopting a Suitable Vocabulary - In this section a list of basic words is suggested for use during the teaching sessions. In some cases it is necessary for staff to supplement these to take account of regional variations in vocabulary.
3. Task Analysis and/or Exercises Provided - If the objective is one which lends itself to task analysis, then one is provided. This also forms the basis of visual aids provided and it is reproduced as a listing in order to ensure consistency by the user when modelling or demonstrating the skill or behaviour concerned. If the objective does not lend itself to

sequential task analysis, then a series of graded exercises are provided. Although these are sometimes intended as alternatives, they are presented in a suggested sequence.

APPLICATION OF THE TEACHING PACKAGE - This section makes specific suggestions about how to introduce the learning objective to the students, the teaching method which may be adopted, and how to make use of the resources provided within the package and by the user. A group size of six is suggested and a series of teaching sessions (or lesson plans) are outlined, usually commencing with an introductory sessions which serves as a basis for motivating the student(s) to want to acquire the knowledge or skill defined in the package objective.

Within the teaching sessions, suggestions are made which involve both *teacher activity* and *student activity*. The results obtained on detailed individual pre-tests (following assignment to the package) enables the teacher to place emphasis on areas of common difficulty. The pre-test results are recorded in the first column of the student's individual record form.

REVIEWING AND RECORDING STUDENT PROGRESS - Where a task analysis is available, then progress is recorded by ticking items correctly performed on successive occasions. These could subsequently be plotted as a *learning curve*. Where exercises are provided, the method of recording also enables a record to be made of the student's progress towards achieving a criterion level of performance. The record form is designed to be suitable for entering into the student's file. It provides a quick visual indicator of progress and serves as a basis for deciding when the individual should proceed to a different objective.

CREATING OPPORTUNITIES FOR STUDENT(S) TO APPLY KNOWLEDGE AND SKILLS - In this section suggestions are made for activities or assignments which aim to ensure that opportunities are created for the student to keep knowledge and skills alive, once they have been acquired. Suggestions are made for ways in which transfer may take place to different but realistic settings. Wherever possible, suggestions are also made of ways in which the student may be given an opportunity to assist in the teaching of others, or to apply new knowledge or skills in a useful way.

DEVELOPMENT OF PACKAGES

Each package has gone through a lengthy development procedure. This is best described in a series of stages.

Stage 1: <u>The development of a task analysis or series of exercises</u>. This was the preliminary stage in the development of any package. A task analysis and/or series of exercises was generated for the objective in question. These were then approved by the Management Consultancy Group. In view of the considerable amount of work involved in drafting these task analyses or series of exercises, responsibility for this was assumed by members of the team, the Group and also by certain more distant *Satellite* Centres (outside the 50 mile radius of the Project) who asked to be involved in some way. The *Satellite* Centres were ususally those which, during our various talks around the country, wanted to be involved in some way. In order to maximise the eventual uptake of the outcomes of the project, to enable staff to feel involved and (hopefully) committed in the long term to use these outcomes, we felt it necessary to provide some opportunity for input of such distant centres during the design phase, not merely during the dissemination phase. They were invited to send in any existing examples of task analyses (or to draft some if necessary) related to any specific teaching objective listed in the Copewell Curriculum, according to local interest and other commitments. These drafts were used by the research team to supplement our drafts, resource materials, etc., in preparing a set of typed versions for approval by the Management Consultancy Group at their monthly meeting. In total, there were approximately 20 such *satellite* centres.

Stage 2: <u>Packages approved by the Management Consultancy Group, and requiring locations</u>. The second stage of the development of a prototype package was the addition of the visual aids. Shot lists were produced, based on the task analyses or exercises prior to arranging a suitable location for taking the colour photographs. This stage of a package was fairly time-consuming, but was facilitated by the cooperation of many ATCs, whose staff often acted as models.

Stage 3: <u>Development of the teaching plans for the prototype packages</u>. Each package, resulting from the Project conforms to the agreed format presented above. A large part of a package consisted of a series of teaching sessions drafted by the members of the research team in collaboration with the Management Consultancy Group. These sessions took acount of a set of teaching principles drawn from research and practice. They suggested the Level of Language to be used, the duration and spacing of learning, the use of small steps, recitation, and overlearning, and so on. A range of alternative activities were outlined to provide for continued interest and involvement, and a *self-evaluation* phase was built in following each learning attempt, during which the individual reviewed the effort with the instructor, encouraged by comments from the group. Sessions included suggestions to the user concerning the use of visual materials provided, and later sessions emphasised the generalisation and transfer of newly acquired skills to other settings.

After a package had gone through these stages, it was then sent for *evaluation* in one or more field settings, in accordance with rigorous procedures agreed with a liaison member of staff within that setting. For the purpose of this field evaluation, 30 ATCs were carefully selected (from the 100 or so within the 50 mile radius) as representing a typical cross-section of ATCs to be found anywhere in the country. An important constraint in selection was that they should be distinct from those ATCs whose managers served on the Management Consultancy Group. This was to ensure a more objective, independent, evaluation of packages, by staff who had not been involved in the design stage.

During evaluation of the packages within the Field Trial Centres, comparisons were made of different techniques of teaching, including various means of presenting the material. A liaison person, appointed within each of these Centres was responsible for collection whatever data was required and for completing a short questionnaire following use of the package. In general, the criteria for evaluation included such factors as relevance, feasibility, validity, and reliability, acceptability, cost-effectiveness and suitability for staff to use even with little training. It was important to know how many other trainees needed such packages, whether it was feasible for staff to teach using these resource materials, whether they actually proved successful, whether the method of use was consistent between users (in such things as recording individual progress, for example), and so on.

Following such field trials (Column 4 of Figure 1) evaluation data was analysed (Column 5) and finally reviewed by the researchers, together with the Management Consultancy Group (Column 6). If the review was favorable, the package was considered ready for widespread dissemination to the field (Column 7).

(c) ASSESSMENT AND RECORDING MATERIALS

An accurate assessment of individual needs forms the basis of any application of teaching packages. A set of criteria for selecting the appropriate assessment tool for a specific use is presented elsewhere (Whelan and Speake, 1981). Project staff and colleagues have developed two scales to assess skill and ability in all areas covered by the curriculum. These are as follows:

The Scale for Assessing Coping Skills

This scale has been specifically designed for use by both parents and staff. It covers 36 areas of knowledge and skill which are central to independent functioning in the community. Each area is described at five levels of independence and the rater indicates by ticks those things able to be done with or without help, and those abilities being used adequately or otherwise. The resulting profile of the individual facilitates the setting of realistic goals and a better use of resources. Two summary sheets enable an individual's rating to be stored conveniently in his/her file (Whelan and Speake, 1980).

The scale first appeared in *Learning to Cope* (Whelan and Speake, 1979). The book describes in considerable detail how assessment serves as the basis for selecting teaching objectives and also provides some 272 activities and exercises for developing self help, social academic and interpersonal skills.

The Work Skills Rating Scale

This scale has been carefully designed to cover all the important areas which research has shown to be related to success as a worker. Twenty-four areas are each clearly defined and described at five levels, one of which is selected as describing the individual's current performance. The resulting profile of work skills can help staff to identify areas where training or counselling may be needed, or to match the individual's current workstyle to the demands of suitable forms of work. Suitable for use with both handicapped and non-handicapped people, the scale form is supplied with a summary sheet for convenient filing (Whelan and Schlesinger, 1980).

At the invitation of Lancashire Social Services Department, keen to enable its ATCs to work more closely together, the project has also been involved in developing, piloting and finalising a complete recording system for individual trainees. This is known as the *Personal Record System*. The system comprises a comprehensive set of standardised forms for use by the Adult Training Centre (or Social Education Centre). The 14 forms, covering background information and assessment results are the product of extensive inter-disciplinary consultation. Their use should lead to improved communications and more effective teamwork (Whelan and Lancashire Social Services, 1980).

RESEARCH OUTCOMES

In addition to the practical outcomes of the Project just described, the design was intended to enable research studies to be carried out on key issues identified by the research team in consultation with the Management Consultancy Group. Descriptive, evaluative, and experimental studies have been completed, mostly related to the initial abilities of trainees, and the effectiveness of the individual packages or specific teaching techniques. Some of the issues studied have, for example, included: attainments of trainees in different sections of the curriculum; attainments in relation to the nature of living accommodation; areas of structured and unstructured teaching in ATCs; the types of learning disability most frequently experienced; the role of anticipation in learning; and the ability to transfer a learning strategy to novel material.

In addition to evaluating *packages*, the intervention strategy of the Project itself has been evaluated. The aim has been to measure changes brought about in the Field Trials Centres which are attributable to their involvement with the Project. The 30 Field Trial Centres were matched for this purpose with another group of 30 Centres not involved in the main project. Detailed information was obtained from all Centres at the beginning and end of the Project, enabling comparisons between the two groups of Centres to be made. Preliminary results show, for example, that Field Trial Centres made greater gains in systematic working (timetabling, use of individual learning plans, etc.) and made more attempts to forge working links with relevant external organisations.

The scope for undertaking research which was both relevant to practice and also of considerable theoretical importance within the framework of the present design is further illustrated by the work completed by a number of attached research students. Three of them obtained Ph.D. degrees and two obtained M.Ed. degrees.

CONCLUSION

It was stated earlier that the authors consider the project's methodology to be as important as its outcomes. We hope that this brief account of our work may persuade others in the future to adopt a similar approach. We intend to monitor the long-term effects of the project, encouraged already by the apparent commitment of practitioners to use the packages which they have not only identified to be necessary but also helped to design, evaluate, and disseminate.

In continuation of our philosophy of partnership, we have recently conducted a national poll of ATCs, inviting their perceptions of priorities for a future research programme. Their priority, also expressed by the DHSS is for a national study of *special care* units (for the profoundly and multiply handicapped). We commenced this work in October, 1983.

SUMMARY

1. The applications of research to practice have not kept pace with other encouraging developments in the field of mental handicap.
2. A National Survey of Adult Training Centres highlighted many of the problems faced by practitioners and emphasised the need for a new approach to the introduction of new ideas and technology.
3. Various earlier attempts to achieve this were found to be only partially successful. Some important criteria were drawn from them.
4. The present project used an *action research* design, within the systematic framework provided by *Lattice Theory*. Its methodology is strongly commended to others.
5. Both practical and research outcomes are briefly described. The former, known as the *Copewell System*, attempts to ensure that the results of the partnership between researcher and practitioner endure long beyond the conclusion of the project.

REFERENCES

Brown, R. I. (1972) 'Research to Practice'. in *International Research Seminar on Vocational Rehabilitation of the Mentally Retarded*, A.A.M.D. Special Publication Series, No. 1, Washington.
Budde, J. F. and Menolascino, F. J. (1971) 'Systems Technology and Retardation: Application to Vocational Habilitation', *Mental Retardation*, *9*, 11.
Clarke, A. D. B. (1977) 'From Research to Practice', in P. J. Mittler (ed.) *Research to Practice in Mental Retardation*, Vol. 1: 'Care and Intervention', University Park Press, Baltimore, Maryland.
Cunningham, B. (1976) 'Action Research: Toward a Procedural Model', *Human Relations*, *29*(3), 215-238.

Hall, J. (1974) 'Survey of Behaviour Modification Training in U.K. Hospitals', Paper given to IRMMH Action Workshop No. 2: *Training and Reorganization for Behaviour Modification in Hospital and Community Settings*, Held at the Ciba Foundation, 24-25 October, London.

Klaber, M. M. (1971) *Retardates in Residence: A Study of Institutions*, University of Hartford, Connecticut.

Martin, G. and Pear, J. (1983) *Behavior Modification, What It Is and How To Do It*, 2nd Ed., Prentice Hall, Englewood Cliffs.

Mittler, P. J. (1976) 'Applying Research to Practice', in T. Fryers and E. Whelan (eds.) *Current Research in Mental Handicap: Applications for Practitioners*, North Western Regional Health Authority, Manchester.

Schlesinger, H. and Whelan, E. (1979) *Industry and Effort*, Spastics Society in association with William Heineman, London.

Speake, B. R. and Whelan, E. (1977) *Young Persons' Work Preparation Courses: A Systematic Evaluation*, Manpower Services Commission: Employment Service Agency, London.

Whelan, E. and Lancashire Social Services (1980) *The Personal Record System*, Copewell Publications, Manchester.

Whelan, E. and Schlesinger, H. (1984) *The Work Skills Rating Scale*, Copewell Publications, Manchester.

Whelan, E. and Speake, B. (1979) *Learning to Cope*, Souvenir Press, Human Horizons Series, London.

Whelan, E. and Speake, B. (1984) *The Scale for Assessing Coping Skills*, Copewell Publications, Manchester.

Whelan, E. and Speake, B. (1981) *Getting to Work*, Souvenir Press, Human Horizons Series, London.

Chapter Five

REHABILITATIVE MODELS AND RESIDENTIAL PROGRAMME SERVICES

John W. Jacobson, Allen A. Schwartz, and Matthew P. Janicki

INTRODUCTION

The past two decades have witnessed many changes in theoretical and applied viewpoints in the social sciences. Among the many prominent concepts to emerge in academic psychology is behaviour analysis, incorporating both behaviour modification practices and the investigation of their ecological validity. At the same time, new methods and philosophies for the care and treatment of mentally disabled persons, particularly those with mental retardation and developmental disabilities, have evolved, leading to applications of psychological and rehabilitative strategies in new settings. Concurrently, there has been an emphasis over the past decade on normalised and community-based service delivery methods, within which framework the new rehabilitative strategies are incidentally rendered.

The concurrence between these two trends in treatment methodologies and service delivery to mentally disabled persons - namely normalisation and community placement on the one hand, and behaviour analysis and ecological psychology on the other - have not yet been sufficiently analysed for their overall compatibility. This chapter attempts to examine and integrate these seemingly diverse notions with an eye toward suggesting ways to make programme models more coherent. Ecological psychology has elucidated ways in which environments naturally encourage and support specific behaviours. Rehabilitative programmes such as group homes for mentally disabled persons are designed to encourage and expedite the acquisition of adaptive behaviours. From the standpoint of ecological validity, the ecology of a group home should incorporate those features which will naturally support (i.e., ordinarily reinforce) desired behaviours. Conversely, activities and rehabilitative strategies should be designed to take advantage of naturally reinforcing features of the social and physical environment. In this way, innovations in service delivery may benefit from recent theoretical advances in branches of the social sciences not normally influencing social policy.

OVERVIEW

Normalisation as a human management model (Bank-Mikkelson, 1969; Nirje, 1969; Wolfensberger, 1972) has been considered critical in stimulating the shift in the focus of developmental disabilities services from custodial care in institutions to active rehabilitation in a variety of community contexts (Landesman-Dwyer, 1981). Residential programmes have been considered from the standpoint of a variety of programme models (Janicki, 1981; Janicki, Jacobson & Schwartz, 1982), the notion of model coherency (Wolfensberger, 1972), and the mutual interdependency of occupant, environmental, and organisational factors as determinants of the programme's service orientation (Jacobson & Schwartz, 1983). Further, some degree of approachment is evident between programme models and normalisation processes, as reflected in Bjaanes, Butler & Kelly's (1981) discrimination between environmental normalisation and client normalisation. Environmental normalisation focuses upon the normalising features of the physical and social environment. Client normalisation, in contrast, is concerned with service provision practices, and activities intended to promote the further personal development of programme occupants. For a programme model to be coherent, both its physical setting and rehabilitative strategy must coincide.

Contemporary developments in the application of operant and classical conditioning techniques (termed behaviour modification in a broad sense) to the remediation of functional deficits found within mentally disabled populations have paralleled trends toward active treatment and community living (Berkson & Landesman-Dwyer, 1977). The availability of effective rehabilitative strategies was undoubtedly a necessary precondition for the growth of community programming. Normalisation concepts provided the philosophical rationale for this growth, while behavioural methods provided the capability to achieve the goals of adaptive growth in community settings. In this context, it should be noted that, although it may by assumed *normal* environments will in some manner elicit normal behaviour, there are little data to support this position. On the other hand, there is substantive evidence from research and everyday life that behaviour must be taught and maintained (Marholin, O'Toole, Touchette, Berger, & Doyle, 1979). While behaviour modification is not intrinsically incompatible with normalisation principles and practices

108

(Epstein, 1982; Roos, 1972), little has been written relating this technology and normalisation. While superficially the option-limiting and highly structured interventions of behaviourism appear incompatible with the *most normal means* premise of normalisation, it must be noted that the normalisation principle encourages use of the most effective treatment available (Wolfensberger, 1980). Finally, behaviour modification can be readily understood as a purposive application of principles that reflect the ongoing transaction and exchange among individuals and the salient characteristics of their environments (Craighead, Kazdin & Mahoney, 1976).

This chapter is intended to provide direction toward the normalised administration and delivery of behaviour management services in a range of residential settings, including foster family care, group home, and institutional settings, the most prominent out-of-home care settings for persons with developmentally disabilities. Each of these environments will be considered from the perspective of ecological congruence as it relates to services (Thurman, 1981), in that each setting should provide only necessary prosthetic supports (Lindsley, 1964) to enhance adaptive functioning, and offer opportunities to move beyond the immediate residential setting to a more independent life-style. Specific attention will be given to the direction and provision of psychological services in these settings. However, many characteristics of suggested service models can be generalised to the allied health professions.

Normalisation. The philosophical perspective of normalisation (Wolfensberger, 1972; Wolfensberger & Glenn, 1975) guides service provision most tangibly through the principles of least restrictive environment and model coherency. Normalisation entails using progressively more normal procedures to bring about greater levels of normal behaviour. Model coherency is defined by the cohesion between programme intent, programme practices, and the programme environment.

The principle of least restrictive environment assumes that the character of the physical setting and, more importantly, the manner in which services are provided should be congruent with occupant abilities and needs. Briefly, occupant participation in planning rehabilitation and recreation activities should be maximised. Correspondingly, unnecessary rigidity of routines, uniformity in formal interventions, and intrusive management practices should be minimised. Individualisation in occupant service receipt, and participation with a view toward promotion of developmental growth and social stimulation are the cornerstones of the least restrictive environment.

Model coherency complements the notion of the least restrictive environment. Model coherency states that internal consistency should be present with regard to specialisation in programme function and content (Wolfensberger, 1972). From this standpoint, the resources (i.e., physical setting, personnel, social system) of a programme should be consonant with the purpose of the programme, which is in turn consonant with the abilities and needs of the occupants. Thus, if a programme serves solely children or adults, variations in resources should reflect the different needs presented by these two groups. Similarly, service intensity and mix should be consistent with the severity and diversity of occupant needs for services. In this regard, consideration of the extent to which the physical environment promotes socialisation, normalisation, and personalisation in everyday routines and activities is especially germane (Gunzburg & Gunzburg, 1973, 1979), regardless of the residential model.

Taken together, the notions of the least restrictive environment and model coherency provide a framework within which programme environments can be designed to promote developmental growth through services and experiences that reflect occupant abilities. These principles allow for the provision of professional services in residential settings when such services are required, in a fashion which both capitalises upon programme resources and draws upon existing programme orientation.

RESIDENTIAL MODEL FACTORS

The structure of a residential programme model can be considered to be a function of three elements:
    the programme's environment,
    the programme's rehabilitative intent,
    the programme's management system.

Programme environment encompasses factors such as its physical design and use, the attitudes, abilities, and activities of its staff, qualitative and quantitative aspects of informal and formal service provision practices, and the interplay of these considerations with occupant characteristics.

Rehabilitative intent defines the goals of occupant change and the process through which rehabilitative technology is applied toward the attainment of these goals (Janicki, 1981; Janicki, Jacobson & Schwartz, 1982). Within developmental disabilities programmes, the context of goal development and service provision is the developmental model, which presumes that disabled persons are capable of growth and skill acquisition. Rehabilitative intent incorporates concerns about programme process and the extent to which model coherency is present.

Management systems subsume both the administrator's or clinician's understanding of the purpose of a programme (the ideological context) and the specific strategies employed for management of ongoing operations. In general, the perspective and strategies employed for management should be consistent with the rehabilitative intent, and with the opportunities and limitations of the programme environment.

Residential Setting Models

The models associated with foster family care, group home, and congregate care settings are surrogate family living, cooperative group living, and therapeutic care, respectively. In this context congregate care refers to any large group living and treatment setting, and would encompass such diverse programmes as residential schools, specialised mental retardation centres, psychiatric facilities, and health care facilities. In foster family, group living, and congregate care settings the following distinctions emerge. The foster family setting relies upon a *natural* family configuration including a *parenting* model for the promotion of occupant development. Interventions in this setting rely upon specialised services provided by day programme centres, or educational services outside the home, complemented by familial socialisation and learning activities and limited formal intervention consistent with a parent training model in the home. The *parent* becomes a participant in the formalised rehabilitation process only on an intermittent basis.

The group home setting relies on a cooperative group living configuration using *mentoring* as a basis for enhancing occupant abilities. Group home staff manage the home, supervise socialisation and community integrative activities, and in addition, carry out components of individual rehabilitation plans. Staff are full participants in the service system, although, as in foster family settings, intensive intervention activities will typically be carried out in programme centre or clinic settings. Limited extension of these services into the group living setting may be desirable to promote generalisation and maintenance of new learning.

The congregate care setting relies upon a therapeutic care model in order to provide supervision and active interdisciplinary health and therapy services. Such

111

settings should include personnel who work directly with occupants as full participants in the interdisciplinary or trans-disciplinary team process (Foley, 1979). Congregate care settings employ structured administrative systems for the purpose of staff role definition, with clear distinction drawn between the prerogatives and responsibilities of supervisory, professional, and direct care staff. Service quality in congregate care settings will be reflected to the extent that comprehensive, structured, and appropriate therapeutic interventions are provided.

BEHAVIOUR MODIFICATION AND ECOLOGICAL VALIDITY

Operant and classical conditioning paradigms have been successfully applied within developmental disabilities service settings in order to address a wide variety of behaviour change issues. The focus of such interventions has included the enhancement of eating, toileting, dressing, grooming, oral hygiene, attention to task, imitation, social behaviour, language use, and vocational skills. Behaviour technologies have contributed to the amelioration of hyperactivity, self-stimulation, stereotypes, self-injurious behaviour, aggression, and tantrums (Whitman & Scibak, 1979). Settings in which implementation of behavioural programmes has been reported include natural homes (Callias & Carr, 1975), foster family care (Kaprowy, 1980), group homes (Haney & Jones, 1982), clinic treatment programmes (Senatore, Matson & Kazdin, 1982), classrooms (Konarski, Crowell, Johnson & Whitman, 1982), sheltered workshops (Schroeder, 1972), and institutions (Reppucci, 1977; Reppucci & Saunders, 1974).

The concerns of ecological psychology have been defined in two ways (Rogers-Warren & Warren, 1977). The term *ecology* has been used to refer to the inter-relatedness or inter-dependency of behaviours and changes in behaviours within individuals (Willems, 1974; Voeltz & Evans, 1982). Ecology has also been used to describe the association between the properties of settings (Price & Blashfield, 1975) and their social character (Insel & Moos, 1974) in influencing, eliciting, and consequating behaviour (Ittelson, Proshansky & Rivlin, 1970; Risley, 1977). The second definition is consistent with the premise that normalised settings offer greater opportunities for the occurrence of adaptive behaviours (i.e., there is a greater likelihood of antecedents which would cue adaptive behaviour). As a consequence, this definition reflects the rationale for much of the research conducted on the behavioural effects of community residential settings (c.f., Bjannes & Butler, 1974; Butler & Bjaanes, 1977, 1978; Close, 1977; Eyman, Demaine & Lei, 1979; Eyman, Silverstein, McLain

& Miller, 1977; Fiorelli & Thurman, 1979; Gilbert & Hemming, 1979; Landesman-Dwyer, Berkson & Romer, 1979; Landesman-Dwyer, Stein & Sackett, 1978).

The efficacy of behavioural techniques has stimulated concern that they be applied in ways, and toward ends, that are socially and ecologically valid (Bernstein, 1981; Kazdin, 1977; Risley, 1970; Schriebman, Koegel, Mills & Burke, 1981). Social validity and relevance can be considered in regard to whether:

1.   the goals selected for behaviour change are important to the person in their natural environment,

2.   the methods used to obtain these goals are acceptable to the person and/or their advocate, and

3.   the amount of behaviour change actually obtained constitutes significant progress or improvement (Kazdin, 1977).   .

Ecological validity, in contrast, is concerned primarily with the utility (and therefore the relevance) of the behaviour change for the individual, and with the capability of the environment to support maintenance and generalisation of the new behaviour (the consonance of the behaviour with the person's environment). In this context Rogers-Warren (1977) has noted:

> *'We arrange and rearrange the contingent relation-*
> *ships between behaviours and their consequences for the*
> *purpose of changing behaviours.   But as behaviour*
> *analysis is extended to more settings and more clients,*
> *it is becoming apparent that behaviour change*
> *procedures do not always yield the same results with*
> *each application.   It is not that the principles of*
> *behaviour are not applicable, but rather that their*
> *application must take into account individual*
> *circumstances...Consideration of individual setting*
> *differences may be critical in the design and*
> *application of behaviour change strategies'* (p. 197).

From an ecological standpoint therefore, the programme environment is to be considered in terms of the impact its structure and process have on the design of an intervention.

Two key constructs which are linked to the expression of ecological validity are *maintenance* (the behaviour's persistence beyond the span of intervention) and *generalisation* (the behaviour's occurrence in settings other than those in which training occurred). Interventions which fail to result in persistence, or generalisation, should be considered as lacking validity and being of questionable functional benefit to the client (Holman, 1977).

IMPLICATIONS FOR SERVICE MANAGEMENT AND PROVISION

Normalisation, residential model factors (rehabilitative intent, programme environment, management systems) and ecological dynamics constitute descriptive frameworks for a matrix within which the process of service provision can be implemented (Bernstein, 1982; Cherniss, 1981).

It can be argued that the effective intervention, aside from its focus on functional and valid behaviours, will have several features. Prominent among these features are: use of existing physical setting elements, antecedent adjustment, response consequation strategies that already facilitate or elicit the behaviour, reinforcement through application of natural contingencies (i.e., the Premack principle), and use of procedures which support the continued provision of the intervention by relevant staff (Rogers-Warren, 1977). Generalisation is promoted through interventions which entail multiple change agents, multiple training methods, multiple reinforcers, and multiple settings (preferably the actual settings in which the behaviour is desired). Similarly, many behaviours evidenced in everyday life are perpetuated by intermittent schedules of reinforcement. Not every occurrence of a behaviour, however positively valued in its context, will be systematically consequated in day-to-day non-clinical settings (Warren, 1977). For new behaviours it will often be necessary to *programme* the environment as part of the intervention for intermittent reinforcement following establishment of the response.

Models for the management and implementation of behaviour interventions exist which include these important considerations. Tharp and Wetzel (1969), and more recently, Bernstein (1982), have advocated a multi-tiered structure for service management. Tharp and Wetzel's quadratic model includes a supervisor (psychologist), behaviour analysts (paraprofessionals trained in applied behaviour analysis), indigenous personnel who actually carry out interventions (parents or teachers), and the focal (i.e., target) individual. Similarly, Bernstein's model assigns these roles to a behavioural consultant (theoretical specialist), behavioural engineers (technical specialists), behaviour managers (implementors), and the focal individual. The role at each level is to guide, monitor, and communicate with the person at the next level. Several noteworthy advantages are inherent in this approach: efficient use of available expertise, limited and clearly defined responsibilities for persons at each level, vestment of responsibility for implementation and follow-up within the rehabilitative environment, and involvement of outside practitioners (Kaprowy, 19890; Lavigneur, 1976; Short, 1980; Vischer, 1982).

Residential Settings and Occupant Characteristics

In general, persons residing in community living situations will be less severely impaired than persons in institutional settings (Hill & Bruininks, 1981). Although there is diversity in the impairment levels of mentally retarded individuals residing in family care and group homes (Jacobson & Janicki, 1983), it has also been noted the most disabled individuals residing in community settings evidence impairments similar to those of the most profoundly multiply-disabled persons living in congregate care settings (Johnson-Silver, Silverman & Lubin, 1984). This dispersion and overlap in occupant abilities has been attributed, in the United States, to the pressure emanating from deinstitutionalisation, the absence of specific admission criteria for community settings (Crawford, Thompson & Aiello, 1981), and stronger advocacy for community residential alternatives regardless of impairment level.

Nevertheless, some systematic variations in characteristics can be identified among persons in different settings. Table 1 summarises some of these variations, as found in a survey of persons in the developmental disabilities service system in the State of New York between 1978 and 1982 (Janicki, Jacobson & Schwartz, 1982). Information is presented on the overt characteristics of individuals in specialised foster family care, group home, and congregate care settings. These characteristics are essentially similar to those of residential setting groups described nationally in the United States by Hill & Bruininks (1981).

Foster Family Care Occupants

Nearly one-fifth of foster family occupants are children or adolescents, while about one-seventh of the group are age 65 or older. This reflects the use of specialised foster family settings for persons who are thought to benefit most from a surrogate family or extended family situation. While few of these individuals evidence psychiatric impairments, the overwhelming majority have a chronic physical impairment or health problem (i.e., cardiovascular and respiratory involvement, diabetes, blindness or deafness). Less than half of these individuals are severely or profoundly mentally retarded and most of them are skilled in self-care areas. However, over one-third of these persons evidence problem behaviours which may impact upon continued stay or inhibit service provision. In general, these problems reflect minor conduct disorders and socialisation deficits, rather than affective or cognitive anomalies. In the absence of a specialised system of family care homes,

TABLE 1: Characteristics of Individuals Residing in Foster Family, Group Living and Congregate Care Settings in New York State (1978-1982)

CHARACTERISTICS	PERCENTAGE OF PERSONS BY LIVING ALTERNATIVE		
	FOSTER FAMILY	GROUP LIVING	CONGREGATE CARE
- Persons age LTE 21 years	18	6	21
- Mental/developmental disability other than, or in addition to, mental retardation present	17	29	58
- Psychiatric diagnosis present	12	26	14
- Physical handicap present	86	80	93
- Proportion severe or profound mental retardation present	43	36	81
- Independent in toileting	86	87	35
- Independent in eating	85	83	33
- Independent in dressing/grooming	63	63	15
- One of more problem behaviours present	37	61	76
- Behaviour (conduct) problem present	15	28	45
- Affective or cognitive problem present	8	16	15
- Reference N	2573	1963	11727

Summarized from Janicki, Jacobson & Schwartz (1982)

it can be anticipated that generic public foster family care systems will also serve a number of young and elderly individuals with developmentally disabilities, similar to those in New York's homes (Adams, 1975).

Group home occupants. In contrast, group home occupants tend to be adults aged 18 to 64 years, with the majority of these persons aged 18-44 years. They are more likely to have multiple developmental disabilities (autism, cerebral palsy or epilepsy in addition to mental retardation) or a psychiatric impairment when compared to family care occupants. Further, while intellectual characteristics and independence in self-care skills are comparable to those of persons in family care, the incidence of behaviour problems among group home occupants is markedly higher, including affective and cognitive problems which are consistent with the presence of characterological disorders.

Congregate care occupants. Although children and adolescents are well-represented in congregate care settings (21 per cent of the occupants), 27 per cent of the occupants are age 45 years or older. A comparison of congregate care occupants with those of family care and group home settings shows that congregate care occupants tend to be more impaired in regard to intellectual factors, physical factors, self-care skills, and incidence of behaviour problems, although there appears to be a lower incidence of psychiatric impairment.

MODEL-BASED SERVICE PROVISION

Building upon the tiered approach to staff and resource allocation, specific recommendations can be developed for the provision of services to persons who reside in different types of settings. In this section, recommendations for specific activities and involvement of professionals are made with the intention of promoting congruence between programme models and intervention characteristics. However, the basic purpose of each type of setting is to offer an environment through which the personal and social growth of occupants is promoted. Consistent with this rationale, the concerns of the professional as an agent in support of this purpose will be similar in responding to each setting's strengths and limitations. Specific approaches are presented in a fashion which is consistent with each model. However, techniques applicable to one setting may also bear upon others. With adaptation, specific techniques, such as those used to promote caretaker involvement in therapeutic activities, must be recognised as useful within a range of programme models.

Foster Family Care

In a foster family care setting the indigenous *personnel* include the foster care parent(s) and the natural children of these parents. Adams (1975) has reported that studies of foster care parents have consistently described a group drawn largely from middle and lower socioeconomic strata, who have a modest life-style and often limited education. This description accurately reflects the composition of the New York family care group (Epple, 1982) in which a high school level of education is predominant among providers.

Eyman (1977) has noted that little research attention has been directed to training foster care parents in behaviour modification, although such applications have been reported (Stein & Gambill, 1976), as has family care parents' participation in providing diverse health therapies (Eyman, 1977). Research suggests that the presence of an organisational model which promotes skill development and maintenance (Cherniss, 1981) may contribute to occupant growth and continued stay in a family care setting (Intagliata, Willer & Wicks, 1981; Willer & Intagliata, 1982).

Involvement of the foster care parent as an implementor of behavioural programmes on an ongoing or episodic basis will necessitate formal training and monitoring. One method to achieve this sort of involvement is an enhanced provider training and supervision programme. Under this type of programme, homes are certified as family care sites and family care parents are certified as special care providers after completing an organised programme of orientation and training. Special care providers receive a greater level of payment than do other family care providers, participate as members of a community services team, and, through the team process, assist in the development and implementation of skill shaping and maintenance activities in the home emphasising occupant acquisition of self-care and self-direction skills.

Another way to achieve caretaker involvement in rehabilitative activities is through foster parent training. Behavioural assistants functioning as case-workers may provide individual formal and informal training in behavioural techniques, or solicit provider participation in group training sessions as part of a skill development process. Extensive research and clinical reports have documented the use and evaluation of natural parents as behaviour change agents. O'Dell (1974), in a review on parent training and behaviour modification, concluded that *like many applied areas of behaviour modification, parent training is being quickly expanded by the volume of the need* and the *usefulness of the area is more promise than fact* (p. 430). However, he also concluded that insufficient evidence was available regarding the permanence of changes in childrens' or parents' behaviour, and the most effective methods for promoting persistence. Since nis review numerous reports have documented the value of parents as behaviour change agents (i.e., Bernstein, 1982; Cunningham, 1975; Forehand & Atkeson, 1977; Lavigneur, 1976; Tennov, Jacobson & Vittucci, 1978), although there are still many concerns about persistence and generalisation of intervention effects, and which procedures best support these. An extensive literature exists on interventions within family settings with immediate applicability to the training and guidance of foster care-based interventions (Becker, 1971; Beltz, 1971; Macht, 1975; Patterson, 1971; Patterson & Gullion, 1968; Watson, 1973).

For children in foster care, classroom settings will offer opportunities for intervention. For adult occupants, day-programme settings, both rehabilitative and sheltered pre-vocational, will also constitute appropriate intervention locales. For elderly individuals, however, who may choose to retire and participate only in non-production oriented or leisure-time activities in the community, opportunities for out-of-home intervention may be more limited. Clinic settings, however, do offer an alternative for selected, and often time-limited, services as the need arises. Callias and Carr (1975), in a report on clinic-based behaviour programmes, have observed that the most common problems dealt with in home and school settings entailed acceleration of self-care skills and deceleration of disruptive behaviours. Interventions in classroom, clinic, and day programme settings are well-reported in the behavioural literature (c.f., Konarski, Crowell, Johnson and Whitman, 1982; Senatore, Matson and Kazdin, 1982; Stacey, Doleys and Malcolm, 1979; Turner, Hersen and Bellack, 1978).

While not focused on developmentally disabled groups, the findings of studies by Ayllon, Garber and Pisor (1975) and Bailey, Wolf and Phillips (1970) underscore the value of communication between the intervention setting and the living situation to assure that interventions in the home are consistent with approaches used elsewhere. For example, Harris & Romanczyk (1976) described the use of over-correction procedures to ameliorate a child's self-injurious behaviour, with treatment in a clinic following applications of contingencies in the child's foster care home.

Commentary

Foster family care should, in its full intent, use a parenting model to bring about the acquisition of new and age-appropriate skills in those mentally disabled individuals under the care of a foster care *parent*. Further,

119

foster care parenting can be seen as no different from parenting done in a natural home or when the disabled individual resides with kin. The goal of parenting is, through modelling and shaping, to produce a range of skills that enhance independent living capability to the greatest possible extent. Although the research literature has not fully addressed when or how to use foster family care toward this end, it has shown that teaching and training procedures can bring about greater levels of skill acquisition. Foster family care homes that are organised and operated in a manner so as to effect growth in occupant skills, and to promote the *parent's* use of systematic and focused training procedures, should show a consistent end result - greater independence - and evidence a greater degree of ecological validity.

Several considerations, however, are noteworthy in relation to this type of residential setting:

1) although a warm, receptive, and caring foster home environment is critically important for nurturing growth, skill acquisition will not occur unless a concerted effort is made to support skill-building interventions. Clinicians working with caretakers, such as foster family care parents, should be aware that they need to assess the parents' abilities to become behaviour modifiers, and be prepared to offer training in effective behaviour change procedures.

2) consultation and supervision are necessary if formal behaviour acquisition programmes are to be effective. Clinicians should be prepared to assess the environment produced by the parents and the home, and construct strategies that would enhance the learning and level of parental skills as behaviour modifiers. Formal behavioural programme designs should be thought out in a manner that builds upon existing parental competencies and willingness to assume such responsibilities.

3) the client's day programme, be it a work or activity environment, and/or clinical services if delivered through a clinic model, must also consider the role of the foster family care parent in the coordination and provision of interventions that cross over into the home. Clinicians must also consider that certain interventions are very appropriate for use in a home environment but others will adversely affect the intent of the home programme. It is critical that rehabilitative interventions that occur in the home, which may have originated within the day programme, have relevance to the context of the home, otherwise they will affect the ecology of the home and its definition as a familial residence.

Group Homes

In order to discuss service provision in group home settings, it is valuable to discriminate between two types of group homes: the supervised residence and the intensive programme residence. The supervised residence is similar to the prototypic group home, in the sense that it is staffed by non-professionals (possibly houseparents) and paraprofessionals, and a manager (i.e., warden) who may be a professional. This type of programme provides limited formal rehabilitative activities and relies heavily upon a socialisation (mentoring) model. In contrast, the intensive programme residence, often certified and funded in the United States as an *intermediate care facility for the mentally retarded*, will include professional staff, through employment or contractural/consultative arrangements, as a component of its on-site personnel. Consequently, the intensive programme residence will more frequently be the site of structured rehabilitative training activities than will the supervised programme. Nevertheless, for occupants of both supervised and intensive programme residences, day programme and clinic services constitute important additional service resources. For the purpose of the following discussion, the term group home will be used to describe supervised residences.

Opportunities for structured behavioural interventions in group homes may be limited as in foster family care settings, but for different reasons. While non-professionals in group homes may, in general, be relatively well-educated compared to family care providers (Janicki, Jacobson, Zigman & Gordon, 1984), the ratio of staff to occupants may be lower than that found in foster homes, even during evening hours when staffing levels may be most enriched. Staff in group homes will generally also be responsible for many of the activities necessary for maintenance of a small group living situation. These activities include meal preparation, provision of transportation, making or overseeing small repairs or improvements to the physical site, supervising and assisting residents, and intervening in episodic *crisis* situations. As noted by Baroff (1980), while the smaller facility offers more individualisation possibilities, group home staff members have a greater degree of immediate responsibility for the care of occupants than do their institutional counterparts. The capability of a group home to support structured interventions is a function of the extent to which the normative structure (values, goals, beliefs and norms that bear upon work), the structure of staff roles, and the power structure (as measured by the extent to which staff participate in decision-making) encompass active rehabilitation (Cherniss, 1981; Cherniss & Egnatios, 1978; Hitzing, 1980). There are several options for defining staff roles in intervention design and implementation, such as designating a single individual responsible for developing and carrying out programming. Alternatively, a *client coordinator* model may be adopted, with each staff member designated as having service coordination, advocacy, and implementation responsibility for a few individuals.

There is evidence of a need for some type of structure to support rehabilitative programming in group homes. Gunzburg (1977) compared changes in occupant social competence in two types of group homes; one of which provided only incidental guidance and assistance to occupants, while the other provided structured guidance and development activities. Gains in social competence were demonstrated in both types of homes; however, occupants of sites which provided structured services evidenced markedly greater gains than occupants of unstructured programmes. The extent to which these gains could be accounted for by programme characteristics alone was indeterminate because of non-systematic variation in occupant histories, abilities, and selection factors. Further, Sandler and Thurman (1981) concluded in a review of behaviour change and anecdotal studies in group homes that, while studies of behaviour change have generally demonstrated improved skills among persons living within small community-based programmes, anecdotal studies suggest a less clear picture. Community programmes appear to vary considerably, with some programmes being rehabilitative and others functioning as little more than *mini-institutions in the community* (Sandler & Thurman, 1981, p. 249). Bjaanes and Butler (1974) have noted that such programmes can be characterised by whether their environments are *custodial*, *maintaining* or *therapeutic*.

Community resources should be readily available to provide for a variety of supports that are required by group home occupants. However, often they are not. In many instances group homes attempt to address these needs but experience difficulties because of:

a) lack of staff experience and expertise,
b) difficulties in finding and retaining qualified staff,
c) difficulties in development of individual plans of care,
d) limited provision of staff training and development activities,
e) problems assessing support services, and
f) necessary preoccupation of staff with household activities, administrative duties, and advocacy (O'Connor & Sitkei, 1975; Jaslow & Spagna, 1977; Felsenthal & Scheerenberger, 1978; Parks, 1978;

Bruininks, Kudla, Wieck & Hauber, 1980; Intagliata, Kraus & Willer, 1980; Cherniss, 1981; Close, O'Connor & Peterson, 1981).

A recent report by Phillips (1982) on the use of staff time in an independent living programme showed only 25 per cent of staff contacts with occupants consisted of occupant training. Further, only 34 per cent of staff time was spent in contact with programme occupants.

These considerations point to the necessity that behavioural interventions in a group home provide maximum benefit with minimal staff allocation, and consequently require assistance and supervision by professionals from outside the home. Outside professionals constitute an important resource for the development of much needed staff expertise. Efforts must be made to assure the availability of a variety of support services to community settings which complement programmes (Short, 1980; Vischer, 1982). Both Short and Vischer have noted that the decision to provide services in a centralised centre, rather than to bring services to community settings where individuals live and work through consultation, may, in the long term, undercut the capabilities of those programmes to meet occupant needs. Consultative activities directed toward the development of staff behaviour management skills can, for example, increase staff ability to independently and appropriately manage client activities and also limit prospective need for outside intervention to cope with behavioural problems. The intent of such training is not to assist a group home to become a more closed environment, but rather to stimulate the setting to become more responsive to occupant needs. Such environments support transactions between the programme, the professional, and the general community which emphasise social support rather than crisis intervention. Training of group home staff in behaviour modification leads to gains in staff experience, and job satisfaction, and improved perceptions of programme occupants (Schinke & Wong, 1977).

Although few formal descriptions have been presented of the socialisation process-model of learning present in the group home, some anecdotal reports are enlightening. For example, Burish (1979) has described learning and vocational activities of group home occupants through development of a home cleaning and lawn care service, food service, and large volume wood-working and car cleaning and refurbishing services. Marlett (1979) has emphasised that training should initially focus on personal routines relating to personal hygiene, clothing care, personal appearance and daily responsibilities, then proceed to areas such as transportation, leisure time, money management, and social behaviour. Crnic and Pym (1979) identified a variety of training areas important to group home occupants' increased independence, including personal maintenance, clothing care, home maintenance, food preparation, time management, social behaviour, community utilisation, communication, and functional academics. Further, they reported on behavioural skills training in these areas, noting that such training was not sufficient for the achievement of greater independence; social support, peer interaction and the availability of intermittent supervision *were* critical. Similarly, Schalock and Harper (1979) have noted selected relationships between formal training and success in independent living. The absence of consistent relationships, however, lends support to Crnic and Pym's findings. Robinson and Cupples (1982) have also presented anecdotal information about approaches which can be employed within a normalised group home setting to promote occupant independence. Their approach encompassed the use of a roster of home maintenance duties, shopping checklists organised according to the locations of items in a supermarket, peer feedback, peer training, self-management routines for personal finances, sequential problem-solving guidelines, modelling, and carefully-selected but naturalistic consequences for progress.

Peck, Blackburn and White-Blackburn (1980) have reviewed literature on interventions in group home settings, citing the use of contingency contracting to increase personal grooming skills (Barry, Apolloni & Cooke, 1977), and special instructional materials to enhance cooking skills (Robinson-Wilson, 1977). They have also described structured behavioural training for group home occupants (or with applicability to this population) in money changing (Bellamy & Buttars, 1975), pedestrian skills (Page, Iwata & Neef, 1976), use of public transportation (Neef, Iwata & Page, 1978), and constructive use of leisure time (Day & Day, 1977; Johnson & Bailey, 1977).

The small group context of group homes also offers the opportunity for peer training (i.e., assistance and direction of less capable occupants by more skilled occupants). Examples of this approach may be found in Dilley (1969) and Wagner and Sternlicht (1975) for interventions targeting self-help skills, and in Wiesen and Watson (1967) for social interaction training. Similarly, Snell (1979) employed programme occupants as trainers of language use by less able occupants. Further, the group home also lends itself to the use of group contingencies (i.e., Frankosky & Sulzer-Azaroff, 1978), wherein reinforcement consequences for all occupants may be contingent on the behaviour of a focal individual, or contingencies for occupants may be tied to minimum performance levels in specific skill areas for all occupants.

One of the few recent studies reporting the use of behavioural techniques in a group home is concerned with enhancing the self-preservation ability of moderately and severely mentally retarded individuals (Haney & Jones, 1982). This study serves as an excellent example of the type of training which is appropriately conducted in a group home setting. In fact, self-preservation ability is an area of group home occupant functioning which has increasingly become a source of concern (Groner, Levin & Nelson, 1981; Coady & MacMillan, 1982; MacEachron & Janicki, 1983), for the ability of an individual to exit rapidly and success- fully from a group home in the case of a fire or other emergency can have life or death consequences.

Commentary. Group homes vary a great deal from each other, as do the occupants and staff of these homes. However group homes, more so than foster family care set- tings, represent a programme type whose purposes have been clearly articulated. In most instances, the programme intent is linked to increased personal growth and greater abilities in independent living. The manifestation of these abilities can be seen either through the transition of individuals to living arrangements with less structure, or through the transition of the whole residence to a less intensive level of care and redefinition of the rehabitative intent.

If the home is to be used as a therapeutic setting, the intent of a group home is to use a home setting to promote cooperative living and acquisition of independence capacity. A human management model, such as normalisation, sets the tone for the definition of both the intent and the means. Behavioural methods lend themselves to these goals because of their proven effectiveness and the manner in which staff can be drawn into the training process. Consequently, the defined ecology of such group home settings should offer little or no contention between the intent, the means of bringing about change, and the outcomes.

Clinicians must be aware of their important role in such settings in promoting behaviour change, constructively shaping expectations, and in observing and managing the gain process. Further, in many instances they will act, not upon the occupants of the homes, but the staff who will serve as the key behaviour modifiers. The diversity of such homes, and the diversity of their occupants and staff, do not offer common approaches for interventions. However strategic rehabilitative planning must involve an assessment of the ecology of each home, acknowledgement of the differences among the occupants (and for that matter the staff members), and the manner in which these will be used to effect change.

Extensive consideration has been given to the support and maintenance of behaviour management services by paraprofessional and non-professional programme staff (Bernstein, 1982). Since much of this work has been carried out in congregate care settings, procedures that have been employed for this purpose are described in the section on congregate care which follows. However, procedures used in congregate care to maintain active treatment have direct applicability to group home and other staffed settings.

Congregate Care Settings

Congregate care settings for developmentally disabled persons are generally populated by severely impaired adults who require an intensive programme model because of chronic medical conditions and secondary physical handicaps. From this it may be inferred that individuals residing in these settings will evidence needs for comprehensive, interdisciplinary services. These settings are usually institutional in nature, provide residential accommodations for from a few to several hundred persons, and offer a wide range of in-house medical, nursing, physical and social therapeutic, and support services (Janicki, Jacobson & Schwartz, 1982).

Reppucci (1977) and Reppucci & Saunders (1974) have noted that a variety of factors impact upon capability to introduce and implement behaviour management regimens in institutional settings. Among the barriers they describe are:

a) institutional constraints including pre-existing caretaker devotion to custodial care,
b) external pressures, which are often administration or regulatory,
c) competing needs of staff and occupants,
d) distancing between professionals and staff because of jargon and the perceived inflexibility of behavioural procedures, and
e) the need to compromise and develop *realistic* rather than *ideal* interventions within the limits imposed by staff and fiscal resources.

In order to manage service provision, congregate care settings use both horizontal and vertical staffing structures. Vertical staffing structures encompass residential unit aides/workers, programme aides, paraprofessionals in specific disciplines, professionals, and clinical/organisational managers and administrators.

This structure is analogous to the tiered model of consultation and direction. The horizontal, linking structure is composed of the inter-disciplinary team

(ACMRDD, 1978, Bernstein, Ziarnik, Rudrud & Czajkowski, 1981; and Crosby, 1980). Crosby (1976) describes the interdisciplinary team process as follows.

> *'In this approach, each participant in the evaluation and planning process, utilizing whatever skills, competencies, insights, and perspective his (her) particular training and experience provide, focuses on identifying the developmental needs of the resident, and on devising ways to meet those needs, without constraints imposed by assigning particular areas of behaviour or development to particular disciplines only'* (p. 6).

The vehicle for the implementation of team findings is the individual programme plan. The steps in programme plan development have been noted by several authors (Findykian, Huff & Miller, 1975; Houts & Scott, 1975; Crosby, 1976, 1980; Sauter, 1977; Throne, Hand, Lankford, Luther, McLennan & Watson, 1977; ACMRDD, 1978; Schachter, Rice, Cormier, Christensen & James, 1978; Bernstein et al., 1981; Maddy & Garvey, 1980) and consist of:

a) discipline-specific assessment of the person's abilities,
b) melding of these assessments into a comprehensive assessment which describes the person's abilities in terms of strengths and needs,
c) determination of goals to be achieved by capitalising on strengths in order to address needs,
d) prioritisation of goals,
e) specification of objectives (activities) to be undertaken to address each goals,
f) implementation of objectives, and
g) formal and informal periodic review and assessment of progress toward goals.

Within this framework professionals will be expected to assess the client in a holistic, developmental manner and integrate intervention strategies with those of other specialists (Foley, 1979). Rehabilitative programming will likely include activities focusing upon physical health maintenance, self-help, communication, social skills, self-direction, and emotional functioning.

The complexity and range of occupant needs in congregate care settings requires that limited and defined available resources should be employed to the greatest degree possible. The high proportion of residential and programme aides in comparison to clinical specialists makes their support of behavioural interventions crucial. Clinicians must also be flexible, because interventions within

127

residential units often are modelled, conducted, supervised, and monitored during evenings and weekends.

Many congregate care facilities will be publicly operated, and in all probability employees will be unionised. Depending upon constraints imposed by contractural agreements, a variety of avenues may be available to involve aides in decision-making and active service provision. One option, and one that may enhance organisational commitment (Cherniss, 1981), entails the participation of aides in the interdisciplinary process, particularly in developing the specifics of behavioural interventions for which different staff may be responsible over time.

A further, and necessary, strategy to support active, consistent intervention is staff training in behaviour management techniques. Although no uniform approach to training paraprofessionals in behaviour management has been demonstrated as most effective (Whitman & Scibak, 1979), the use of non- and para-professionals as behaviour therapists has been amply demonstrated in studies by Bricker, Morgan and Grabowski (1971), Iwata, Bailey, Brown, Foshee and Alpern (1976), Gladstone and Sherman (1975), Montegar, Reid, Madsen and Ewell (1977), and Panyon, Boozer and Morris (1970). Recently, support for the effectiveness of direct care staff as therapists was provided by Page, Iwata and Reid (1982), who found small but noticeable improvement by residents in training tasks using direct care staff whose behaviour management training and activities were overseen by their immediate supervisors.

Extensive effort has also been made to assure that once acquired, skills covered in behaviour management training programmes for direct care staff will be employed. Mansdorf, Burick and Judd (1977) found, in an observational study, that, out of a possible ten key behavioural techniques, residential unit staff who were untrained in behaviour management utilised only two, verbal and physical prompts. Without supports to encourage the persistence of behaviour management activities by staff it is probable that, in the face of conflicting responsibilities, direct care staff's use of techniques would return to a similarly low level following training. Bernstein (1982) has described the wide variety of supports that have been employed to induce persistence in active treatment, including the public posting of performance, feedback and contingent approval, supervisory staff reinforcement contingent on direct care staff performance, tokens, money, work schedule rearrangement opportunities, and competition among peers for prizes. Clearly, there is a consensus that in implementing behavioural interventions, knowledge alone is insufficient to insure that interventions will be instituted and carried through.

Fielding (1972) has described methods that can be used to phase behavioural programming into an institutional environment. Considerations to be addressed during the introduction of behaviour management procedures include:

1) application of procedures which require a minimum number of direct care or middle management staff,
2) devotion of as little staff time as possible to the use of procedures,
3) use of small groups for occupant training to maximise efficient use of staff time,
4) selection of target behaviours that hold promise for rapid modification and thereby a source of reinforcement for staff, and
5) selection of target behaviours which reflect common and pervasive occupant deficits, thereby permitting a degree of uniformity in the application of techniques.

A more client-centered model for institutional settings, with greater differentiation in training goals and more individually structured interventions, has been presented for persons with severe and profound mental retardation by Bigelow and Griffiths (1972). Their model for an intensive training unit relied heavily upon a combination of a token economy system providing differential reinforcement for non-disruptive behaviour and structured teaching to promote adaptive skills.

Within congregate care settings, the interdisciplinary team, and specifically the psychologist, will often be called-upon to develop interventions to facilitate decreases in maladaptive and self-injurious behaviour. The clearly defined boundaries of this setting, the relative abundance of staff, and the corresponding ability to alter both the antecedents and consequences of behaviours are valuable supports to such interventions, although institutional settings are not the sole locale where these may be conducted.

Examples of approaches which may be used to obtain behaviour change in congregate care settings include interventions to suppress self-stimulatory behaviour in an institutional unit and related day school programme, by Coleman, Whitman and Johnson (1979) and in a center-based classroom by Shapiro, Barrett and Ollendick (1980). Other examples of institution-based approaches to modifying undesired behaviours include reports by Azrin and Wesolowski (1975), and Foxx (1976) which specifically dealt with behaviours interfering with programme participation. In these reports overcorrection, positive practice, and compliance training are presented as applicable techniques.

Consideration should also be given to both gains in behavioural control and increased opportunities for training made possible by altering the physical plant of a facility. For example, Levy and MacLeod (1977) found that conversion of an institutional day room to a less open structure that lent itself to use by smaller groups was associated with reduced stereotypies and increased *productive* behaviour. Similarly, Harris, Veit, Allen and Chinsky (1974) found that ward aides worked more effectively when alone and assigned to a small group of individuals; consistent with these findings, small group involvement could be encouraged through physical plant and programme design.

Commentary. Congregate care facilities are often ideal settings in which to design and implement behaviour interventions. However, there are limitations that constrict rehabilitative strategies and confound means to define ecological validity. Such facilities usually provide for multi-handicapped persons and are designed to provide residential care with a full range of professional and clinical services. The environment is less a function of the overall programme intent than in community care settings. Here the environment is set to maximise the provision of specialised services. In most instances, also, the settings are employee-centered and not client-centered. However, rehabilitative methods and behavioural interventions are very appropriate. Their absence or misapplication in such settings remains a defining characteristic of custodial care.

CLOSING COMMENTS

The consideration of rehabilitative means and their application to residential programme services is a critical aspect of a clinician's work. Persons, dependent because of mental or physical handicap, are the consumers of a myriad of services that for the most part, if judiciously applied, can support movement toward less dependence and the acquisition of more functional capabilities. Rehabilitative technologies have a specific purpose: *the restoration or integration of a disabled individual.* This purpose must be considered when defining the role of a residential programme and constructing interventions to apply within that programme. In this regard, this chapter has attempted to interweave fundamental notions prevalent in a human management model with a framework for defining residential models and the application of effective behavioural methodologies. The key notions are:

1. Rehabilitative practices must draw upon a framework for designing a rehabilitative plan that encompasses the total person. Consideration of a human management model such as normalisation, which is structured to promote social, physical, and psychological integration, is pertinent.

2. Rehabilitative practices will be more functional if they are designed to operate within the various residential models available and take into account the purpose of using one model over another. This must extend to matching an individual with an appropriate environment that is conducive to accommodating the overall rehabilitative plan.

3. The residential model of a programme encompasses the programme's environment, its rehabilitative intent, and management system. To the extent that consultation and professional service activities are tailored to capitalise on the strengths and minimise the limitations inherent within a residential model, these activities will be supportive of the programme's purpose.

4. The principles of behavioural intervention, as well as alternative theoretical orientations, demonstrate clear applicability across a range of residential models. Variations in implementation strategies and the structure of supports are required, however, to ensure caregiver participation in programming and beneficial therapeutic outcome.

5. Consultative and clinical services must be provided with a recognition that the setting as a rehabilitative system, as well as staff and occupants, is best understood as a *focus* of intervention. Strategies directed at enhancing the programme environment and its management will, in turn, enhance the capabilities of staff. Enhanced staff capabilities will, in turn, promote a positive prognosis for occupant rehabilitative growth.

6. Congregate care systems represent social and service systems which are not readily amenable to intervention by external agents. Change in congregate care settings is externally imposed primarily through administrative practices which determine absolute levels of resource availability. In contrast, foster care and group home settings are intrinsically linked to, and dependent upon, the larger service system and general community in which they are embedded. These considerations are primary determinants of the capabilities of each residential model.

7. Rehabilitative practices should be built upon technologies with proven effectiveness and ease of use. These include building interventions based upon social learning principles, whether the applications are directly or indirectly behavioural (for example, using humanistic approaches but structured according to learning principles).

In summary, rehabilitative practices will be more effective when consideration is given to the residential ecology and when designing interventions (or the overall rehabilitation plan), consideration is given to the validity of using interventions in the context of the residential model.

REFERENCES

Accreditation Council for Services for Mentally Retarded and Other Developmentally Disabled Persons. (1978) *Standards for Services for Developmentally Disabled Individuals*, Joint Commission on Accreditation of Hospitals, Chicago.

Adams, M. (1975) 'Foster Family Care for the Intellectually Disadvantaged Child: The Current State of Practice and Some Research Perspectives', in M. J. Begab & S. A. Richardson (eds.), *The Mentally Retarded and Society: A Social Science Perspective*, University Park Press, Baltimore.

Ayllon, T., Garber, S. & Pisor, K. (1975) 'The Elimination of Discipline Problems through a Combined School-Home Motivational System', *Behaviour Therapy, 6*, 616-626.

Azrin, N. H. & Wesolowski, M. D. (1975) 'The Use of Positive Practice to Eliminate Persistent Floor Sprawling by Profoundly Retarded Persons', *Behaviour Therapy, 6*, 627-631.

Bailey, J., Wolf, M. & Phillips, E. (1970) 'Home-Based Reinforcement and the Modification of Pre-Delinquents' Classroom Behavior', *Journal of Applied Behavior Analysis, 3*, 223-233.

Bank-Mikkelson, N. E. (1969) 'A Metropolitan Area in Denmark: Copenhagen', in R. B. Kugel & W. Wolfensberger (eds.), *Changing Patterns in Residential Services for the Mentally Retarded*, President's Committee on Mental Retardation, Washington, D.C.

Baroff, S. (1980) 'On "Size" and the Quality of Residential Care: A Second Look', *Mental Retardation, 18*, 113-117.

Barry, K., Apolloni, T. & Cooke, T. (1977) 'Improving the Personal Hygiene of Mildly Retarded Men in a Community-Based Residential Training Program', *Corrective Social Psychiatry, 23*, 65-68.

Becker, W. C. (1971) *Parents are Teachers: A Child Management Program*, Research Press, Champaign, Illinois.

Bellamy, T. & Buttars, K. L. (1975) 'Teaching Trainable Level Retarded Students to Count Money: Toward Personalized Independence through Academic Instruction', *Education and Training of the Mentally Retarded, 10*, 18-26.

Beltz, S. E. (1971) *How to Make Johnny Want to Obey*,
   Prentice-Hall, Englewood Cliffs, New Jersey.
Berkson, G. & Landesman-Dwyer, S. (1977) 'Behavioral
   Research on Severe and Profound Mental Retardation
   (1955-1974)', *American Journal of Mental Deficiency*,
   81, 428-454.
Bernstein, G. S. (1981) 'Research Issues in Training
   Interpersonal Skills for the Mentally Retarded',
   Education and Training of the Mentally Retarded, *16*,
   70-73.
Bernstein, G. S. (1982) 'Training Behavior Change Agents:
   A Conceptual Review', *Behavior Therapy*, *13*, 1-23.
Bernstein, G. S., Ziarnik, J. P., Rudrud, E. H. &
   Czajkowski, L. A. (1981) *Behavioral Habilitation
   Through Proactive Programming*, Paul H. Brookes,
   Baltimore.
Bigelow, G. & Griffiths, R. (1972) 'An Intensive Teaching
   Unit for Severely and Profoundly Retarded Women' in
   T. Thompson & J. Grabowski (eds.), *Behavior Modific-
   ation of the Mentally Retarded*, Oxford University
   Press, New York.
Bjaanes, A. T. & Butler, E. W. (1974) 'Environmental
   Variation in Community Care Facilities for Mentally
   Retarded Persons', *American Journal of Mental
   Deficiency*, *78*, 429-439.
Bjaanes, A. T., Butler, E. W. & Kelly, B. R. (1981) 'Place-
   ment Type and Client Functional Level as Factors in
   Provision of Services Aimed at Increasing Adjustment',
   in R. H. Bruininks, C. E. Meyers, B. B. Sigford & K. C.
   Lakin (eds.), *Deinstitutionalization and Community
   Adjustment of Mentally Retarded People*, American
   Association on Mental Deficiency, Washington, D.C.
Bricker, W. A., Morgan, D. G. & Grabowski, J. G. (1972)
   'Development and Maintenance of a Behavior Modification
   Repetoire of Cottage Attendants through T.V. Feedback',
   American Journal of Mental Deficiency, *77*, 128-136.
Bruininks, R. H., Hill, B. K. & Thorsheim, M. S. (1980) *A
   Profile of Specially Licensed Foster Homes for Mentally
   Retarded People in 1977*, Department of Psycho-
   educational Studies, University of Minnesota,
   Minneapolis, Minnesota.
Bruininks, R. H., Kudla, M. J., Wieck, C. A. & Hauber, F. A.
   (1980) 'Management Problems in Community Residential
   Facilities', *Mental Retardation*, *18*, 125-130.
Butler, E. W. & Bjaanes, A. T. (1977) 'A Typology of
   Community Care Facilities and Differential
   Normalization Outcomes', in P. Mittler & J. deJong
   (eds.), *Research to Practice in Mental Retardation:
   Care and Intervention*, University Park Press,
   Baltimore.

Burish, T. G. (1979) 'A Small Community Model for Develop-
    ing Normalizing Alternatives to Institutionalization',
    Mental Retardation, 17, 90-91.
Callias, M. & Carr, J. (1975) 'Behavior Modification
    Programs in a Community Setting', in C. C. Kiernan &
    F. P. Woodford (eds.), *Behaviour Modification with the
    Severely Retarded,* American Elsevier, New York.
Cherniss, C. (1981) 'Organizational Design and the Social
    Environment in Group Homes for Mentally Retarded
    Persons', in H. C. Haywood & J. R. Newbrough (eds.),
    *Living Environments for Developmentally Retarded
    Persons,* University Park Press, Baltimore.
Cherniss, C. & Egnatios, E. (1978) 'Participation in
    Decision-Making by Staff in Community Mental Health
    Programs', *American Journal of Community Psychology,
    6,* 171-190.
Close, D. W. (1977) 'Community Living for Severely and
    Profoundly Retarded Adults', *Education and Training of
    the Mentally Retarded, 12,* 256-262.
Close, D. W., O'Connor, G. & Peterson, S. L. (1981) 'Util-
    ization of Habilitation Services by Developmentally
    Disabled Persons in Community Facilities', in H. C.
    Haywood & J. R. Newbrough (eds.), *Living Environments
    for Developmentally Retarded Persons,* University Park
    Press, Baltimore.
Coady, D. & MacMillan, R. (1982) *Fire Safety Training
    Materials for Adults with Mental Handicap,* A paper
    presented at the 6th International Congress of the
    International Association for the Scientific Study of
    Mental Deficiency, August, Toronto, Canada.
Coleman, R. S., Whitman, T. L. & Johnson, M. R. (1979)
    'Suppression of Self-Stimulatory Behavior of a
    Profoundly Retarded Boy Across Staff and Settings: An
    Assessment of Situational Generalization', *Behavior
    Therapy, 10,* 266-280.
Craighead, W. E., Kazdin, A. E. & Mahoney, M. J. (1976)
    *Behavior   Modification: Principles,   Issues   and
    Applications,* Houghton Mifflin, Boston.
Crawford, J. L., Thompson, D. E. & Aiello, J. R. (1981)
    'Community Placement of Mentally Retarded Persons:
    Clinical and Environmental Considerations', in H. C.
    Haywood & J. R. Newbrough (eds.), *Living Environments
    for Developmentally Retarded Persons,* University Park
    Press, Baltimore.
Crosby, K. G. (1976) 'Essentials of Active Programming',
    Mental Retardation, 14(2), 3-9.
Crosby, K. G. (1980) 'Implementing the Developmental
    Model', in J. F.Gardner, L. Long, R. Nichols & D. M.
    Iagulli (eds.), *Program Issues in Developmental
    Disabilities: A Resource Manual for Surveyors and
    Reviewers,* Paul H. Brookes, Baltimore.

Crnic, K. A. & Pym, H. A. (1979) 'Training Mentally Retarded Adults in Independent Living Skills', *Mental Retardation, 17*, 13-16.

Cunningham, C. (1975) 'Parents as Therapists and Educators', in C. C. Kiernan & F. B. Woodford (eds.), *Behavior Modification with the Severely Retarded*, American Elsevier, New York.

Day, R. & Day, M. (1977) 'Leisure Skills Instruction for the Moderately and Severely Retarded: A Demonstration Program', *Education and Training of the Mentally Retarded, 12*, 128-131.

Dilley, G. M. (1969) 'Retarded Women Teach Self-Help Skills', *Hospital & Community Psychiatry, 20*, 44-45.

Epple, W. (1982) *Personal Communication*, Program Research Unit, New York State Office of Mental Retardation and Developmental Disabilities. Albany, New York.

Epstein, H. R. (1982) 'Means, Ends, and the Principle of Normalization: A Closer Look', *Education and Training of the Mentally Retarded, 17*, 153-156.

Eyman, R. K. (1977) *Review of Foster Care Literature*. UCLA Neuro-Psychiatric Institute, Pacific State Hospital, Pomona, California.

Eyman, R. K., Demaine, G. C. & Lei, T. (1979) 'Relationship Between Community Environments and Resident Changes in Adaptive Behavior: A Path Model', *American Journal of Mental Deficiency, 83*, 330-338.

Eyman, R. K., Silverstein, A. B., McLain, R. & Miller, C. (1977) 'Effects of Residential Settings on Development', in P. Mittler & J. deJong (eds.), *Research to Practice in Mental Retardation: Care and Intervention*, University Park Press, Baltimore.

Felsenthal, D. & Scheerenberger, R. C. (1978) 'Stability and Attitudes of Primary Caregivers in the Community', *Mental Retardation, 16*, 16-21.

Fielding, L. (1972) 'Initial Ward-Wide Behavior Modification Programs for Retarded Children', in T. Thompson & J. Grabowski (eds.), *Behavior Modification of the Mentally Retarded*, Oxford University Press, New York.

Findykian, N., Huff, T. M. & Miller, P. H. (1975) *A Manual of Instruction for Preparing and Recording Documents for the Goal Planning System* (Goal Planning System Technical Document GP 75-02), Tennessee Department of Mental Health and Mental Retardation, Nashville.

Fiorelli, J. S. & Thurman, S. K. (1979) 'Client Behavior in More and Less Normalized Settings', *Education and Training of the Mentally Retarded, 14*, 85-94.

Foley, G. M. (1979) *Family-Centered Resources Project-Outreach*, Paper presented at the 103rd Annual Meeting of the American Association on Mental Deficiency, June, Miami Beach.

Forehand, R. & Atkeson, B. M. (1977) 'Generality of Treatment Effects with Parents as Therapists: A Review of Assessment and Implementation Procedures', *Behavior Therapy, 8*, 575-593.

Foxx, R. M. (1976) 'Increasing a Mildly Retarded Woman's Attendance at Self-Help Classes by Overcorrection and Instruction', *Behavior Therapy, 7*, 390-396.

Frankosky, R. J. & Sulzer-Azaroff, B. (1978) 'Individual and Group Contingencies and Collateral Social Behaviors', *Behavior Therapy, 9*, 313-327.

Gilbert, K. A. & Hemming, H. (1979) 'Environmental Change and Psycho-Linguistic Ability of Mentally Retarded Adults', *American Journal of Mental Deficiency, 83*, 455-459.

Gladstone, B. W. & Sherman, J. A. (1975) 'Developing Generalized Behavior Modification Skills in High-School Students Working with Retarded Children', *Journal of Applied Behavior Analysis, 8*, 169-180.

Groner, N. E., Levin, B. M. & Nelson, H. E. (1981) 'Measuring Evacuation Difficulty in Board and Care Homes', *Fire Journal, 75*(5), 44-50.

Gunzburg, H. (1977) 'Guided or Unguided Adjustment to Life in the Community: An Evaluation', *Journal of Practical Approaches to Developmental Handicap, 1*, 31-36.

Haney, J. I. & Jones, R. T. (1982) 'Programming Maintenance as a Major Component of a Community-Centered Preventive Effort: Escape from Fire', *Behavior Therapy, 13*, 47-62.

Harris, J. M., Veit, S. W., Allen, G. J. & Chinsky, J. M. (1974) 'Aide-Resident Ratio and Ward Population Density as Mediators of Social Interaction', *American Journal of Mental Deficiency, 79*, 320-326.

Harris, S. L. & Romanczyk, R. G. (1976) 'Treating Self-Injurious Behavior of a Retarded Child by Over-Correction', *Behavior Therapy, 7*, 235-239.

Hill, B. K. & Bruininks, R. H. (1981) *Physical and Behavioral Characteristics and Maladaptive Behavior of Mentally Retarded People in Residential Facilities* (Project Report No: 12), Department of Psycho-Educational Studies, University of Minnesota, Minneapolis.

Hitzing, W. (1980) 'ENCOR and Beyond', in T. Apolloni, J. Cappucilli & T. P. Cooke (eds.), *Achievements in Residential Services for Persons with Disabilities: Toward Excellence*, University Park Press, Baltimore.

Holman, J. (1977) 'The Moral Risk and High Cost of Ecological Concern in Applied Behavior Analysis', in A. Rogers-Warren & S. R. Warren (eds.), *Ecological Perspectives in Behavior Analysis*, University Park Press, Baltimore.

Houts, P. S. & Scott, R. A. (1975) *Goal Planning with Mentally Disabled Persons*, Department of Behavioral Sciences, Pennsylvania State University, Hershey, PA.

Insel, P. M. & Moos, R. H. (1974) 'Psychological Environments: Expanding the Scope of Human Ecology', *American Psychologist, 29*, 179-188.

Intagliata, J., Kraus, S. & Willer, B. (1980) 'The Impact of Deinstitutionalization on a Community Based Service System', *Mental Retardation, 18*, 305-307.

Intagliata, J., Willer, B. & Wicks, N. (1981) 'Factors Related to the Quality of Community Adjustment in Family Care Homes', in R. H. Bruininks, C. E. Meyers, B. B. Sigford, & K. C. Lakin (eds.), *Deinstitutionalization and Community Adjustment of Mentally Retarded People* (Monograph No. 4), American Association on Mental Deficiency, Washington, D.C.

Ittelson, W. H., Proshansky, H. M. & Rivlin, L. G. (1970) 'The Environmental Psychology of the Psychiatric Ward', in H. M. Proshansky, W. H. Ittelson & L. G. Rivlin (eds.), *Environmental Psychology: Man and his Physical Setting*, Holt, New York.

Iwata, B. A., Bailey, J. S., Brown, K. M., Foshee, T. J. & Alpern, M. (1976) 'A Performance-Based Lottery to Improve Residential Care and Training by Institutional Staff', *Journal of Applied Behavior Analysis, 9*, 417-431.

Jacobson, J. W. & Janicki, M. P. (1983) *Clinical Need Variations of Disabled Persons in Group Homes*, Unpublished Manuscript, State Office of Mental Retardation and Developmental Disabilities, New York.

Jacobson, J. W. & Schwartz, A. A. (1983) 'Evaluation of Community Living Alternatives', in J. Matson & J. Mulick (eds.), *Handbook of Mental Retardation*. Pergamon Press, Elmsford, New York.

Janicki, M. P. (1981) 'Personal Growth and Community Residence Environments: A Review', in H. C. Haywood & J. R. Newbrough (eds.), *Living Environments for Developmentally Retarded Persons*, University Park Press, Baltimore.

Janicki, M. P., Jacobson, J. W. & Schwartz, A. A. (1982) 'Residential Care Settings: Models for Rehabilitative Intent', *Journal of Practical Approaches to Developmental Handicap, 6*, 10-16.

Janicki, M. P., Jacobson, J. W., Zigman, W. B. & Gordon, N. A. (1984) 'Characteristics of Employees of Community Residences for Retarded Persons', *Education and Training of the Mentally Retarded, 19*.

Jaslow, R. I. & Spagna, M. B. (1977) 'Gaps in a Comprehensive System of Services for the Mentally Retarded', *Mental Retardation, 15*, 6-9.

Johnson, M. S. & Bailey, J. S. (1977) 'The Modification of Leisure Behavior in a Half-way House for Retarded Women', *Journal of Applied Behavior Analysis, 10,* 273-282.

Johnson-Silver, E., Silverman, W. & Lubin, R. A. (1984) 'Community Living for Severely and Profoundly Retarded Persons', in J. M. Berg & J. deJong (eds.) *Perspectives and Progress in Mental Retardation: Proceedings of the 6th Congress of IASSMD, Toronto (Vol. I: Social, Psychological and Educational Aspects*), University Park Press, Baltimore.

Kaprowy, E. A. (1980) 'A Program Evaluation of a Community Behavioural Support Service for the Retarded', *Journal of Practical Approaches to Developmental Handicap, 4,* 4-9.

Kazdin, A. E. (1977) 'Assessing the Clinical or Applied Importance of Behavior Change Through Social Validation', *Behavior Modification, 1,* 427-451.

Konarski, E. A., Crowell, C. R., Johnson, M. R. & Whitman, T. L. (1982) 'Response Deprivation, Reinforcement, and Instrumental Academic Performance in an EMR Classroom', *Behavior Therapy, 13,* 94-102.

Landesman-Dwyer, S. (1981) 'Living in the Community', *American Journal of Mental Deficiency, 86,* 223-234.

Landesman-Dwyer, S., Berkson, G. & Romer, D. (1979) 'Affiliation and Friendship of Mentally Retarded Residents in Group Homes', *American Journal of Mental Deficiency, 83,* 571-580.

Landesman-Dwyer, S., Stein, J. G. & Sackett, G. P. (1978) 'A Behavioral and Ecological Study of Group Homes', in G. P. Sackett (ed.), *Observing Behavior, Vol. 1: Theory and Applications in Mental Retardation,* University Park Press, Baltimore.

Lavigneur, H. (1976) 'The Use of Siblings as an Adjunct to the Behavioral Treatment of Children in the Home with Parents as Therapists', *Behavior Therapy, 7,* 602-613.

Levy, E. & MacLeod, W. (1977) 'The Effect of Environmental Design on Adolescents in an Institution', *Mental Retardation, 15,* 28-32.

Lindsley, O. R. (1964) 'Direct Measurement and Prosthesis of Retarded Behavior', *Journal of Education, 141,* 62-81.

MacEachron, A. E. & Janicki, M. P. (1983) 'Self-Preservation Ability and Residential Fire Emergencies', *American Journal of Mental Deficiency, 88,* 157-163.

Macht, J. (1975) *Teaching Our Children,* John Wiley & Sons, New York.

Maddy, B. J. & Garvey, B. (1980) *Individual Program Plans: A Practical Guide for County Care Facilities.* University of Iowa, University Affiliated Program, Division of Developmental Disabilities, Iowa City.

Mansdorf, I. J., Burick, D. A. & Judd, L. C. (1977)
'Behavioral Treatment Strategies of Institutional Ward
Staff', *Mental Retardation, 15,* 22-24.
Marholin, D., O'Toole, K. M., Touchette, P. E., Berger, P.
L. & Doyle, D. A. (1979) '"I'll have a Big Mac, Large
Fries, Large Coke, and Apple Pie,"....or Teaching
Adaptive Community Skills', *Behavior Therapy, 10,*
236-248.
Marlett, N. J. (1979) 'Incentive for Independence in
Residential Training for the Developmentally Handi-
capped', *Journal of Practical Approaches to
Developmental Handicap, 3,* 9-13.
Montegar, C. A., Reid, D. H., Madsen, C. H. & Ewell, M. D.
(1977) 'Increasing Institutional Staff to Resident
Interactions Through In-Service Training and Supervisor
Approval', *Behavior Therapy, 8,* 533-540.
Neef, N. A., Iwata, B. A. & Page, T. J. (1978) 'Public
Transportation Training: *In Vivo* versus Classroom
Instruction', *Journal of Applied Behavior Analysis, 11,*
331-344.
Newman, E. S. & Sherman, S. R. (1979-80) 'Foster-Family
Care for the Elderly: Surrogate Family or Mini-
Institutions?' *International Journal of Aging and
Human Development, 10,* 165-176.
Nirje, B. (1969) 'The Normalization Principle and its Human
Management Implications', in R. B. Kugel & W.
Wolfensberger (eds.), *Changing Patterns in Residential
Services for the Mentally Retarded,* President's
Committee on Mental Retardation, Washington, D.C.
O'Connor, G. & Sitkei, E. G. (1975) 'Study of a New
Frontier in Community Services', *Mental Retardation,
13,* 35-38.
O'Dell, S. (1974) 'Training Parents in Behavior Modifica-
tion: A Review', *Psychological Bulletin, 81,* 418-433.
Page, T. J., Iwata, B. A. & Neef, N. A. (1976) 'Teaching
Pedestrian Skills to Retarded Persons: Generalization
from the Classroom to Natural Environments', *Journal of
Applied Behavior Analysis, 9,* 433-444.
Page, T. J., Iwata, B. A. & Reid, D. H. (1982) 'Pyramidal
Training: A Large-scale Replication with Institutional
Staff', *Journal of Applied Behavior Analysis, 15,*
335-351.
Panyon, M., Boozer, H. & Morris, N. (1970) 'Feedback to
Attendants as a Reinforcer for Applying Operant
Techniques', *Journal of Applied Behavior Analysis, 3,*
1-4.
Parks, A. W. (1978) 'A Model for Psychological Consultation
to Community Residences', *Mental Retardation, 16,*
149-152.

Patterson, G. R. (1971) *Families: Application of Social Learning to Family Life*, Research Press, Champaign, Illinois.

Patterson, G. R. & Gullion, M. E. (1978) *Living with Children*, Research Press, Champaign, Illinois.

Peck, C. A., Blackburn, T. & White-Blackburn, G. (1980) 'Making it Work: A Review of the Empirical Literature on Community Living Arrangements', in T. Apolloni, J. Cappucilli & T. P. Cooke (eds.), *Achievements in Residential Services for Persons with Disabilities: Toward Excellence*, University Park Press, Baltimore.

Phillips, R. (1982) 'The Use of Independent Living Staff's Time', *Journal of Practical Approaches to Developmental Handicap, 6*, 17-21.

Price, R. H. & Blashfield, R. K. (1975) 'Explorations in the Taxonomy of Behavior Settings: Analysis of Dimensions and Classification of Settings', *American Journal of Community Psychology, 3*, 335-350.

Provencal, G. & MacCormack, J. P. (1979) 'Adult Foster Care: Paradox and Possibility', *DD Polestar, 1*(7), 4.

Public Interest Law Center (1979) *Working Paper on Uses of Title XIX to Sustain Community Residential Services for Developmentally Disabled Persons*, Public Interest Law Center of Philadelphia, Philadelphia, Pennsylvania.

Reppucci, N. D. (1977) 'Implementation Issues for the Behavior Modifier as Institutional Change Agent', *Behavior Therapy, 8*, 594-605.

Reppucci, N. D. & Saunders, J. T. (1974) 'Social Psychology of Behavior Modification: Problems of Implementation in Natural Settings', *American Psychologist, 29*, 649-660.

Risley, T. R. (1970) 'Behavior Modification: An Experimental-Therapeutic Endeavor', in L. A. Hammerlynck, P. O. Davidson & L. E. Acker (eds.) *Behavior Modification and Ideal Mental Health Services*, University of Calgary Press, Calgary, Alberta.

Risley, T. R. (1977) 'The Ecology of Applied Behavior Analysis', in A. Rogers-Warren & S. F. Warren (eds.) *Ecological Perspectives in Behavior Analysis*, University Park Press, Baltimore.

Robinson, D. & Cupples, J. (1982) 'Normalization as Process and Outcome: A Case Study of a Community Residence', *Journal of Practical Approaches to Developmental Handicap, 3*, 9-14.

Robinson-Wilson, M. (1977) 'Picture Recipe Cards as an Approach to Training Retarded Adults to Cook', *Education and Training of the Mentally Retarded, 12*, 69-73.

Rogers-Warren, A. (1977) 'Planned Change: Ecobehaviorally Based Interventions', in A. Rogers-Warren & S. F. Warren (eds.), *Ecological Perspectives in Behavior Analysis*, University Park Press, Baltimore.

Rogers-Warren, A. & Warren, S. F. (1977) 'The Developing Ecobehavioral Psychology', in A. Rogers-Warren & S. F. Warren (eds.), *Ecological Perspective in Behavior Analysis*, University Park Press, Baltimore.

Roos, P. (1972) 'Reconciling Behavior Modification Procedures with the Normalization Principle', in W. Wolfensberger (ed.), *Normalization: The Principle of Normalization in Human Services*, National Institute on Mental Retardation, Toronto.

Sandler, A. & Thurman, S. K. (1981) 'Status of Community Placement Research: Effects on Retarded Citizens', *Education and Training of the Mentally Retarded, 16*, 245-251.

Sauter, R. C. (1977) 'Elements for Developing Competency-based Programs for the Mentally Retarded', *Mental Retardation, 15*, 40-42.

Schachter, M., Rice, J. A., Cormier, H. J. G., Christensen, P. M. & James, N. J. (1978) 'A Process for Individual Program Planning Based on the Adaptive Behavior Scale', *Mental Retardation, 16*, 259-263.

Schalock, R. L. & Harper, R. S. (1979) 'Training in Independent Living Can Be Done', *Journal of Rehabilitation Administration, 3*, 129-132.

Schinke, S. & Wong, S. (1977) 'Evaluation of Staff Training in Group Homes for Retarded Persons', *American Journal of Mental Deficiency, 82*, 130-136.

Schriebman, L., Koegel, R. L., Mills, J. I, & Burke, J. C. (1981) 'Social Validation of Behavior Therapy with Autistic Children', *Behavior Therapy, 12*, 610-624.

Schroeder, S. R. (1972) 'Parametric Effects of Reinforcement Frequency, Amount of Reinforcement, and Required Response Force on Sheltered Workshop Behavior', *Journal of Applied Behavior Analysis, 5*, 431-442.

Senatore, V., Matson, J. L. & Kazdin, A. E. (1982) 'A Comparison of Behavioral Methods to Train Social Skills to Mentally Retarded Adults', *Behavior Therapy, 13*, 313-324.

Shapiro, E. S., Barrett, R. P. & Ollendick, T. H. (1980) 'A Comparison of Physical Restraint and Positive Overcorrection in Treating Stereotypic Behavior', *Behavior Therapy, 11*, 227-233.

Short, R. (1980) 'From Institution to Comprehensive Community Services: A Realistic View or a Nightmare.' *Journal of Practical Approaches to Developmental Handicap, 4*, 9-13.

141

Snell, M. E. (1979) 'Higher Functioning Residents as Language Trainers of the Mentally Retarded', *Education and Training of the Mentally Retarded, 14*, 77-84.

Stacey, D., Doleys, D. M. & Malcolm, R. (1979) 'Effects of Social Skills Training in a Community-based Program.' *American Journal of Mental Deficiency, 84*, 152-158.

Stein, I. J. & Gambill, E. D. (1976) 'Behavioral Techniques in Foster Care', *Social Work, 21*, 34-39.

Tennov, D., Jacobson, J. W. & Vittucci, M. (1980) 'Token Economies and Unpredictable Reward in Family Settings: A Descriptive Report', *Psychotherapy: Theory, Research and Practice, 17*, 220-226.

Tharp, R. G. & Wetzel, R. J. (1969) *Behavior Modification in the Natural Environment*, Academic Press, New York.

Throne, J. M., Hand, R. J., Hupka, M. L., Lankford, C. W., Luther, K. M., McLennan, S. L. & Watson, J. B. (1977) 'Unified Programming Procedures for the Mentally Retarded', *Mental Retardation, 15*, 14-17.

Thurman, S. K. (1981) 'Least Restrictive Environments: Another Side of the Coin', *Education and Training of the Mentally Retarded, 16*, 68-70.

Turner, S. M., Hersen, M. & Bellack, A. S. (1978) 'Social Skills Training to Teach Prosocial Skills in an Organically Impaired and Retarded Patient', *Journal of Behavior Therapy and Experimental Psychiatry, 9*, 253-258.

Vischer, J. C. (1982) 'Problem Analysis in Planning a Community-based Behaviour Management Program', *Journal of Practical Approaches to Developmental Handicap, 6*, 22-27.

Voeltz, L. M. & Evans, I. M. (1982) 'The Assessment of Behavior Inter-Relationships in Child Behavior Therapy', *Behavioral Assessment, 4*, 131-165.

Wagner, P. & Sternlicht, M. (1975) 'Retarded Persons as "Teachers": Retarded Adolescents Tutoring Retarded Children', *American Journal of Mental Deficiency, 79*, 674-679.

Warren, S. F. (1977) 'A Useful Ecobehavioral Perspective for Applied Behavior Analysis', in A. Rogers-Warren & S. F. Warren (eds.), *Ecological Perspectives in Behavior Analysis*, University Park Press, Baltimore.

Watson, L. S. (1973) *Child Behavior Modification: A Manual for Teachers, Nurses and Parents*, Pergamon Press, New York.

Whitman, T. L. & Scibak, J. W. (1979) 'Behavior Modification Research with the Severely and Profoundly Mentally Retarded', in N. R. Ellis (ed.), *Handbook of Mental Deficiency, Psychological Theory and Research* (2nd ed.), Lawrence Erlbaum, Elmsford, New Jersey.

Wiesen, A. E. & Watson, E. (1967) 'Elimination of Attention-Seeking Behavior in a Retarded Child', *American Journal of Mental Deficiency, 72,* 50-52.

Willems, E. P. (1974) 'Behavior Technology and Behavior Ecology', *Journal of Applied Behavior Analysis, 7,* 151-165.

Willer, B. & Intagliata, J. (1982) 'Comparison of Family-Care and Group Homes as Alternatives to Institutions', *American Journal of Mental Deficiency, 86,* 588-595.

Willer, B. & Intagliata, J. (1981) 'Social-Environmental Factors and Predictors of Adjustment of Deinstitutionalized Mentally Retarded Adults', *American Journal of Mental Deficiency, 86,* 252-259.

Wolfensberger, W. (ed.) (1972) *Normalization: The Principle of Normalization in Human Services,* National Institute on Mental Retardation, Toronto, Ontario.

Wolfensberger, W. & Glenn, L. (1975) *Program Analysis of Service System Handbook* (3rd ed.), National Institute on Mental Retardation, Toronto.

Wolfensberger, W. (1980) 'The Definition of Normalization: Update, Problems, Disagreements, and Misunderstandings', in R. J. Flynn & K. E. Nitsch (eds.) *Normalization, Social Integration, and Community Services,* University Park Press, Baltimore.

Chapter Six

BEHAVIORAL AND EMOTIONAL ASPECTS OF TRAINING FOR
ADOLESCENTS AND ADULTS WHO ARE DEVELOPMENTALLY HANDICAPPED

E. Anne Hughson

INTRODUCTION

Over the last 15 years in Canada attempts to meet the needs
of individuals with developmental handicaps have led to a
variety of more humane, normalising training programmes and
living environments. The development and application of
effective teaching techniques in special education and adult
rehabilitation settings have been made available to adolescents and adults, with the result that an increasing number
of individuals with handicapping conditions are gaining
competence and, with this, access to the range of daily
activities experienced by the average citizen. Increased
success in teaching functional skills, corresponding changes
in values and tolerance for those individuals considered to
be deviant, have encouraged greater accountability for
service delivery and resulted in the rise of consumer
advocacy in the delivery of educational, vocational and
residential services.

Professional personnel have increased their competence
and degree of participation with handicapped individuals and
their families. Furthermore, collaboration between
professionals from a variety of health, behavioural and
social science disciplines has fostered a multidisciplinary
and transdisciplinary approach to assessment and training
techniques, which has affected the sophistication of theoretical knowledge and the range of practical approaches to
rehabilitation.

The development of Individualized Program Planning
which requires that consumers, families and professionals
jointly set goals and objectives and carry out the teaching
of functional skills, has had encouraging results (Wehman &
McLaughlin, 1981). Some government departments at the level
of societal planning, policy making and fiscal control
articulate beliefs, under the umbrella of normalisation, in
deinstitutionalisation, regionalisation and community

144

operation of facilities. All of these factors have markedly affected the growing field of Rehabilitation Education and challenged our communities to increase the qualitative aspects of life for individuals with developmental handicaps. Such challenges include increased concern for evaluation of programme effectiveness, and conscious willingness to accept all individuals into education and training programmes.

In the last few years structured training environments have been established which systematically present tasks in a developmental sequence, leading to a continua of training phases for social-education, vocational and home-living skills (Gold, 1973; Marlett & Hughson, 1978; Brown & Hughson, 1980). Perhaps this technology has even lulled teachers and trainers into assuming that such structure is tailor-made for all individuals who are developmentally handicapped, regardless of their varied personalities. However, evaluation studies have critically examined reasons for failure in training competence and independence. Gunzburg & Gunzburg (1973) query the inappropriate application of the normalisation principle for those not equipped for independence, i.e. deficits do not disappear by merely placing the individual in more normal environmental circumstances. They propose a far more expansive model of socialisation, normalisation and personalisation. Rosen and Kivitz (1973) emphasise that normalisation is an ideology not a psychological principle and that adequate training in independent living skills is vital. More importantly, it must be emphasised that learning adaptive behaviours such as personal hygiene, transportation skills and assembling industrial tasks, although indisputably important criteria for functioning, represent minimal criteria. Adaptive behaviour represents dimensions of performance not of personality. A construct which implies the teaching of adaptive behaviours only does not take into account the many psycho-social, motivational and environmental variables that may determine a person's maladaptive or adaptive behaviours. Acceptance of a repertoire of trained adaptive behaviours as the sole criterion of social adjustment could be as detrimental as the acceptance of intelligence quotients alone as the criterion. It is suggested that efforts must be made to provide supportive educational programmes conducive to higher order needs than those necessary for merely surviving in our communities.

Historically, researchers have acknowledged the importance of the emotional life of individuals who are developmentally delayed, but have minimised the application of personality theory or structure in intervention strategies. Mazland, Sarason and Gladwin's (1958) authoritative account of biological, psychological and cultural factors in predicting non-academic problem-solving behaviours, suggests that personality or emotional factors rather than cognitive deficiencies may be the primary determinants of behavioural and social adjustment. Teachers and trainers cannot afford to ignore the basic dimensions of personal adjustment as essential aspects of each individual. This includes the following:

- self-concept,
- independence and responsibility for one's own behaviours,
- accurate perception of reality,
- ability to feel and express affect appropriately,
- job satisfaction,
- ability to maintain goal-directed behaviour,
- ability to maintain satisfying interpersonal relationships, and
- the capability for appropriate sexual relationships.

Some investigators such as Sternlicht (1965) and Rosen, Clark and Kivitz (1977) have produced theoretical constructs with empirical findings that have potential for developing criteria for adjustment. These would facilitate education and training for adolescents and adults, by making goals more explicit. However, these efforts often remain isolated and untried as rehabilitation and education personnel ignore these dimensions. Some professionals continue to value only intellectual measures or other cognitive constructs as the key to diagnosis and training. On the other hand, rehabilitation practitioners working with adults now use work samples, vocational aptitude tests and task analysis, and appreciate the necessity to teach money-handling skills or provide exposure to the *world of work*. Yet, it is rarely asked how a history of failure may have conditioned acceptance of lowered aspirations, or how limited intellect or physical disability may affect self-concept. How often do professionals query whether structured and protected training environments condition patterns of helplessness and dependency? How willing are professionals to explore and develop the permanent networks of social relationships necessary to support individuals in coping with daily stresses in an uniquely personal fashion while reducing the dangers of loneliness and isolation? The results of follow-up studies such as the work of Brown and Bayer (1982) demonstrate the need for increased emphasis on such issues of personal adjustment, and the long-term nature of the rehabilitation process that implies varying degrees of intensity over time.

146

SOCIAL EMOTIONAL FACTORS

It is with these concerns and the advancing effectiveness of
our educational technology in mind that many professionals
have begun to explore interventions and training methods for
the more maladapted developmentally handicapped individual.
It appears that many communities are not adequately serving
those individuals who become more severely behaviourally
disturbed. Those with more severe levels of mental retardation and deviant or bizarre behaviours often reside in
custodial institutions, whereas adolescents and adults who
are mildly and moderately retarded and experience difficulties in psychosexual development, understanding the
increasingly symbolic abstractions of advancing school work
and the allied complexities of social-adaptive expectations
from family and peers live in the normal community. These
individuals are labelled as emotionally disturbed, and thus
alienated from typical Rehabilitation Education. They are
frequently unwelcome in vocational and other day training
centres and are often turned away from group home facilities. Such individuals tend to be perceived as highly
vulnerable, frustrated, unmotivated and failures in society.
It is also observed that this group tend to be rejected by
family and peers, because of these undesirable behavioural
traits, even though there is often a fairly close approxim-
ation to developmental expectations. The loss of interpersonal contacts exacerbates the handicapping conditions
and leaves many individuals desperate and feared as highly
deviant by others in society.

    In addition to the description of the above-mentioned
individuals, another group of persons seems to be ill-served
by Rehabilitation Education. This group, more popularly
called the *dual-diagnosis* population by some researchers
(McGee & Menolascino, 1982), shows mental retardation as the
primary diagnosis, with psychiatric disorder as secondary.
The latter include schizophrenic and organic brain disorders, adjustment reactions, non-specific mental disorders,
personality disorders, affective disorders of one kind or
another, neurotic disorders and special symptoms. The
knowledge and treatment of mental illness in mentally
retarded people has led to dilemmas in developing quality
services. As Wortis (1977) has stated, the skills of
psychiatry are needed as part of the multidisciplinary
treatment team, especially when considering that perhaps 25
per cent of the mentally retarded population show psychiatric disorders.

    Confusion and fragmentation in services appear to have
stemmed from misconceptions of the early history of the
field. It has only been in this century that the impact of
mental testing has differentiated the concept of mental
retardation from mental illness, and community services have

separated responsibilities for treating each group in different facilities, with different professionals, and often with different stated goals. Those individuals with a dual diagnosis have frequently been shunted from one facility to another as they do not fit the criteria for treatment.

In summary, the attitude of many professional personnel towards the maladjusted individual has been represented by restricting their environments and assuming that segregated, controlled settings are the safest answer to the problem. It does not seem uncommon that when such adolescents are diagnosed as emotionally disturbed their disruptive behaviour is seen as too detrimental for the vocational or classroom setting and rejection follows. This results in the individual remaining at home with families who are highly stressed and have limited or no support. It often leaves the individual further devalued, isolated and perhaps more disturbed. When these individuals and their families seek professional services additional problems may arise during the assessment phase. Frequently the assessment of the individual is biased by staff perceptions of deviancy. For example, an individual who is shy, withdrawn, or very anxious may be perceived as unmotivated and deliberately trying to frustrate the trainer. Many trainers and teachers question whether new skills can be learned or whether, with lowered intelligence, there will be a change in the social-emotional level of functioning. Often there is a sense of hopelessness and lowered expectations with regard to the usefulness of intervention. Thus, the assessment of an individual's ability to benefit from training is clouded by these negative attitudes. This lack of optimism seems more pronounced if the individual has also engaged in anti-social behaviours that put them in conflict with the legal system. Eventually the circumstances of many individuals lead to requests by parents and/or professionals for institutionalisation.

TREATMENT ISSUES

Barbara

Barbara is a 29 year old woman who has lived, most recently, in her own bachelor apartment. She attended special classes in a small town, and left school at 15 years of age. Her parents sent her to a vocational and residential programme in the city when she was 20 years old. From the time she left home she was diagnosed as mentally retarded (IQ reported as 65) and schizophrenic. Over the last nine years she has attended four different vocational programmes, but has been terminated from each of them due to poor motivation, disruptive behaviour (yelling and crying for 'no reason'), and poor attendance. She has lived in two group homes, a room-and-board situation, a shared apartment with another woman and now in her own apartment. She receives social assistance but her financial arrangements are confusing to her. She has her own bank account. She has been hospitalized on five occasions over the last five years to the psychiatric unit of an acute-care hospital. On all but one occasion Barbara admitted herself, as she felt confused, lonely and frightened. On the last occasion she was escorted by police to hospital, as she became very disruptive and demanding in a neighbourhood bank.

After a period of assessment, the psychiatric staff felt that Barbara required long-term treatment. An Outreach Team has been contacted to discuss whether there are any community options to which Barbara can return. The hospital staff insist that if Barbara lives in the community she must have constant supervision otherwise she should be placed in an institution for long-term treatment of the mentally ill.

John

John is a good-looking adolescent, 15 years of age. He lives at home with his adoptive parents and one younger sister. They moved to the city one year ago. John has always attended special education classes but has had great difficult adjusting to a new city and his new school. He has left behind a girlfriend whom he misses a great deal and telephones whenever the family can afford the long distance phone bills. John looks and tries to behave like a typical teenager; he likes current music, movies, a few beers and is curious about marijuana.

His parents are very involved with John and have concerns about his teenage interests. They feel he should be protected from negative influences as they feel he cannot make sound social judgements about people or about choices of leisure activities. He has been brought home several times by a policeman who found him wandering drunk on the streets.

John has been assessed as mildly mentally retarded. However, he has many appropriate social skills so he is not easily identified as handicapped. John has difficulty reading all but a few public signs and cannot make change or budget his money. He is very anxious at school, is shy with his teachers and has a nervous laugh whenever he talks or asks questions. This habit is irritating to authority figures and John is often perceived as a 'smart-aleck' who does not take anything seriously. The Outreach Team has been contacted by John's teacher because he has just been terminated from school as he was suspected of physically

*attacking another student.   The teacher also hinted that
John had sexual problems but would not elaborate or provide
evidence to support this statement.   The teacher has
requested that the Team help the family deal with John more
effectively.*

*When the Outreach Team met John and his family, they
reported great concern over the attitude of the school,
John's lack of daytime activities and his increasingly
rebellious behaviour. He has been sneaking out of the house
in the evening and going downtown to drink in the bar with
older men who pay for his beer and then leave him wandering
the streets.*

*The family want him to return to school and to stay
home in the evenings or participate in supervised leisure
activities.   The school states that John is seriously
disturbed, requires intensive therapy and is a danger to
other students.*

Alternative Service Models

In order to increase the quality of rehabilitative training
for those individuals who demonstrate either transitory or
chronic emotional/behavioural difficulties, additional
aspects of service have been considered. Some communities
have recognised the need to enhance the programme content
and staffing ratios to meet the individualised needs of
adolescents and adults in day training programmes.

In examining the service gaps that exist for individuals with behaviour problems the concept of an Outreach
Team has emerged as one model of support service which can
meet a range of individual problems. There are several
features to developing such a team within a community
setting.   Because the numbers of individuals who are
developmentally handicapped and have behavioural/emotional
problems may be small in any one classroom or vocational
centre, an Outreach Team should be designed to meet the
needs for a wide range of individuals participating in one
or more programmes. A team of professionals with a multidisciplinary background of education and experience offers a
wide range of skills to such individuals for consultation
and training. Such a team of staff must be available to
carry out individual and environmental assessments, design
the programme implementation phase and provide follow-up for
each client within each setting that is relevant to the
client's daily activities.

An effective Outreach Team should:

1) provide objective assessment and effective intervention strategies and consultation for the family and/or
staff working directly with the referred client;

2) provide specific interventions and advocacy to the client directly; and

3) engage in data collection, evaluation and monitoring of services in order to research methods that will improve the overall objectives and services to individuals with emotional/behavioural difficulties.

In order to enhance the effectiveness of such a service an Outreach Team should be prepared to observe and participate in all environments that are relevant to the client. A frequent problem for a client is the artificial separations that professionals create when individuals participate in more than one programme e.g. vocational, residential, leisure education programmes. Differing expectations and conflicting goals and interactions occur in different settings and these can lead to frustration for both client and staff which, in turn, lead to perceived or actual behavioural disturbances. Both staff and clients may have difficulty in transferring skills across settings.

Staffing

The success of an Outreach Team lies in the skill of the team members. Their roles should include the provision of specific assessments and interventions suitable for the client. They should extend advocacy and consultation skills to a wide range of people who may or may not always wish to co-operate in achieving effective environments and changing the functioning level of the client. An effective team will have a range of competencies and a belief in combining skills co-operatively for the client's benefit. Knowledge from the fields of education, social work, psychology, psychiatry, medicine, rehabilitation, recreation, law and management are all required in the provision of comprehensive programming to clients, families and agencies. The team's level of experience in front-line work should be extensive in order to understand client needs practically and to implement specific interventions effectively. The ability of the team to model specific strategies must be emphasised, for it is a very efficient and meaningful method of implementing change in the environment and teaching the use of practical behavioural tools to other relevant people in the client's life.

Intervention

The degree of success of an Outreach Team also lies in its ability to assess, implement, monitor and provide follow-up to the intervention programmes and this should include the manner in which other relevant staff and family actively participate in each stage of the plan. The aim is to ensure the Team can realistically withdraw involvement, provide follow-up consultation, and become accessible for new clients. A programme philosophy that believes people can change and learn new behaviours that are not dependent for maintenance on the Outreach staff can help ensure such goals are achieved by the team. Clear objectives can lead to serving more clients without creating helpless dependence and prolonged treatment. An outreach programme that encourages the involvement of natural social networks and provides social training through group therapy experiences has proven, in the author's experience, to be effective in reducing the length of such specialised involvement. Many adolescents and adults are desperate for social interactions where there is acceptance and natural experiences that encourage a more positive, competent self-image. An outreach team that promotes such strategies can often motivate individuals to engage in a wide range of appropriate behaviours that reduce the perception of disturbance or deviance.

In establishing an Outreach Team it should be realised that varying levels of severity of client problems will be referred. This should lead to a flexible plan for implementing varying levels of programme intensity. Intervention may need to be so intensive at some stages in the client's life that alternate residential treatment models may have to be considered for the older adolescent or adult. It has been the author's experience that a small number of clients (perhaps 6-12 clients from a referral pool of over 300 people) may require specialised residential group home settings for intensive training for varying lengths of time (6 months to 2 years). Such programming, with the support of an Outreach Team at the time of intake to and at discharge from such intensive units, can increase the likelihood that clients will not remain in segregated, restrictive setting indefinitely. At the least intensive level, an Outreach Team may be involved in promoting self-help groups and teaching specific self-management skills. At this level periodic personal support may be all that is required to maintain behavioural change. Such contact can often be left to the client's discretion, particularly if the team has developed a trusting relationship with the client.

Many aspects of clinical intervention must be ethically examined and skillfully applied to a wide range of problem behaviours by an Outreach Team such as the one described here. Skills as behaviourists, family therapists, counsellors and consultants with a knowledge of different theories about human behaviour, and a willingness to apply and assess results systematically are essential to the development of an effective team. A team that relies on one methodology or treatment strategy may become only useful to those clients who fit the treatment model. Ideally an outreach team, by the very nature of being a *team* of competent professionals, should be able to match an effective treatment strategy to need for a wide range of problems. It has been the author's experience that, too often, developmentally handicapped individuals with emotional/behavioural problems are either too *retarded* or too *disturbed* to fit standard treatment/ rehabilitation models provided by many agencies. This group then become society's worst failures, often living in the most harsh circumstances until some professional labels them and requests custodial institutionalisation or incarceration to protect society. For example, the Outreach Team in Calgary lost six individuals out of 65 new referrals over one year to large institutions away from their community.

Staff Training Model

In developing an alternative model such as an Outreach Team for those with emotional/behavioural problems it is essential to consider where to locate and to whom to attach such a team. Consideration of easy access, valued status, neutral territory and a location that provides well-developed resources should all be factors to consider. In the author's experience it has been most valuable to develop such a clinical service within a teaching setting such as a university or college programme. This setting is usually attributed with status, and other agencies usually consider it to be a neutral setting, with all the advantages that educational resources can offer. As such, this arrangement has proven to be beneficial in developing an alternative service model that does not require building a new facility or fitting into existing programme models. The tremendous advantage of such an affiliation within an educational setting is the link with pre-service training of potential rehabilitation personnel. The practical clinical setting operated by a member of the teaching staff who can then make meaningful practicum experiences available for students seems to be a highly desirable means of enhancing the theoretical and clinical skills of future personnel. Furthermore, the supervised relationship of students with some clients expands the Outreach Team's potential resources to clients. Another advantage of this arrangement experienced by the author is the interest of other rehabilitation services and agencies in taking advantage of the teaching resources provided through the Outreach Team. By developing a credible programme within an accepted educational setting the team members can also be available to provide in-service training workshops/seminars for rehabilitation personnel concerned with individuals with developmental handicaps. Such on-site training is an efficient and practical method of upgrading the competencies of many front-line staff, and reduces the need for more specialised services for clients who have major behavioural difficulties.

When the front-line staff of training programmes have confidence in their ability to handle difficult learning problems and have support to increase competence and measure their success practically, there seem to be fewer clients within their agencies labelled as *behaviour problems*. Such a reduction of perceived deviance by front-line staff increases the quality of service that an Outreach Team can provide. Practical in-service training for existing staff and well-trained new personnel, represents attempts to be more proactive in meeting the needs of individuals who are developmentally handicapped. If staff have a useful model for understanding and interpreting human behaviour, and have been trained to apply good training techniques for success-ful learning, then it seems that fewer adolescents and adults appear to have behavioural problems that disrupt the typical group settings for vocational, residential and educational training. In effect staff will create a supportive environment that enhances positive social/emotional growth. The individual will then be considered as an unique personality whose rehabilitation needs are specifically planned for him or her within the individual's natural social network.

Over-Riding Issues in Service Provision

The following issues are highlighted as essential in con-sidering social-emotional factors related to Rehabilitation Education.

1. In attempting to address the social/emotional needs of individuals with developmental handicaps this chapter has discussed the concerns of those with more severe disturbances. It should be emphasised that this is a particularly specialised service within the rehab-ilitation training model. Throughout all facets of Rehabilitation Education, programmers must be cognisant of promoting a teaching environment that engages indiv-iduals in positive social experiences, encourages positive self-regard and enhances competence, independ-ence and social maturity. Specific experiences in practicing adaptive behaviours must incorporate oppor-tunities for individuals to express feelings and atti-tudes as well as perform functional skills. Training in making social judgements and personal decisions, and strategies for solving typical daily problems, must be

the major goals of adequate programme plans. Without attention to teaching these abstract, but most essential, features of social adjustment, the more vulnerable individual with handicapping conditions will be considered deviant or difficult. It is a major challenge in Rehabilitation Education to develop teaching models that produce staff skilled enough to create meaningful interactions and environments in which individuals can practice social skills successfully. Environments that promote social adjustments must extend to the communities beyond the training setting. Bearing this in mind, the pressing question for the practical researcher of social/emotional development is the examination of environmental factors that will create more effective communities within which *all* individuals can flourish.

2. Continued concern for social/emotional development in conjunction with adaptive training for individuals with developmental disabilities represents a proactive preventative approach to successful social rehabilitation. Such prevention is, of course, an overriding issue in ensuring fewer individuals require the more specialised support service or more intensive, highly costly programmes such as restricted settings for the severely disturbed. Proactive approaches must include active development of support services and programmes for families and children as soon as problems have been identified. Although the normal stresses of adolescence and young adulthood may create social/emotional problems of a transitory or more chronic nature, it must be emphasised that many behavioural difficulties can be avoided if consistent practices and experiences are available to the younger child and the family structure. Practical information on social/emotional as well as cognitive development, and specific practical teaching techniques, can support many families through early difficulties and promote positive social development in later years.

3. Another issue that threatens the quality of rehabilitative services concerns the development of a continuum of integrated services. It must be stressed that educational planning must be an ongoing process that does not stop when an individual becomes 16 or 18 years of age. A number of adolescents with learning difficulties will be particularly vulnerable to environmental and social stresses during these years. Thus, a continuum of training options must be accessible to, and developmentally appropriate, for the individual as he matures and grows older chronologically. Co-ordination

of services that promote the next stage of social development must be smooth, as the transition into adulthood is a highly stressful experience. Many individuals will need supportive help in both educational, vocational and residential planning. Individuals of 18 years of age and older are also often having to face leaving home for some other accommodation, and many adjustments are necessary. This type of support should begin well before the actual move to a new setting is made. Early planning and participation in assessing and matching the individual to the best environment is crucial in avoiding potential behavioural maladjustments. As logical as these statements appear, it is common for major problems to develop at this stage of an individual's life. Often this is exacerbated by the artificial divisions that service delivery models delineate. Services for children usually stop at 16 or 18 years of age. Adult services are usually more fragmented and professionals know less about the services with which they are not affiliated. Unfortunately, early planning is neglected and crises develop when an individual *suddenly* becomes an adult chronologically.

4. Behavioural deviance is often perceived to be a frightening, unchangeable and/or highly unacceptable fact in our communities. Many doors are therefore closed to individuals who exhibit social maladjustments. This fact seems to be true even within settings that are designed to train or educate those with special needs. Consumer and professional advocacy for better services, access to appropriate treatment, and qualitative evaluation to improve services becomes an increasingly important issue. Such advocacy is concerned with human rights and issues of legal and social responsibilities as well as standards of treatment.

Sometimes programmes which treat severe emotional and behavioural disturbances are segregated and isolated from community monitoring and participation. This can lead to questions regarding the ethical nature of treatment practices, and concerns over the reduction of rights and freedoms of the client. Community-operated boards with advisory members from many disciplines should be essential components of any human service model, but are crucial if such segregated programmes must exist. Furthermore, clearly identified standards for treatment that protect human rights and provide opportunities for participation by guardians and/or clients in treatment decisions are essential to humanistic services. Specific treatment procedures, goals and measures of results should be part of the expected written standards available for monitoring by clients, guardians and other professionals. Consumers of specialised services for emotional/behavioural disturbances may not be able to advocate for or protect their interests, and therefore greater responsibilities lie with the guardian, and professional and community members to ensure that ethical procedures are adopted and maintained. When restrictive procedures are introduced there must be clear mechanisms in place to monitor effectiveness and to insist on the lessening of restrictions as quickly and consistently as possible. The lack of such vigilance will only prolong the costly effects of segregation and institutionalisation with further detriment to an individual's potential for growth and change.

5. Continuing issues for the field of Rehabilitation Education are the study of social/emotional development and the application of research to the training of adolescents and adults. Theoretical models of human behaviour must be examined and tested. Systematic monitoring of treatment strategies and their effects must be studied. Retrospective studies that examine the identified population and its characteristics, in conjunction with longitudinal prospective projects that explore factors relating to treatment as well as community and allied environmental affects over time, are necessary if individual quality of life is to be enhanced. Studies of cost benefit, models of service delivery, and administrative structure are also critical in the development of behavioural services.

    The evaluation of existing programmes must be stressed, particularly in areas of social training. Programs are becoming more sophisticated and greater emphasis on accountability is being demanded by funding sources. This demand is very timely. Each client deserves to participate in programmes that have proven to be successful in enhancing social and emotional development. Program evaluation must include examination of such factors as staff competence, programme structures and processes, intervention strategies and their results, environmental influences and administrative procedures. More evaluation should be conducted into the comparison of treatment models for different individuals. To date, we commonly assume that everyone will benefit from *treatment* or *training* without specifying or matching the *helping* strategies to the types of problems individuals are experiencing.

6. Over the last decade advances in education programmes preparing rehabilitation personnel for employment in the

field have been tremendous. Most practitioners now have had training opportunities that provide a common base of competencies. However, many practitioners do not feel competent to deal with social/emotional difficulties particularly if individuals are labelled as *deviant* or *disturbed*. A recent study by the Rehabilitation Programme, University of Calgary, shows that a large proportion of people returning for further study in rehabilitation request knowledge and skills in this area. The issue of increased competence for present and new rehabilitation personnel must be considered at all levels within the staffing structure. Administrators and management personnel who have a detailed knowledge of rehabilitation practice are more likely to risk tackling difficult problems. With competence there is increased confidence within a staffing model to try new methods and explore more comprehensive and individual-ised programmes.

7. The dilemma of assessment and diagnosis is a constant issue for individuals with emotional/behavioural prob-lems. Commonly the professional who diagnoses the problem will be labelling the individual on the basis of their chosen theoretical framework or model of human behaviour. Such labelling usually implies a particular treatment model. For example, if an individual is labelled as schizophrenic, a medical model will often be the chosen treatment modality, whereas if someone is said to have severe temper tantrums, a behaviour modification technique may be the chosen intervention strategy. Not only does the choice of label imply treatment prescription, it can also imply in what treatment environments an individual will be placed; e.g. group home vs. hospital ward. Further research and documented clinical experience is crucial to the client and professional. Assessment tools that provide useful prescriptive techniques are almost totally lacking. Diagnosis, based on such limited resources, are often detrimental and even damaging to the future of the individual. In practice, an individual who becomes labelled under some category of behavioural or emotional problem will have great difficulty losing the stigma of such a name. The professionals' attitudes about emotional problems can be rigid and associated with specific and lowered behavioural expectation. General optimism for behavioural change is replaced with negative predictions. Attributing unchanging negative behaviours to individuals who are perceived to be mal-adjusted can be the major barrier to developing creative treatment/training approaches in rehabilitation.

SUMMARY

Knowledge and practice in Rehabilitation Education have made considerable advances in the development and provision of increasingly systematic and humanistic programmes. However, the techniques for teaching adaptive behaviour to individuals who require such structured education relate only to some of the dimensions of behaviour. Greater efforts must be placed on developing theoretical models and training/treatment strategies for higher-order needs such as the social and emotional development of individuals with handicapping conditions. The lack of practical expertise in this area has led to the exclusion of a particular group of adolescents and adults from typical educational and rehabilitation settings. In recognising the pressing needs of such individuals and their families an alternative service model described as an Outreach Team is proposed to bridge the gaps in services. Major roles of such a multi-disciplinary team include:

- hands-on training in conjunction with consultation,
- emphasis on strengthening of natural social networks for the client,
- clearly identified treatment goals that are monitored,
- responsibility for the collection of data and documentation of intervention practices,
- provision of training to existing and new rehabilitation personnel, and
- integration of a continuum of services within the client's community.

Seven major issues were identified as crucial to the social/emotional aspects of Rehabilitation Education:

1) expansion of specialised training of social skills,
2) proactive approaches to the training and promotion of psycho-social development,
3) the development of integrated planning for a continuum of services for clients,
4) advocacy of human rights and concerns for standards of treatment in the least restrictive manner,
5) increased research endeavors,
6) increased professional training,
7) a resolution to the dilemma of assessment and diagnosis that limits quality rehabilitation.

REFERENCES

Brown, R. I. & Bayer, M. B. (1982) *A Follow-Up Study of Developmentally Handicapped Adults - An Examination of Later Life Experience in Canada*, Paper presented at the International Association for the Scientific Study of Mental Deficiency, Toronto, Canada.

Brown, R. I. & Hughson, E. A. (1980) *Training the Developmentally Handicapped Adult*, C. C. Thomas, Springfield, Illinois.

Gold, M. W. (1973) 'Research on the Vocational Rehabilitation of the Retarded: The Present, the Future', in N. R. Ellis (ed.), *International Review of Research in Mental Retardation*, Vol. 6., Academic Press, New York.

Gunzburg, H. C. & Gunzburg, A. L. (1973) *Mental Handicap and Physical Environment*, Bailliere, Tindall and Cox Ltd., London.

Mazland, R. L., Sarason, S. B. & Gladwin, T. (1958) *Mental Subnormality: Biological, Psychological and Cultural Factors*, Basic Books, New York.

McGee, J. & Menolascino, F. (1982) *Types and Prevalence of Mental Illness in Mentally Retarded Persons*, Paper presented at the International Association for the Scientific Study of Mental Deficiency, Toronto, Canada.

Marlett, N. J. & Hughson, E. A. (1977) *Rehabilitation Programs Manual*, Vocational and Rehabilitation Research Institute, Calgary, Canada.

Rosen, M., Clark, G. R. & Kivitz, M. S. (1977) *Habilitation of the Handicapped*, University Park Press, Baltimore.

Sternlicht, M. (1966) 'Psychotherapeutic Procedures with the Retarded'. in N. R. Ellis (ed.), *International Review of Research in Mental Retardation*, Vol. 2, Academic Press, New York.

Wehman, P. & McLaughlin, P. J. (1981) *Program Development in Special Education*, McGraw-Hill Co., New York.

Wortis, J. (1977) 'Introduction: The Role of Psychiatry in Mental Retardation Services' in J. Wortis (ed.), *Mental Retardation and Developmental Disabilities*, IX, Brunner/Mazel, New York.

Chapter Seven

INTERPERSONAL RELATIONSHIPS: SELF-ESTEEM, SEXUAL INTIMACY, AND LIFE-LONG LEARNING

Peter R. Johnson

INTRODUCTION

Until about 1975, sex education for handicapped people usually meant the provision of information (AAPHER 1971; Fischer, Krajicek & Borthick, 1973), often with the fervent hope that it would not be used! During the next few years, attempts were made to put sex education in a social behaviour framework (Kempton, 1978; Johnson, 1981), sometimes with little commitment to students becoming sexually active. However, experience seems to indicate that these approaches may be somewhat superficial, and that they would be more meaningful to the person who has already experienced close relationships.

Jim Smith

Jim Smith [*] *appears to be very conscious of his masculinity. He usually wears cowboy boots, sturdy denim jeans, and battered leather jackets which emphasise the width of his shoulders. In addition, the practised scowl on his weather-tanned face enhances the machismo image he values so highly.*

Jim is an outdoorsman who works as a forest ranger in a large national park. His hobbies include mountaineering and hang-gliding. In fact, it was while hang-gliding that Jim sustained a serious spinal cord injury, when a gust of wind blew him against the face of a cliff and he plummeted 70 feet to the valley floor below.

However, in the three years following the accident, he has made a spectacular recovery. The only permanent physical damage seems to be a lack of sensation on the medial aspect of his lower right leg. Unfortunately, Jim is extremely fearful that he will no longer be able to perform sexually, and it is this concern which finally caused him to seek help. Since the accident, he has avoided close relationships with both women and men, but now the other forest rangers are beginning to tease him about being gay! In addition, his employers are seriously concerned about his work performance which is increasingly marked by forgetfulness, irritability, and a lack of attention to detail.

Melvin and Brenda Fields

Melvin Fields and his partner have just finished leading a workshop on human sexuality. People seem attracted by Melvin's warmth, sincerity and ready smile, and he is now surrounded by a group of people who wish to ask further questions. As each person speaks, it appears that they have his complete attention, while his supportive responses both challenge and stimulate the questioners.

In between questions, Melvin glances across the room to where his partner, Brenda, stands in animated conversation with another group, and looks forward to the time when they will be alone. Later that evening, they will discuss the effectiveness of their teaching and smile about the sexual invitations which they each occasionally receive from members of their audiences.

Melvin has lived with a severe handicap since he was 20 years old. At that time, he was struck down by a truck whose driver was subsequently charged with driving while under the influence of alcohol. Melvin's legs are completely paralysed, while he retains little use of his arms. In fact, he wears finger splints in order to retain a modicum of fine motor control in his upper limbs. He cannot control either his bowel or bladder and wears a bag which collects the waste produced by the reflex action of his urinary system. In addition, his anus must be manually stimulated each day in order to remove faeces. Obviously, Melvin is very dependent upon the assistance of others in the routines of daily living.

Brenda met Melvin two years after his accident. She relates that as she got to know him, she noticed less of the handicap and more of the person. As their friendship grew and deepened, they made a lifelong commitment to each other. In their teaching and writing, Melvin and Brenda take pains to explain that theirs is a complete relationship containing a sexual component which is deeply satisfying to both partners.

These two vignettes illustrate the importance of sexual intimacy and self-esteem in rehabilitation. In the first one, Jim has only a minor handicap yet his inability to form intimate relationships appears to be having a negative effect in other areas of his life. However, in spite of a severe disability, Melvin has an intense relationship with

Brenda, and seems to have maximised his remaining abilities in both his career and interpersonal skills.

The relationship between sexual activity and intimacy is another facet of the vignettes. One might predict that if Jim was involved in a sexual relationship, he would focus on performance rather than intimacy. In fact, there might be very little emotional contact between Jim and his partner. On the other hand, Melvin and Brenda would probably say that they have an intimate relationship in which sexual activity forms one important component. In many societies, people are confused by the relationship between sexual activity and intimacy, and this misunderstanding can cause much unhappiness in the lives of the handicapped and non-handicapped people alike.

This situation can be remedied by relationship education in its broadest form. This education utilises many techniques, ranging from class teaching to group counselling, and from information-giving to sex therapy. It utilises many teachers from parents and helping professionals to friends and lovers. It is a life-long education which begins in infancy and ends in preparation for death.

The balance of this chapter contains a more detailed discussion of the three issues raised by the experiences of Jim and Melvin:

(1) The relationship between love needs and a self-concept which facilitates the process of rehabilitation.
(2) The role of sexual activity in an intimate relationship.
(3) Education for intimacy.

Thus the case is made for the inclusion of relationship education as an integral, rather than peripheral, component of the rehabilitation process. Consequently, it seems that learning to be a friend may enhance the ability to become a lover.

LOVE NEEDS AND SELF-ESTEEM IN THE REHABILITATION PROCESS

In the second edition of his book, *Motivation and Personality*, Maslow (1970) postulates that the basic needs of humans can be arranged in a hierarchy which commences with the physiological and culminates in the aesthetic. Generally speaking, needs which are lower in the hierarchy must be fulfilled before those at a higher level. Thus a steady supply of food must be accessible before people can focus upon their need for safe and secure dwelling places, and this desire must, in turn, be satisfied before those concerning love and self-esteem. (See Figure 1.)

FIGURE ONE

Maslow's Hierarchy of Human Needs

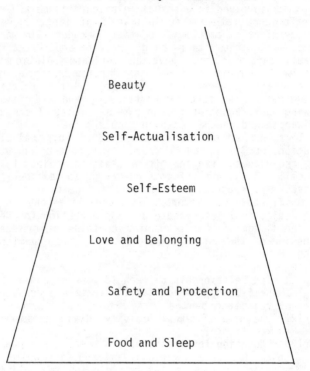

Beauty

Self-Actualisation

Self-Esteem

Love and Belonging

Safety and Protection

Food and Sleep

Love and Belonging

However, in western countries, the basic needs for food and
sleep and for safety and protection have largely been met.
Most handicapped people have a secure place in which to live
and few are literally starving. Consequently, it is the
higher needs of Love and Belonging and Self-Esteem which are
our current concern.

Maslow points out that at the stage of Love and
Belonging, people will feel keenly, as never before, the
absence of friends, or a lover, or children. They will
hunger for affectionate relationships with others, for
intimacy, for the giving and receiving of love, and for a
place in a group or family. They will be especially
sensitive to the pangs of loneliness, of ostracism, and of
rejection. In fact, one could argue with some conviction

that the neglect of this need can lead to maladjustment and even serious pathology.

Perhaps of all people in our societies, those who live with handicaps are particularly vulnerable to deficits of this kind. In adults, trauma or the onset of illness may precipitate both the overt and covert withdrawal of intimacy by friends or lovers, and rejection by formerly-accepting groups. For example, the young children of a father disfigured by burns may now be afraid of him, while the woman whose hands are deformed by arthritis may feel her lover's subtle withdrawal from her touch.

People with developmental disabilities often have somewhat different experiences. In many cases, as they will have lived at home with a loving, caring family, their needs for love and belonging may have been fully met during childhood. However, some may not have had the opportunity to experience and develop peer friendships; a lack which may produce difficulties in adulthood when love needs cannot be met by the family.

Unfortunately, many people have been denied a loving family home. They may have spent their early lives in impersonal institutions, or a succession of rapidly-changing foster homes in which there was little chance to develop loving relationships or a sense of belonging. When one considers Bowlby's (1969) work on attachment or studies of the *attic children* (Davis, 1940, 1947), it is surprising that more developmentally disabled people have not been permanently damaged by the lack of loving relationships in their early years. Perhaps for many, these needs were met at a minimal level by a particularly affectionate ward orderly or foster parent, but, nevertheless, it appears that some people have become seriously maladjusted due to these deficits.

Bobby Green

Bobby Green is a 20 year old, native Indian who has a mild mental handicap. Although he looks several years younger than his age, he carries none of the obvious signs of mental retardation. His speech and movements are very rapid, and he seems to have difficulty in attending to learning tasks for more than a couple of minutes.

On leaving the maternity hospital, Bobby was placed in a foster home because his mother was unable to keep him. Since then, he has had very little contact with his natural family, and has lived in a succession of foster homes and residential institutions for the mentally handicapped. In at least one of these locations, he was sexually abused on a regular basis.

Currently, he is enrolled in a semi-custodial programme, where he is receiving treatment for his anti-social behaviours. Bobby has a history of sexually molesting little boys. Whenever the opportunity arises, he will seek out children who are about 8 years old and take them to a secluded place. Then he will undress them and manipulate their genitals, while he himself masturbates. Bobby reports that this is a strong drive.

The psychologist who is working with Bobby has two major concerns. The first is that Bobby shows little motivation to change his behaviour. The second is that he appears to care little for other people, including two of his former social workers who have become his friends and advocates. Bobby's prognosis is poor. Unless there is a major breakthrough, he is likely to continue to abuse children and to spend considerable amounts of time in jail where he, in turn, will be abused by the other prisoners due to the nature of his crime.

Could it be that Bobby's unmet needs for Love and Belonging have resulted in his seriously maladjusted behaviour, and are his attacks on children attempts to take the love which was never given?

In summary, there seem to be two main issues concerning the love needs of handicapped people. For those who have become handicapped as adults, the task is likely to be the restoration of intimate relationships, while people with developmental disabilities may need to learn how to develop loving friendships. However, as many non-handicapped people have difficulties with close relationships, many of the former group may also require education for intimacy.

Self-Esteem

The terms self-esteem, self-concept, and self-image appear to be largely synonymous. For example, in the *Dictionary of Behavioural Science* (Wolman, 1973), self-concept is defined as the individual's appraisal or evaluation of himself, and Evans (1978) sees self-image as the view of oneself as one believes others see one. With the possible addition of a qualitative component, either could stand as a passable definition of self-esteem! Consequently, for the purposes of clarity in this discussion, the term self-esteem will be used exclusively, and it will mean the value which each individual places on a personal appraisal of him- or herself. In this respect, social interaction is particularly important. As Mead (1934) proposed, people tend to conceive of themselves as they believe significant others conceive of them, and they often act in accord with the expectations projected by significant others.

Maslow (1970) proposes that when the need for Love and Belonging has been met, humans will focus on the need for Self-Esteem. He believes that all people have the need for a stable, firmly-based and high evaluation of themselves, and that this need has two components. The first is a desire for achievement, adequacy, mastery and competence, while the second relates to the need for recognition, status, and appreciation. Satisfaction of the Self-Esteem need leads to feelings of self-confidence, but the thwarting of these desires produces feelings of worthlessness, helplessness, and a resulting lack of motivation.

Research in the field of rehabilitation indicates a recognition of the value of self-esteem, particularly as it relates to effective behavioural performance (Fitts, 1972). For example, Wolf and Wenzl (1982) have shown a positive relationship between self-esteem and academic performance in mildly mentally handicapped-emotionally disturbed children, and McGarry (1979) has related improved behavioural competence to higher self-esteem and internal locus of control in 42 mildly mentally handicapped adults. In addition, Morgan and Leung (1980) demonstrated that an assertiveness training programme increased the self-esteem of 14 physically handicapped college students, while Simpson and Meaney (1979) reported a similar effect when a group of trainably mentally handicapped children learned to ski.

In the area of developmental handicaps, much of the recognition of the importance of self-esteem is probably derived from the Principle of Normalization (Wolfensberger, 1972), where the concept of the *least restrictive environment* allows for the optimisation of behavioural competence. Consequently, much careful and painstaking work has been done to facilitate the acquisition of new skills (Brown, 1975; Brown & Hughson, 1980). Working within a framework of research, demonstration and practice, initial interest focussed on employment and home-living skills, but more recent programmes have considered the learning of leisure-time and social skills (Johnson, 1981; Beck-Ford & Smith, 1979; Ryba, 1979;).

Body image or schema is another important aspect of self-esteem. This refers to the mental idea and/or basic attitudes people have toward their own bodies and reflects the physical, aesthetic, and even social self-perceptions (Singh & Magner, 1975). In reference to parapalegic patients, Berger (1952) has pointed out the importance of the integration of the physical disability into the body image, and this point is emphasised in self-help books such as *Toward Intimacy* (Shaul, Bogle, Harbough, & Norman, 1978). Unfortunately, many of the early clinical observations were not supplemented by objective evidence. However, more recent research seems to re-affirm the relationship between body schema, self-esteem, and handicapping conditions. For example, Starr and Heiserman (1977) assessed 72 teenagers who had oral-facial clefts, and discovered that those who accepted their disability scored higher on measures of self-esteem than those who did not. Abelson and Paluszny (1978) found that mentally handicapped children had a less-developed sense of body gender identity than their non-handicapped peers, but Margalit (1979) showed that a structured gross motor and verbal training programme advanced the development of body schema in a similar, but slightly older group.

While behavioural competence and body image have been explored, there appears to be little research concerning the effect of intimate relationships upon the self-esteem of handicapped people. This may be a serious lack, given Mead's social interactionist viewpoint along with Singh and Magner's emphasis on significant others. Certainly, it would be difficult to argue that the relationship between the adult, monogamous couple did not have considerable effect on the self-esteem of both partners. The effect could, of course, be positive, as when one is selected as the sole, sexual partner of a widely-respected person, or negative, as in the battered wife syndrome.

However, there is also some indirect evidence from studies of mentally handicapped married couples (Craft & Craft, 1979; Mattinson, 1970). These books mention the stability of the relationships, the partners' expressed wishes to stay together, and the focus marriage has given to their lives. The companionship between the partners, and their social isolation from others are mentioned on several occasions. Consequently, one is led to speculate on a comparison between the self-esteem of the minority of handicapped people who have just one intimate friend and the majority who have none.

Interdependence in the Needs Hierarchy

In presenting his concept of a needs hierarchy, Maslow (1970) comments on the interdependence of the components. While it is necessary that the lower needs should be largely satisfied before the individual's attention turns to a higher level, complete gratification is not required. He further comments that this phenomenon is most often seen in the inter-dependence between the needs of Love and Belonging and Self-Esteem! Evidently, he is referring to the cycle in which love provides the self-esteem necessary for perform-ance which, if successful, increases self-esteem and love.

Nevertheless, in spite of some interdependence between needs, many rehabilitation practitioners may well have the wrong priorities. In the present state of the discipline, it is easier to concentrate upon the relationship between concrete behavioural performance and self-esteem than it is to struggle with the traditionally esoteric concepts of Love and Belonging. And yet this may be a grave error. How many people are currently learning vocational skills when they live in a desert of impersonality with its mirages of love and intimacy? It is suggested that we become more sensitive to the need for Love and Belonging, to the role of inter-personal relationships in the development of self-esteem, and to innovative methods of teaching handicapped people to meet their needs for intimacy.

Deborah White

Deborah White lives in a group home with four other handicapped young adults. Each day she commutes to the downtown core of the city where she works in the photo-copying department of a large company. While her salary is modest yet competitive, her union membership and seniority provide her with a substantial amount of job security. Like many other young people, she is exploring relationships and freedom, sometimes making poor choices in male companions, style of dress, and alcohol consumption. 'Don't worry,' she tells her counsellor, 'I'm learning! I'm learning!'

Deborah was brain-damaged at birth. She has a learning disability, a speech impediment, and has been diagnosed as mildly mentally handicapped. Fortunately, Deborah had a loving and supportive family with whom she spent all her childhood. They expected her to take on responsibilities, to stand up for herself in the inevitable sibling rivalries, and eventually to move into her own home.

When Deborah was 18, she surprised everybody by announcing that she had won a nation-wide competition in poster design! On her own initiative, she had designed a road safety poster and entered it in the competition. The public announcement of the results brought the usual media attention, including television and newspaper interviews for the designer.

A year later, Deborah and a close female school friend decided they wanted to live together in a group home. The local association for the mentally handicapped was able to meet this request, and they subsequently moved into their present home. On graduating from school, Deborah refused placement in a sheltered workshop, and, following a series of temporary jobs, has now obtained a permanent position.

While Deborah's life has not been without stress and pain, it readily illustrates the influence of well-met needs of Love and Belonging and Self-Esteem on the rehabilitation process.

It is worth noting that the next need in the hierarchy is that of Self-Actualisation. When this has been achieved,

a human being has become the person that he or she has the
potential to be. Surely this is the ultimate goal of all
rehabilitation.

SEX AND INTIMACY

In addition to the constraints imposed upon the learning
process by handicapping conditions, disabled people face an
additional problem in trying to meet their needs for
friendship and sexual intimacy. This relates to society's
general confusion and unhappiness about these two important,
inter-personal areas. In an environment in which many
people seem unable to form close, supportive relationships
with others, consistent role-modelling is not available to
people with handicaps.

There is even confusion about the meaning of the word
intimacy. For example, Webster (1964) defines it both as a
close personal relationship marked by affection or love, and
as an uninvited sexual liberty such as fondling or
intercourse. As Morris (1971) points out, these dual
meanings probably have their origin in the coy and sexually
repressive Victorian England when in many cities *intimacy*
became an euphemism for sexual intercourse. For our
purposes, intimacy is defined as a close personal relationship marked by love and affection.

Developmental Aspects of Intimacy

Morris (1971) speaks of a strong desire for intimacy among
humans. He believes this has a biological basis as
illustrated by the similarities between the stages of
courtship in both humans and animals. Furthermore, he cites
evidence from prisoners in solitary confinement and young
people alone in a strange city that death by suicide might
be preferable to a prolonged lack of close human contact.
Such a statement is quite devastating in terms of the unmet
needs of many handicapped people.

Successful intimacy appears to develop along two
parallel axes. One axis relates to intimacy within the
family unit, while the other focuses on relationships with
peers (See Figure 2). The former begins with the intense
intimacy between the parents and the infant child, before
gradually diminishing through the rest of the lifespan. The
latter begins with the shallow, temporary friendships of the
2-year old, develops into the reciprocal companionship of
adolescence, and culminates in the intense bonding of the
mature adult (Rubin, 1980). Of course, the two axes are
interdependent, especially in terms of the child's ability
to transfer family-learned intimacy skills to peer

relationships. Infants who have experienced strong, intimate bonding with their parents will be better equipped to make strong peer attachments as young adults (Morris, 1971).

FIGURE TWO

Intimacy Needs: Family and Peer Components

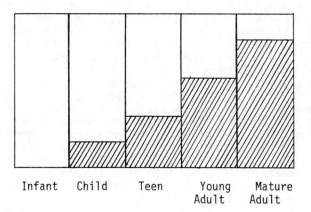

Infant   Child   Teen   Young   Mature
                            Adult   Adult

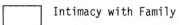 Intimacy with Family

Intimacy with Peers

Such a framework can provide a useful frame of reference in assessing the intimacy needs of handicapped people. For those who are developmentally delayed, stages rather than chronological age will be of more importance. Therefore, if people are independently employed in the community yet meeting all their intimacy needs within the family, this may indicate a need to develop peer friend-ships. Similarly, the same conclusion may be drawn if formerly-independent adults who have become handicapped are also meeting all of their intimacy needs within the primary family unit.

There appears to be a fairly complex relationship between a developmental view of intimate relationships and sexual behaviour. Young children's sexual explorations may be one of the more obvious signs of the establishment of gender identity, but the observation of familial relationships and peer social interactions are also ways in which people learn about sexuality. However, the behaviours usually become more directly sexual with age. For example, while two 7 year olds might play games like *Doctors and Nurses*, it is not unusual for pubescent boys to engage in mutual masturbation. During childhood, sexual behaviour may occur with siblings or outside the family, but adult intrafamilial sexual relationships are considered aberrant in most societies. Consequently, adults tend to form sexual liaisons with peers. Nevertheless, it must be pointed out that for a short time, many young adults have sexual relationships which involve a minimum of intimacy.

For people with developmental handicaps, the relationship between sexuality and intimacy can produce difficulties. For many, it appears that the concept of gender identity emerges slowly, especially in the absence of appropriate male role models (Johnson, 1981), and subtle cues to social behaviour may be unheeded without sensitive instruction. The result could be a mentally handicapped teenager who becomes involved in the exploratory sexual behaviour of young children. Discovery frequently results in accusations of child molesting, and the removal of the handicapped persons from an environment where so much can be learned about relationships.

Fred and Brenda

At 8:15 a.m. on a sunny June day, the driver of a passing special bus was shocked to see two handicapped adults apparently engaged in anal intercourse on a grassy area adjoining the bus stop. As soon as she could, the driver notified her supervisor who called a sheltered workshop in the area. Later, the driver went down to the shop and identified the two people who were subsequently interviewed by the manager.

Fred Gomez who is 42 and lives in a large institution, was somewhat shamefaced about the incident. He had attended a sex education class at the institution and knew he would get in trouble if he was discovered engaging in sexual activities. However, when he suggested it to Brenda, she seemed willing, and the opportunity was too good to miss. Interestingly, Fred had little knowledge of the vagina, and appeared to believe that the female rectum was the appropriate place for his penis.

Brenda is 37 years old and has Down's Syndrome. She is considerably larger than Fred and indicated that she was an enthusiastic participant in the activity which progressed from kissing and fondling to attempted intercourse. Brenda lives with her aging mother who has actively prevented her daughter from gaining sexual knowledge, and told her that sex is bad. In a surprisingly articulate manner, Brenda expressed her confusion by asking how anything that felt so good could be bad. She also requested further sexual information from the staff people at the workshop.

As far as anybody remembers, neither Fred nor Brenda have ever had any close friendships. Can their behaviour be explained in terms of a need for intimacy, and what is the significance of Fred's knowledge of anal intercourse?

Aberrant behaviour may also occur if developmentally handicapped adults cannot meet their sexual and intimacy needs by culturally normative means. However, there are now many examples of adults with mental handicaps who have met these needs with peers in appropriate ways, and enough studies of marriages, e.g. Mattinson (1970), Craft & Craft (1979), to demonstrate that this is a viable life-style for many handicapped people. This alternative must now be considered as a right and not a privilege.

Living Up to Community Standards?

One often hears the admonition that handicapped people must live up to community standards or they will not be allowed to remain at large. This seems to mean they must comply with the publicly-stated, middle-class values of people over 40. Little allowance is made for the fact that we are all exposed to a bewildering array of messages which both directly and indirectly flout the moral standards we claim to espouse.

What are the unspoken community standards? Alcohol abuse, family violence and petty theft seem to be an accepted way of life for a considerable minority. Pornography, i.e. the sexual victimisation of one person by another, is increasingly available, while erotica, sexual intimacy between loving and consenting partners is comparatively rare. On television, one can frequently watch people being murdered, but rarely see two people making love.

Perhaps pornography represents a perversion of the drive for intimacy. Men are the consumers, while women and children tend to be the victims. Magazines, films, video-tapes and strip clubs display their wares behind a facade of intimacy. Newstand booklets purporting to contain readers' intimate letters reveal masturbatory fantasies of anal sex, bestiality, bondage, incest, orgies and sadomasochism in alphabetical order!

For women, the false image of intimacy is displayed more subtly. For example, the quest for eternal youth and physical beauty seems to embody the pursuit of intimacy.

173

Women are also the major consumers of romantic novels where
details and locations change but the handsome, strong-
willed, silent but passionate hero always carries off the
sweet, young heroine in the end. Ironically, one can easily
imagine these heroes as the brutal, self-centered and
inarticulate men who become wife-beaters and child-abusers,
e.g. Peake (1983).

Then, of course, there is the question of sexual abuse
within the family. In the past, parents warned their
children about the sexual advances of strangers, but it is
now clear that they are in more danger with adult friends
and family members (Meiselman, 1979). While over 95 per
cent of the offenders are male, so are about 40 per cent of
the victims. In other words, both boys and girls can become
the victims of men who sexually molest children. At
present, it is not clear if this type of crime is on the
increase, or if it is simply that more victims are now
speaking out.

Children who are handicapped may be considered perfect
victims of this type of crime. Many cannot speak, others
may have memory deficits which prevent accurate recall of
the abuse, and finally, in a court of law, the testimony of
a handicapped person is usually suspect (Seattle Rape
Relief, 1981). Clearly, the prevention of the sexual abuse
should be a major goal of sexuality training and intimacy
education.

Why do men become sexual offenders? While it is
difficult to provide definitive answers, some facts are
emerging. For example, many of these men have, as children,
lived in cold, uncaring families, where they too were the
victims of physical and sexual abuse. As adults, they
appear to have difficulties in forming intimate relationships with other grown-ups and thus seek out children who
are non-threatening. Although one may feel some compassion
for these unfortunate men, the fact remains that they have
engaged in criminal acts which have traumatised their
innocent victims.

Masters and Johnson (1970) have stated that there is an
epidemic of sexual dysfunctions among married couples in
North America. However, it is interesting to note that the
resulting sex therapy seems to focus on increasing the
intimacy between the partners (Kaplan, 1974; Annon, 1974).
It seems that in the context of a deeply trusting relationship, sexual dysfunctions disappear with unexpected rapid-
ity. This is another illustration of the complex relationship between the two factors under discussion.

Pornography, petty crime, escapist novels, incest,
sexual dysfunctions and family violence represent community
standards in relation to sexuality and intimacy. They also
represent the widespread unhappiness of people who are

having difficulties in forming close, trusting relationships. It must be recognised that it is within this confusing environment that the handicapped person has to learn
about interpersonal relationships. In addition, it may well
be that the teachers are themselves experiencing difficulties with their own sexuality and intimate relationships.

RELATIONSHIP EDUCATION

As discussed in the first section of this chapter, all
people, including those who have a handicap, need to love
and be loved, and to develop feelings of self-esteem. These
needs can be met through intimate relationships with others.
Unfortunately, most community environments provide ambivalent and contradictory messages about ways of developing
these relationships. However, as relationship skills can be
learned, competent, creative and sensitive teaching can help
in the development of mutually-supportive partnerships
between people.
    In the past, relationship education has either been
ignored or taught in a piecemeal fashion. Typically, it is
only after the occurrence of a crisis that an individualised
programme is implemented or a person gains access to an
existing course. While these programmes may prove successful in the short-term, they fall far short of helping people
to recognise their needs for intimacy and to understand how
these can be met in an interpersonal relationship.
    Therefore, relationship education should be comprehen-
sive, systematic, and based upon developmental principles.
It must recognise that handicapped people are qualitatively
similar to others, and will pass through the same developmental stages. However, this may be at a slower rate or in
a more fragmented form. In this educational process, chronological age will mean little, while the concept of developmental delay is of prime importance. For example, a profoundly handicapped young adult may come to recognise
herself as female, and be ready to learn the appropriate
greeting rituals between family, friends and strangers.

General Learning Principles

In many human service agencies and community colleges, the
sporadic attempts at teaching interpersonal skills have
illustrated an additional perplexing fact. General learning
principles are often not applied in this area. For example,
while vocational skill training has incorporated features
such as task analysis, jig construction and schedules of
reinforcement, sex education may still use only verbal

instruction, perhaps aided by line drawings (Johnson, 1979). Consequently, it appears necessary to point out some of the learning principles that are especially important in relationship education.

(a) <u>The Planning Process</u>: For both ethical and motivational reasons, it is important that the handicapped person has an active role in the planning process. This includes the power of veto in situations where the consumer does not wish to participate. In the case of children or adults who cannot comprehend the process, similar rights reside with the parents or their designated substitutes. By now, staff people should be aware of the power of the consumer-professional partnership and the importance of families in the teaching of handicapped people (Mittler, 1983).

Plans for relationship education should not be developed in isolation from other aspects of the consumer's life such as leisure activities or medical needs. Consequently, it forms an important part of the general service and individual programme planning process. The general service plan identifies and describes the services and environments in which relationship education will take place, while the individualised programme identifies the teaching methods and strategies which will be used.

(b) <u>Functional Assessments</u>: When it became apparent that the IQ score had little relevance in the teaching of handicapped people, a number of assessment scales were developed in order to measure the functional skills of the individual (Gunzburg, 1969; Vulpe, 1969; Marlett, 1971). As these focussed on the concrete skills needed for independent community living, the area of interpersonal relationships was somewhat neglected. While there is still a lack of functional assessment scales which deal with relationships, more recent efforts have focussed on basic social skills.

The Sexuality Development Index (Johnson, 1979) is an example of this kind of scale. It consists of a series of videotaped vignettes which deal with the gender identity, socio-sexual behaviours and sexual knowledge of developmentally handicapped adults and adolescents. Obviously, knowledge and awareness in these basic areas are prerequisites for adult intimacy.

In addition, some researchers have developed interesting, informal assessments of social behaviours. For example, Ryba (1979) used simulated social situations in his programme. Students were asked to sign documents, take pills and lend money by adults who were perceived as being in positions of authority, with their resistance to these requests being used as a measure of assertiveness. It seems likely that socially assertive behaviour is another prerequisite for successful intimate relationships.

There is a great need for further work in the development of a functional assessment scale which measures interpersonal skills. A creative approach to the problem may well overcome the ethical and practical problems involved in the measurement of traditionally abstract concepts such as love and intimacy. Until such a large task is completed, informal practical assessments will remain an important component of the learning process.

(c) <u>Teaching Methods</u>: It is of the utmost importance that assessments are linked to a teaching plan. The teacher must work from the current skills and knowledge of the student, in order to build upon them. Reassessments at regular intervals may provide a measure of progress which is rewarding to both teacher and student alike. Conversely, a lack of positive change can emphasise the need for different training strategies. While the concept of assessment-training-reassessment is a simple and important one, it is often neglected by teachers of handicapped people. This is especially true in the areas of sexuality and complex social skills.

Generally speaking, several short lessons are more effective than one long one. Consequently, when teaching a student to shake hands with a new acquaintance, it is often more effective to repeat the short, role-playing exercise on five consecutive days rather than devoting one hour-long session to the task.

Task analysis, i.e. the reduction of a task to a sequence of small steps, is a very important teaching strategy which can also be applied to relationship education. For example, within many marital relationships, intimacy fails to develop due to poor communication skills during lovemaking. Consequently, some therapists have task analysed the mutual sensual exploration of lovers in order to facilitate communication. A typical sequence might go as follows: -

- female strokes inside of male's thigh
- female asks, 'How does that feel?'
- male responds
- female scratches inside of male's thigh
- female asks, 'How does that feel?'
- male responds
- etc.

Rewards and schedules of reinforcement have been shown to be critical components in the learning process (Ferster & Skinner, 1957). However, many teachers still neglect the use of positive reinforcers, relying instead on punishment or the withdrawal of privileges. Consequently, it is not surprising that handicapped people are not usually required to be the dispensers of positive rewards. When they learn to sincerely thank others for dinner or a gift, they enhance their value as friends because they can now dispense verbal rewards.

Particular attention should be paid to the student's preferred mode of learning. As Brown and Hughson (1980) mention, many developmentally handicapped people learn most efficiently through the visual and tactile modes rather than by listening. This probably accounts for the lack of progress in cases such as that of the teenager who had sexually molested a young niece and nephew. While his parents had repeatedly warned him not to touch them, the threesome were allowed to share the same bed. Clearly, the tactile message was stronger than the verbal one!

Nor should the kinesthetic mode be neglected. Learning by doing should be an important part of relationship education. Practising the acceptance of social invitations or the rejection of unwanted sexual advances appears to be an effective means of generating adaptive responses in real-life situations (Johnson, 1983).

(d) <u>Generalisation</u>: Many people who work with handicapped students are aware of their difficulties in transferring learning concepts from one situation to another (Brown & Hughson, 1980; Robinson & Robinson, 1976). For example, a man who has learned socially assertive responses in the classroom may be unable to apply them at home or in a restaurant. Consequently, it is important to ensure that the generalisation of learning is included in the overall teaching plan.

This can be accomplished in two ways. The first is to ensure that the desired responses are <u>over</u>-learned, i.e. practised beyond the point where the student is achieving a satisfactory proportion of correct responses. In new and anxiety-provoking situations, most people temporarily forget some of their previous learning. However, the responses which are least likely to be forgotten are those that have been over-learned to the point of becoming almost automatic.

In addition, the generalisation of behaviour is enhance if the desired response is practised in a variety of settings. Consequently, the young woman who has learned in class how to respond to the sexual propositions of strangers, now needs to practise the response in a variety of environments. Not only should she get the opportunity to practise at a number of bus-stops, but also in the same locations at night! In this way, the teacher attempts to ensure that the desired response has become generalised in both location and time.

(e) <u>Differential Development</u>: It is important to remember that development is not constant across all domains; that is

why we see some very large men with considerable intellectual deficits. In the area of interpersonal relationships,
some people with cerebral palsy may have the ability to be a
valued friend while not being completely independent in
self-care. Conversely, people with psychosis may have
advanced vocational skills and yet be relatively insensitive
to the feelings of others.

A Developmental Approach

In order to counter the lack of relationship education, a
new approach is suggested. (It is hoped that this model
will encourage parents and professionals to approach
relationship education in a positive and systematic way, as
opposed to making ad hoc responses to crisis situations.)
The model indicates that humans pass through seven phases of
intimacy during a normal lifespan. This is not to suggest
that the phases are discrete, for clinical observation shows
that overlap, omission, and incomplete development are
apparent in many people. However, the sequence will not be
unfamiliar to the reader.

An overview of the model is presented in Figure 3. The
seven developmental phases - Security, Exploration, Friends,
Lovers, Commitment, Maturity and Resolution - are presented
along the horizontal axis, while the vertical is occupied by
eight important components of the learning process. These
are the identification of the Primary and Secondary
Relationship Tasks, their Cognitive, Affective and
Psychomotor components, the Sexual factor, Specific Skills
to be learned, Teachers and Resources. The interactions
between the developmental phases and the components of
learning occupy the body of the table and are described
below.

FIGURE THREE: RELATIONSHIP EDUCATION - LIFESPAN ISSUES

	(1) Security	(2) Exploration	(3) Friends	(4) Lovers	(5) Commitment	(6) Maturity	(7) Resolution
(A) Primary Relationship Tasks							
(B) Secondary Relationship Tasks							
(C) Cognitive							
(D) Affective							
(E) Psychomotor							
(F) Sexual Component							
(G) Skills to Be Learned							
(H) Teachers							
(I) Resources							

Phase One: Security

Primary Relationship
Tasks:

In this phase, the developing person forms an intense attachment to the parent(s). This begins, of course, with warmth, security, love, and physical care provided by the parent(s).

Secondary Relationship
Tasks:

None at this level.

Cognitive:

To distinguish self from non-self.
To distinguish between people, animals and objects.
To distinguish between parent(s) and other people.
To begin to understand the verbal communication of others.
To begin to develop a vocabulary of single words.

Affective:

To feel secure and optimistic, i.e. the experienced world is a nurturing, non-hostile environment.

Psychomotor:

To be frequently held and cuddled.
To be warm, safe, and well-fed.
To explore own body and immediate environment.

Sexual Component:

The developing person is in a state of extreme physical dependence upon the parent(s). The complete physical intimacy between parent and child is thought to be a preparation for sexual intimacy in adulthood (Morris, 1971).

Skills to be
Learned:

Rudimentary control of own sensory and motor systems, e.g. turning head in response to a sound and voluntary movement of hands in order to touch objects. Active responses to parents, e.g. smiling and cooing.

	Exploration of immediate environment.
Teachers:	Parents with support from professionals. In this model of service delivery, the professional person helps the parent to teach skills such as large muscle exercises or hand-eye coordination, and suggests positive ways to deal with feelings like frustration and despondency.
Resources:	-Infant Development Programmes of British Columbia: Brynelsen, (1983) -Pilot Parents (self-help groups) Perske, R. (1980).

Phase Two: Exploration:

Primary Relationship Tasks:	While the strong attachment to the parents remains supreme, the developing person now begins to form relationships with people in the extended family. In this phase, the establishment of an appropriate gender identity assumes prime importance.
Secondary Relationship Tasks:	The developing person forms brief, casual friendships with peers.
Cognitive:	To distinguish between parent(s), extended family, friends, and strangers. To distinguish between males and females. To begin to see peers as *like me*. To expand knowledge of environment. To expand capabilities in both the receptive and expressive aspects of verbal communication.
Affective:	To feel secure with members of the extended family. To experience a range of positive and negative feelings, e.g.,

happiness, affection, hurt, pain
and anger.
To begin to be attracted to peers.

Psychomotor:
To show verbal and nonverbal
affection to family and peers,
e.g., Pats, hugs and kisses.
To express a range of emotions both
verbally and non-verbally.
To interact with peers in culturally normative settings, e.g.,
preschools, infant schools, homes
of parents and their friends.

Sexual Component:
A clear sense of gender identity
becomes established. Gratification
is obtained from self-stimulation
of the body, including the
genitals. It should be noted that
male gender identity seems to be
enhanced by the presence of a warm,
nurturant father (Hetherington,
1970).

Skills To Be
Learned:
The names and appearances of
extended family members. The
dimensions of maleness and
femaleness.
The sensual stimulation of own
body.
The labelling of emotions.
The cause and effect relationship
between own behaviours and the
reactions of others.

Teachers:
(i)   Parents
(ii)   Preschool and kindergarten
        teachers
(iii)   Peers.

Resources:
-Preschools and kindergartens.
-Day care centres.
-Elementary Sexuality programmes.
Baker, Brightman & Hinshaw (1981);
McClennen, Hoekstra & Bryan (1981);
Johnson & Davies (1979).

Phase Three: Friends:

Primary Relationship
Tasks:
The importance of the relation-
ship with the parents begins to

183

decline. It is gradually replaced by intense peer relationships, usually with people of the same gender.

Secondary Relationship Tasks:

However, the relationship with the parent(s) and extended family does not disappear, but continues to play an important secondary role through much of the remaining lifespan.

Cognitive:

To understand the concept of reciprocity in friendships.
To realise the importance of friendships.
To become increasingly sensitive to the needs of others.
To know the source of love feelings towards family members.

Affective:

For the first time, to feel *cared for* by a person outside the family. As this person has no previously-vested interest in the relationship and has freely chosen the special friend, self-esteem is greatly enhanced.
To feel affection/love for friends.
To be vulnerable to hurt from peers.
To feel the importance of belonging to a group.

Psychomotor:

To show concerned and affectionate behaviours towards friends and family, e.g. helps friend who is sick, sends birthday cards, and shares chocolate bar.
To demonstrate appropriate greeting rituals, e.g. hugs parent(s), shakes hands with acquaintances, and ignores strangers.
To spend much time in the company of friends.
To dress in the *uniform* of the peer group.
To use the rituals of the peer group in speech and behaviour.

Sexual Component:

In this phase, there is an increased interest in sexual concerns, which begins with a clearer understanding of sex role behaviours. It is not uncommon to note an increase in masturbation and even sexual experimentation with friends of the same gender. There may be much peer discussion of the opposite sex, and a search for information in books and magazines. The prevention of sexual abuse begins to assume more importance.

Skills to be Learned:

Dressing and behaving like peer group.
Social skill rituals, e.g. introductions, riding the bus, and shopping.
Ways in which to demonstrate caring for friends and family.
Sexual knowledge, especially in relation to human reproduction, and the prevention of abuse.

Teachers:

(i)   Parents
(ii) Peers
(iii) Schoolteachers

Resources:

-Integrated school programmes.
-Books for non-handicapped children:-
 Ominsky (1977); Sobol (1977); Brightman (1976).
-Books for parents:- e,g, Perske (1980); Whelan & Speake (1979)
-Integrated community college programmes.
-Curricula:- e.g. Foden (1982a); Davies & Johnson (1982a); Johnson (1981); Edwards & Wapnick (1980).
-Prevention of sexual abuse:-
 e.g. Seattle Rape Relief (1981).

Phase Four: Lovers:

Primary Relationship Tasks:	Although peer relationships continue to become increasingly intimate, relationships with the opposite sex begin to develop. These relationships are often marked by intense romantic feelings and an important sexual component. Many of them are of short duration, but others last longer with a resulting increase in intimacy.
Secondary Relationship Tasks:	While relationships with parent(s) and the extended family remain important, the developing person may become somewhat rebellious, hostile, and resentful. For some people, this seems to be a way of establishing themselves as independent adults.
Cognitive:	To begin to understand the concept of personal integrity, and how it relates to intimate relationships. To begin to evaluate behaviours which facilitate and block intimacy. To begin to understand the relationship between sexuality and intimacy. To become knowledgeable about contraception and venereal disease.
Affective:	To feel supported by friends. To feel intense romantic and passionate feelings for prospective sexual partner(s). To be devastated by the termination of romantic relationships. To begin to integrate sexuality and intimacy.
Psychomotor:	To find private places in which to be alone with sexual partner. To experience sexual intimacy, possibly including sexual intercourse, for the first time. To use contraceptives in a responsible manner.

	To continue to spend time with a number of group of same sex peers.
Sexual Component:	In this phase, sexual expression may well be the over-riding relationship concern. In addition, the peer group may be used as a reference point for the comparison of sexual experiences.
Skills To Be Learned:	The role of personal integrity in a sexual relationship. The use of contraceptives. Safeguards against venereal disease.
Teachers:	(i) Peers - many people learn a good deal about relationships directly from their partners. (ii) Teachers, including counsellors and health professionals. (iii) Parents.
Resources:	-Peers. -Health Services, e.g., Public health Department, Birth Control Clinic, Venereal Disease Clinic, Women's Health Collective. -Community Colleges, Adult Education Centres. -Curricula:- e.g. Foden (1982b); Davies & Johnson (1982b, c); Comfort & Comfort (1981); Kempton (1978).

Phase Five: Commitment:

Primary Relationship Tasks:	The formation of a committed and intimate relationship with a person of the opposite gender. This most important relationship has the potential to reach intense levels of intimacy as it makes great demands on the emotional maturity and communication skills of each partner. It is not unusual for these relationships to fail. However, many people try again with a new partner.

Secondary Relationship Tasks:	Relationships with parents, peers, and extended family continue to be important.
Cognitive:	To understand the dynamics of personal relationships. To be aware of own emotional needs. To increase understanding of personal integrity. To become more aware of unconventional relationships.
Affective:	To experience the personal affirmation of being *the special one* in the life of another. To integrate sexual passion, love and friendship. To experience *interdependence* in an intimate relationship. To experience deeper feelings of care for old friends.
Psychomotor:	To obtain own private place in which to be intimate with partner. To use communication skills in interpersonal relationships. To become more experienced in lovemaking.
Sexual Component:	Paradoxically, sexual expression may become physically less urgent yet emotionally more satisfying as the relationship progresses. This phenomenon is often accompanied by the growing importance of friendship between the partners. In this phase, the couple may continue to use contraceptives or decide to have children.
Skills To Be Learned:	Interpersonal communication with partner. Moral and ethical issues of committed relationships. The balance between intimacy and independence. The behavioural components of being responsible for the well-being of another person.

Teachers: (i) Peers
                             (ii) Adult education teachers,
                             including counsellors, psychol-
                             ogists, etc.

Resources: -Continuing education courses and
                              workshops through colleges and
                              community groups.
                             -Marriage counselling and sex
                              therapy, provided by a variety
                              of community agencies and
                              private clinics.
                             -Curricula:- e.g. Davies &
                              Johnson (1982d).
                             -Books:- e.g. Carrera (1981);
                              Craft & Craft (1979).

Phase Six: Maturity:

Primary Relationship   In this phase, the committed
Tasks: personal relationship often forms
                             the basis for child-rearing.
                             Consequently, the intimacy has come
                             full circle and the adult now
                             becomes the parent to a child who
                             is at the beginning of the
                             relationship sequence.

Secondary Relationship   Some peer friendships of many
Tasks: years standing may now become
                             increasingly valued.
                             Adults usually become increasingly
                             concerned about their aging
                             parents, sometimes assuming a more
                             nurturing role with them.

Cognitive: To understand the importance of the
                             parental role in child rearing.
                             To give consideration to the
                             permanent forms of birth control.
                             To be aware of the finiteness of
                             life.
                             To begin to evaluate own life in
                             terms of interpersonal relation-
                             ships.

Affective: To become intimate with own
                             children.
                             To experience increasingly deeper
                             feelings for partner.

	To feel responsible for well-being of aging parents.
Psychomotor:	To physically nurture own children. To teach own children many things, from self-care to academics.
Sexual Component:	Throughout this phase, people can remain sexually active. Although the pace may be more leisurely, it can be accompanied by increased physical intimacy. Cultural and religious values may seriously curtail sexual intimacy in middle-aged couples.
Skills To Be Learned:	Parenting skills. Maintenance of communication skills with partner. Reflection on past relationships.
Teachers:	(i) Public health professionals (ii) Parents (iii) Peers
Resources:	-Parenting courses, offered by schools, community colleges, and other local agencies. -Parents (i.e. grandparents) can pass on useful information on child rearing. -Extended family can provide respite care when parents need a break from the children. -Mental health services for families in stress.

Phase Seven: Resolution:

Primary Relationship Tasks:	In this phase, the developing person prepares for death. There is a keen awareness of the time limitations on relationships with partner and old friends. If these people die first, there will be a consequent increase in loneliness.
Secondary Relationship Tasks:	None.

190

Cognitive: To understand that own children
                              have become independent adults.
                              To be aware of own physical
                              deterioration and imminence of
                              death.
                              To prepare for own death and that
                              of partner.
                              To reflect upon, understand, and
                              resolve the course of own life.

Affective: To increasingly value time spent
                              with partner and old friends.
                              To resent unwanted dependence on
                              children or other family members.
                              To grieve the deaths of partner and
                              old friends.
                              To accept the existential feelings
                              of aloneness, and helplessness.

Psychomotor: To spend more time in leisure
                              activities of a social nature, such
                              as visiting friends or belonging to
                              recreational groups.
                              To be involved in the care and
                              teaching of grandchildren.
                              To make formal arrangements for
                              disposition of self and property.
                              To become increasingly dependent on
                              others in the requirements for
                              daily living.

Sexual Component: The developing person continues to
                              be sexually active and to need
                              intimacy. However, cultural and
                              religious values may increasingly
                              prevent sexual expression. For
                              example, people in residential
                              institutions for senior citizens
                              are often considered to be asexual.

Skills To Be   Making a will.
Learned:

Teachers: (i)   Lawyers
                              (ii) Adult Educators
                              (iii) Social Service
                                    Professionals

Resources: -Legal firms.
                              -Community college or continuing
                               education courses on *Estate*

> *Disposition* and *The Process of Aging*.
> -Social service agencies for health, social, financial, and counselling services.

This model has several uses in relation to the planning process. First it serves as a reminder that intimate relationships should be an integral rather than peripheral parts of the handicapped person's life. In a broad sense, it is an aid in identifying the developmental stage of the individual, along with the relationship tasks that he or she is likely to be facing. These tasks have been reduced to behavioural terms and a number of resource materials have been identified, with the aim of facilitating the learning process. However, it should be remembered that curricula and audio-visual aids are merely resources, for little will be attained without the thoughtfulness, creativity, and interpersonal skills of the various teachers.

Perhaps a word of caution is needed with regard to secondary handicaps which can be caused by the environment in which the person lives. For example, if an institution is three miles from the nearest bus stop and winter temperatures fall to -30°C., the residents have an additional, secondary handicap in their integration into a normalised community environment. It is probably impossible for adequate relationship education to take place in settings where handicapped people are separated from their families and non-handicapped peers.

Mention should also be made of sexual preferences. As most people are sexually intimate with members of the opposite gender, heterosexual relationships have been used to illustrate the primary relationship tasks of adults. However, a minority of handicapped people will choose to have sexual relationships with adult members of their own gender. It should be recognised that this is not a symptom of psychiatric illness, and that gay men and lesbian women are capable of sustaining intimate and mutually-supportive relationships.

Research Findings

The above-mentioned model is the result of several years of research, clinical observations, and discussions with a large number of handicapped people and their families. While the several research projects have been described in more detail elsewhere (Johnson, 1981, 1983; Miller, Mannula, Parker & Brouillet, 1981; Johnson, Grant & Wilson, 1983), a summary of the major findings may provide further specific information which is useful in the planning process.

The Sexuality Development Index (SDI), a functional assessment of gender identity, social behaviours and sexual knowledge has now been used with 77 developmentally handicapped adults. Interviews were conducted with 38 men and 39 women who were in receipt of services from community-based agencies. Their mean chronological age was 24.5 years with a range from 17 to 40, while IQ scores fell between 50 and 89 with a mean of 66.7. The main findings were:

1. Females appear to have a stronger sense of appropriate gender identity than do males.
2. The majority of the handicapped people sometimes saw themselves as children rather than adults.
3. In more than 75 per cent of the assessments, performance was inhibited by anxiety aroused by viewing sexually explicit materials.
4. While women appeared to have a better understanding of the concept of public and private behaviours, few could provide reasons why certain behaviours should not be exhibited in public places.
5. Generally, men were aware that they should not touch strangers of the opposite sex, but only a few women demonstrated a similar awareness.
6. More than three quarters of the 77 students said they would not indulge in *necking* or sexual intercourse with a long-time partner. Approximately 40 of them said they should not do these things even if they were married!
7. Conversely, it appeared that a large number of people could be persuaded to comply with requests for sexual favours.
8. About 80 per cent of the group lacked even basic knowledge about birth control.
9. The majority of people knew names for the breast and penis.
10. However, they were largely unsuccessful in describing the uses of the various sexual organs.
11. Items concerning intercourse, masturbation and menstruation proved too difficult for the majority of the group.
12. A considerable minority lacked basic information even about their own bodies.
13. As a whole, the group seemed to be less sexually active than their non-handicapped peers. However, there were more sexually experienced women than men in this population.
14. Unfortunately, sexual pleasure, i.e. masturbation and orgasm, appeared to be outside the experience of 70 per cent of the women.

In addition to the functional assessment, a teaching programme has been developed. It is entitled Group Sexuality Counselling and differs from traditional sex education in that it incorporates the affective and psychomotor domains, as well as providing information. On several occasions, the programme has been evaluated using the SDI as a pre- and post-test measure. The results indicate that not only is Group Sexuality Counselling an effective programme, it is also more powerful than traditional didactic sex education in producing positive changes.

Groups usually consist of four men and four women with both male and female leaders. From the assessments, the leaders know the strengths and needs of the students and try to make sure these are incorporated into the programme. Initially, participation is voluntary, but after making a commitment to attend, students are expected to be active and to demonstrate a concern for other members of the group. In addition, they are expected to participate in decision-making relating to the content of each session, and to complete homework assignments which are largely social in nature.

A sex education slide set (Kempton, 1978) is used extensively for the provision of information on topics as diverse as sexual anatomy and venereal disease. However, it is supplemented by other teaching aids including sets of contraceptives. Discussion of the slides always begins with the student's contributions which are elicited by open-ended questions such as, *'What do you see on this slide?'* It is crucial that the trust level in the group is sufficient for students to risk making errors. Indeed, in a well-functioning group, the slides can be an effective stimulus for the discussion of personal concerns.

Role playing is another important component of the programme. Students begin by pretending to invite a partner to a social event. When they have achieved a measure of success in this, they are encouraged to transfer the behaviour to a real situation. Next, the role-playing takes the form of assertively rejecting both polite and persuasive invitations to social events. Finally both males and females learn assertive behaviours in the face of threatened sexual coercion of various kinds.

The sharing of personal experiences is an elusive, yet potentially powerful teaching technique. Skilled counsellors can sometimes create a milieu which is supportive enough for students to discuss personal concerns. For example, a female leader's self-disclosure of her feelings about pelvic examinations can legitimise similar expressions of concern from the female students. Occasionally, concerns about sexual functioning or abuse are raised, and the associated intense feelings must be accepted, discussed and understood. And in one recent group, two female students confronted each other about the pros and cons of sterilis- ation. The sharing of feelings perhaps forms the basis of the truly integrated learning which involves the cognitive, affective and psychomotor domains.

SUMMARY

Love Needs and Self Esteem

- Insufficient attention has been paid to the interpersonal relationships of people who are handicapped.
- While the needs for Love and Belonging have often been recognised in children, many handicapped adults live in an impersonal world.
- When the needs for Love and Belonging are unmet, this tends to have a negative effect on self-esteem.
- Many training agencies have focussed on the vocational and self-care programmes associated with self-esteem to the exclusion of the teaching of interpersonal skills.
- It is suggested that relationship education become an integral part of the individualised programme plan.

Sex and Intimacy

- The tasks of relationship education are complicated by the ambiguity of community standards regarding sex and intimacy.
- Many non-handicapped people are confused by the covert messages they receive about intimacy, and are unhappy in their close relationships.
- Increases in the sales of pornography, the incidence of incest, and the consumption of romantic novels are all symptoms of this general malaise. In such an environment, extraordinary care, clarity of purpose, and sensitivity to individual needs are the hallmarks of the effective teacher.

Relationship Education

- General learning principles apply to relationship education.
- A developmental model of relationship education seems to encompass seven phases, i.e. Security, Exploration, Friends, Lovers, Commitment, Maturity, and Resolution.
- Each phase has its primary task, be it the intense bonding between parent and child, or preparation for death.

- At each step, consideration must be given to the cognitive, affective and psychomotor aspects of the primary task, along with its sexual component.
- The goal of relationship education is interpersonal self-actualisation, i.e. to help individuals reach their true potential in a range of intimate relationships.

REFERENCES

Abelson, G. & Paluszny, M. (1978) Gender Identity in a Group of Retarded Children, *Journal of Autism and Developmental Disorders, 8*(4), 403-411.

American Association for Health, Physical Education and Recreation. (1971) *A Resource Guide in Sex Education for the Mentally Retarded*, AAPHER, Washington, D.C.

Annon, J. S. (1974) *The Behavioural Treatment of Sexual Problems*, Enabling Systems, Honolulu.

Baker, B. L., Brightman, A. J. & Hinshaw, S. P. (1981) *Toward Independent Living: A Skills Training Series for Children with Special Needs*, Research Press, Champaign, Illinois.

Berger, S. (1952) 'The Role of Sexual Impotence in the Concept of Self in Male Paraplegics', *Dissertation Abstracts, 12*(4), 533.

Beck-Ford, V., & Smith, N. (1979) 'Leisure Training with Developmentally Handicapped Adults, in R. I. Brown & M. B. Bayer (eds), *Research, Demonstration and Practice: Ten Years of Progress*, Vocational & Rehabilitation Research Institute, Calgary, Alberta.

Bowlby, J. (1969) *Attachment and Loss*, Hogarth Press, London.

Brightman, A. (1976) *Like Me*, Little, Brown, Boston, Mass.

Brown, R. I. (1975) 'Vocational and Social Training', in K. Wedell (ed.), *Orientations in Special Education*. John Wiley & Sons, London.

Brown, R. I., & Hughson, E. A. (1980) *Training of the Developmentally Handicapped Adult*, Charles C. Thomas, Springfield, Massachusetts.

Brynelsen, D. (1983) 'Infant Development Programmes in British Columbia,' in P. Mittler & H. McConachie (eds.), *Parents, Professionals, and Mentally Handicapped People: Approaches to Partnership*, Croom Helm, London.

Carrera, M. (1981) *Sex. The Facts, the Acts and Your Feelings*, Crown, New York.

Comfort, A. & Comfort, J. (1981) *The Facts of Love: Living, Loving and Growing Up*, Crown, New York.

Craft, A., & Craft, M. (1979) *Handicapped Married Couples*, Routledge and Kegan Paul, London.

Davies, R. & Johnson, P. R. (1982) (a) 'Appreciate the Significance of Conventional Sexual Identification, (b) Understand the Expectations of a Sexual Relationship, (c) Appreciate Personal Integrity in a Sexual Relationship, (d) Appreciate the Significance of Unconventional Sexual Relationships,' in D. Oakes (ed.), *An Alternative Route Toward Independent Living*, Ministry of Education, Vancouver, British Columbia.

Davis, K. (1940) 'Extreme Social Isolation of a Child,' *American Journal of Sociology, 45*, 554-565.

Davis, K. (1947) 'Final Note on a Case of Extreme Isolation,' *American Journal of Sociology, 52*, 432-437.

Edwards, J. P. & Wapnick, S. (1980) *Being Me*, Ednick, Portland, Oregon.

Erikson, E. H. (1963) *Childhood and Society* (2nd ed.), Norton, New York.

Evans, C. (1978) *Psychology: A Dictionary of the Mind, Brain and Behaviour*, Arrow Books, London.

Ferster, C. B. & Skinner, B. F. (1957) *Schedules of Reinforcement*, Appleton-Century, New York.

Fischer, H. L., Krajicek, M. J., & Borthick, W. A. (1973) *Sex Education for the Developmentally Disabled: A Guide for Parents, Teachers, and Professionals*, University Park Press, Baltimore, Maryland.

Foden, S. (1982) '(a) Enter Personal Relationships, (b) Conduct Personal Relationships', in D. Oakes (ed.), *An Alternative Route Toward Independent Living*. Ministry of Education, Vancouver, British Columbia.

Gunzburg, H. C. (1969) *Progressive Assessment Charts and Manual*, National Society for Mentally Handicapped Children, London.

Hetherington, E. M. (1970) 'Sex Typing, Dependency, and Aggression', in T. D. Spencer & N. Kass (eds), *Perspectives in Child Psychology*, McGraw-Hill, New York.

Johnson, P. R. (1979) 'The Sexuality of the Mentally Retarded Person: A Dragon with Two Heads', in R. I. Brown & M. B. Bayer (eds.), *Research, Demonstration, and Practice - Ten Years of Progress* Vocational and Rehabilitation Research Institute, Calgary, Alberta.

Johnson, P. R. (1981) 'Sex and the Developmentally Handicapped Adult: A Comparison of Teaching Methods', *British Journal of Mental Subnormality, 27*(1), 8-17.

Johnson, P. R. (1983) 'Community-Based Sexuality Programmes for Developmentally Handicapped Adults', in J. Berg (ed.), *Proceedings of the VI World Congress of the International Association for the Scientific Study of Mental Deficiency*, Charles C. Thomas, Springfield, Illinois.

Johnson, P. R. & Davies, R. (1979) 'Explain Physical Growth
    and Development', in M. Belke (ed.), *An Alternative
    Route Toward Independent Living*, Ministry of Education,
    Vancouver, British Columbia.
Johnson, P. R., Grant, D. & Wilson, J. S. T. (1983) 'Group
    Sexuality Counselling: Further Research Findings',
    *Journal of Practical Approaches to Developmental
    Handicap* (in press).
Kaplan, H. S. (1974) *The New Sex Therapy: Active Treatment
    of Sexual Dysfunctions*, Brunner-Mazel, New York.
Kempton, W. (1978) *Sexuality and the Mentally Handicapped*,
    James Stanfield Film Associates, Los Angeles.
Margalit, M. (1979) 'Comparison of Two Training Programs to
    Advance Body Schema of Trainable Mentally Retarded
    Children', *Israel Annals of Psychiatry and Related
    Disciplines, 17*(4), 298-304.
Marlett, N. J. (1979) *The Adaptive Functioning Index*,
    The Vocational and Rehabilitation Research Institute,
    Calgary, Alberta.
Maslow, A. H. (1970) *Motivation and Personality* (2nd
    edition), Harper and Row, New York.
Masters, W. H., & Johnson, V. E.(1970) *Human Sexual Inade-
    quacy*, Little Brown, Boston, Massachusettes.
Mattinson, J. (1970) *Marriage and Mental Handicap*,
    Duckworth, London.
McClennen, S. E., Hoekstra, R. R. & Bryon, J. E. (1981)
    Social Skills for Severely Retarded Adults. Research
    Press, Champaign, Illinois.
McGarry, M. S. (1979) 'An Exploration of Personality Change
    as a Function of Skill Acquisition in Adult
    Retardates', *Rehabilitation Psychology, 26*(2), 57-60.
Mead, G. H. (1934) *Mind, Self and Society from the Stand-
    point of a Social Behaviourist*, University of Chicago
    Press, Chicago.
Meiselman, K. C. (1979) *Incest: A Psychological Study of
    Causes and Effects with Treatment Recommendations*,
    Jossey-Bass, San Francisco.
Mittler, P. & McConachie, H. (1983) *Parents, Professionals
    and Mentally Handicapped People: Approaches to
    Partnership*, Croom Helm, London.
Morris, D. (1971) *Intimate Behaviour*, Jonathan Cape,
    London.
Morgan, B., & Leung, P. (1980) 'Effects of Assertion Train-
    ing on Acceptance of Disability by Physically Disabled
    University Students', *Journal of Counselling Psych-
    ology, 27*(2), 209-212.
Ominsky, E. (1977) *Jono: A Special Boy*, Prentice-Hall,
    Englewood Cliffs, New Jersey.
Peake, L. (1983) *Passionate Intruder*, Harlequin, Stratford,
    Ontario.

Perske, R. (1980)   *New Life in the Neighbourhood*, Parthenon, Nashville, Tennessee.

Robinson, N. M. & Robinson, H. B. (1976)   *The Mentally Retarded Child* (2nd edition), McGraw-Hill, New York.

Rubin, Z. (1980)   *Children's Friendships*, Harvard University Press, Cambridge, Massachusettes.

Ryba, K. A. (1979)   'Practical Approaches to Teaching Socially Assertive Behaviour', in R. I. Brown & M. B. Bayer (eds.), *Research, Demonstration and Practice: Ten Years of Progress*, Vocational & Rehabilitation Research Institute, Calgary, Alberta.

Seattle Rape Relief (Developmental Disabilities Project) (1981)   *Special Education Curriculum on Sexual Abuse, (I) Elementary Level, (II) Secondary Level*, Comprehensive Health Education Foundation, Seattle, Washington.

Seattle Rape Relief (1981)   *The King County Developmental Disabilities Project*, Seattle Rape Relief, Seattle, Washington.

Shaul, S., Bogle, J., Harbaugh, J. H., & Norman, A. D. (1978)   *Toward Intimacy: Family Planning and Sexuality Concerns of Physically Disabled Women*, Human Sciences Press, New York.

Simpson, H. M., & Meaney, C. (1979)   'Effects of Learning to Ski on the Self-Concept of Mentally Retarded Children', *American Journal of Mental Deficiency, 84*(1), 25-29.

Singh, S. P., & Magner, T. (1975)   'Sex and Self: The Spinal Chord-Injured', *Rehabilitation Literature, 36*(1), 2-10.

Sobol, H. L. (1977)   *My Brother Steven is Retarded*, Collier Macmillan, London.

Starr, P., & Heiserman, K. (1977)   'Acceptance of Disability by Teenagers with Oral-Facial Clefts', *Rehabilitation Counselling Bulletin, 20*(3), 198-201.

Steinem, G. (1980)   'Erotica and Pornography: A Clear and Present Difference', in L. Lederer (ed.), *Take Back the Night: Women on Pornography*, William Morrow, New York.

Vulpe, S. G. (1977)   *Vulpe Assessment Battery* (2nd edition), National Institute on Mental Retardation, Toronto.

Webster.   (1964)   *Third New International Dictionary*, Merriam Co., Springfield, Massachusettes.

Whelan, E. & Speake, B. (1979)   *Learning to Cope*, Souvenir Press, London.

Wolf, T. M., & Wenzl, P. A. (1982)   'Assessment of Relationship Among Measures of Social Competence and Cognition in Educable Mentally Retarded-Emotionally Disturbed Students, *Psychological Reports, 50*(3), 695-700.

Wolfensberger, W. (1972)   *The Principle of Normalization*, National Institute on Mental Retardation, Toronto, Ontario.

Wolman, B. C. (ed.) (1973) *Dictionary of Behavioral Science*, Van Nostrand-Reinhold, New York.

FOOTNOTE

*While the vignettes in this chapter are essentially factual, names and some details have been changed in order to protect the anonymity of the people concerned.

Chapter Eight

TRANSITION FROM SCHOOL TO ADULT LIFE

Robin Jackson

INTRODUCTION

The aim of this chapter is to describe some of the main
findings of past research and to discuss some of the
important philosophical and practical implications which
arise from these findings. Particular attention is paid to
examining some of the assumptions on which both past
research and present practice in the fields of education and
rehabilitation are based. Through an appreciation of the
questionable nature of some of these assumptions, it is
hoped the reader may be encouraged to think of ways in which
to improve the quality of research and present provision and
practice.

The second aim of the chapter is to analyse the nature
of the predicament currently facing the mentally handicapped
young person and adult. This was a predicament overlooked
by the British Government Committee of Enquiry into the
Education of Handicapped Children and Young People (Warnock
Committee). The implications of this oversight are
discussed.

PAST RESEARCH

Windle (1962) in his classic review *Prognosis of Mental
Subnormals* asserted that predictive studies in the field of
mental retardation, by comparison with similar predictive
studies in penology and psychiatry, were immature in concept, design, procedure and execution. He also expressed
the view that although prognostic work with mentally
handicapped people was less well advanced, it might present
fewer problems than predictive studies in penology and
psychiatry. He based his view on the belief that retarded
persons are less complicated psychodynamically than those of

normal intellect, and thus one might anticipate that fewer factors would be involved in their adjustment.

Since the publication of Windle's monograph a succession of critical reviews have appeared which have clearly, and at times mercilessly, exposed the many methodological deficiencies of past studies (Goldstein, 1964, Wolfensberger, 1967, Cobb, 1972). The apparent decline in the number of predictive studies undertaken in the two last decades may owe something to the impact of these reviews and a belated recognition of the fact that prediction in the field of mental retardation is a much more complex process than either Windle or other commentators had hitherto supposed.

In one of the most incisive and comprehensive reviews of past research undertaken, Cobb (1972) noted that no formulae for predicting success of mentally handicapped adults had been found. Indeed the conclusion which emerges from this review is that no simple formula for predicting vocational success may ever be possible. Cobb indicated that studies which sought to examine the post-school adjustment of retarded people tend to fall into two broad categories. First, there are studies of a longitudinal or follow-up nature. Second, there are studies which seek to examine in a systematic manner the relationship between predictor (eg, IQ) and criteria (eg, outcome) variables. Although most of the follow-up studies have been descriptive in nature, Cobb noted that some have attempted to identify the factors that characterise *successful* and *unsuccessful* groups. While the second kind of study usually employed more rigorous design and sophisticated procedures, Cobb drew attention to the persistence in many of these studies of design flaws, conceptual ambiguities and non-sequiturs in the conclusions drawn from the data. Cobb's verdict on the quality of past research is unambiguous:

> *'With few exceptions, they constitute isolated*
> *investigations, with little attempt to develop*
> *a coherent body of knowledge, to replicate or*
> *cross-validate, to expand the basis of general-*
> *isation from small local population samples to*
> *wider populations, to systematise and standardise*
> *the measurement of independent and dependent vari-*
> *ables, or to fit predictive investigation to*
> *coherent development of theory.'*

Until these kinds of deficiency were remedied, Cobb saw little progress in the development of useful predictive methods in the rehabilitation of retarded persons.

Despite the many limitations in design and procedure of past studies, Cobb was able to identify certain important findings. Some of these are briefly described and their significance assessed.

1) Past studies appear to show that a high proportion (two-thirds to three-quarters) of those identified as mildly mentally handicapped make satisfactory adjustment, i.e., adjustment without any special supporting services or treatment.

2) While studies involving retarded people have made it clear that their identification as retarded is closely linked with school failure, failing on leaving school appears to result from other factors. In Cobb's view this finding is important as it challenges the common assumption that the reasons for post-school failure arise from the same causes as school failure.

3) Studies of the value of special school/class placement on subsequent adjustment have also proved inconclusive. One reason for this may be, as Cobb has suggested, that most follow-up studies have been poorly controlled and the educational variables and adaptive criteria have been too loosely defined. Nevertheless the proportion of *successes* claimed for the effects of special education is, in most of the studies, little different from the proportion of retarded reported to *succeed* without the benefit of attendance at special school or class.

4) Although many investigations have sought to examine the relationship between measured intelligence and adjustment outcome, its effect still remains unclear (Jackson, 1968).

5) The only predictive indices which have shown some stability are measures of manual dexterity. However, as most of these studies have been confined to workshop training centres and schools in which industrial training programmes were employed, we have no evidence that such measures have any predictive validity in the long term in relation to adjustment to work.

6) While attempts to establish the predictive validity of measures of personality and social behaviour have been more successful than measures of intellectual functioning, they too have to be accepted with some reservation. As Windle (1962) noted, the measures of personality which are conventionally adopted usually consist of staff ratings on various characteristics of differing specificity. The relative absence of studies using more refined personality measures is probably due to the lack of an instrument which is both easy to apply and to interpret. The inadequate verbal and self-reporting skills of mentally handicapped persons are a further obstacle.

7) The few longitudinal studies which have sought to determine adjustment after some time has elapsed since school leaving appear to show a clear shift from a period of

initial instability to relatively increased stability with the passage of time (eg, Baller, Charles and Miller 1967). Thus, although mentally handicapped people may experience a higher incidence of marital, social and occupational failure than non-retarded controls in the early stages, Cobb concluded that this difference diminishes with time.

SOME CONCERNS RELATING TO LONG TERM SUCCESS

Cobb's conclusion that the majority of mentally handicapped adults eventually make satisfactory adjustment in employment and the community needs to be treated with caution. A critical weakness in most of the studies undertaken in North America and Britain is that they have examined only the first few years in the transition from school to adult life. This has meant that factors which usually become operative later in a retarded person's life are overlooked. The possible significance of some of these factors is briefly outlined.

LOSS OF PARENTAL SUPPORT

There can be no doubt that the successful adjustment of some retarded people in the community is wholly or partly dependent on support received from parents (Bayer & Brown, 1982). A characteristic feature of this support is that it cannot be sustained indefinitely. There comes a time when either because of unwillingness, inability or death, it is withdrawn or lapses. Some parents feel that when their children have reached adulthood they are freed of any familial obligation to continue maintaining them. Others, while not sharing this narrow interpretation of their familial role, have insufficient financial resources to look after them. Such a situation can easily occur where the handicapped person is earning too low a wage to achieve financial independence. Finally, some parents find the physical and psychological strain of caring for a retarded adult so overwhelming that, either from their own choice or on professional advice, they are reluctantly forced to discontinue their support. The real crisis occurs when one or both parents die, for in the absence of any developed form of residential provision for the retarded in the open community, dependent children are quite likely to be referred to a mental subnormality hospital.

MARRIAGE AND FAMILY COMMITMENTS

Two simple facts need to be stressed. First, the age at which retarded people tend to marry falls outside the time period examined by most follow-up studies. Second, it is apparent from research evidence that retarded people encounter more problems in their marriage than their normal peers. Some of the factors which appear to promote marital instability have been identified by Floor, Baxter, Rosen and Zisfein (1975):

(a) a lower than average income and job status,
(b) minimal social education and experience,
(c) the absence of a family model or family support, and
(d) the intense struggle to exist on a day-to-day basis without any awareness to do otherwise.

As the basic wage earned by many retarded workers is often insufficient to meet the needs of one person, attempts to support a wife and children can easily run into difficulty. A low family income is also likely to complicate still further problems of household management, for it requires greater not less skill to budget within the constraints of a limited income. No less important than the more obvious kinds of financial and managerial problems confronting the retarded are problems of a psychosexual nature. As Fisher and Krajicek (1974) have pointed out few retarded people are adequately prepared in this area. Apart from the general reluctance of parents in our culture to discuss sexual matters with their children, there may be an additional reason why parents of retarded children may be more than usually reticent. Our society still holds somewhat ambivalent attitudes towards retardation. On the one hand, there is the manifest and sympathetic recognition of the rights of retarded people to special treatment and support, yet on the other hand, and at a different level, there exists a latent and specific fear that they are innately predisposed to commit sexual crimes (Farber, 1968; Wolfensberger, 1970). It is still commonly believed, as indeed it was in the Victorian Age, that retarded men are prone to commit sexual offences and to act *indecently*, whilst retarded women are likely to be promiscuous. The reality is usually ignored that retarded persons are more often sinned against than sinning. Nevertheless the way in which retarded children are brought up by their parents is likely to be influenced by the extent to which these popular myths are held in their own community. Thus parental reaction may take the form of ignoring, concealing or disguising sexual issues when they arise, strategies which may be effective and convenient for the parents but which are hardly likely to enlighten or prepare the retarded.

A further important factor that may contribute to marital instability is the individual's experience of family life. Research evidence has repeatedly shown that retarded children tend to be drawn from families in which there has been a greater prevalence of divorce and separation (Stein and Susser, 1960), greater frequency of referrals of family members to hospital for psychiatric treatment (Kennedy, 1948) and a much lower level of integration into the community (Meyerowitz and Farber, 1966). As Farber (1968) has indicated, if retarded individuals tend to come from homes that reflect instability and insufficiency then even without the assumption of mental retardation, their own families can be expected to have characteristics comparable to their parental families.

WITHDRAWAL OF AFTER-CARE SUPERVISION

For several years after leaving school, local authority or voluntary social workers may supervise the progress made by some leavers and by so doing prevent failure. After a few years this supervision usually ceases even though the importance of continuing it may be officially recognised:

> '...the problem of the school-leaver with special difficulties should not be thought of as one that can readily be dealt with in one year or two from leaving school. It can persist, and be aggravated by drifting; but the time when effective action can be taken may be a man's twenty-third birthday rather than his seventeenth.' (Department of Employment, 1972)

There are two main reasons for the withdrawal of supervision:

1) it may be felt that there is a limit to the amount of intrusion into the life of a retarded individual that can be justified, and that, with the approach of adulthood, supervision should be discontinued. While the doubtful ethical propriety of maintaining open-ended follow-up programmes may be cited as a legitimate reason for terminating supervision, a second more compelling reason exists.
2) A long period of supervision would impose intolerable strains on already over-burdened social work departments. Thus it is often the case that within a short time of leaving school and with the exception of those

youngsters who have been categorised as being *at risk*, most leavers disappear from any form of supervision.

There are two important points here worth brief comment. There is no reliable evidence to suggest that it is possible to predict with any degree of accuracy which leavers are going to adjust successfully and which are going to experience adjustment breakdown (Cobb, 1972). Therefore, attempts by schools, the school psychological service, social work departments, careers service, either individually or collectively, to identify those most in need of supervision are of questionable value and effect.

There is also the paradox that supervision often appears to be withdrawn when it is most needed. As a consequence, when faced with a minor difficulty or a major crisis, the retarded adult frequently does not know what to do or to whom to turn for appropriate advice and guidance. This is a point which is clearly underlined in the findings of the follow-up survey conducted by Matthew (1964):

> *'Many of the failures... ...left school with every promise of a successful career. They met a bad patch, and had an interested agency or adult been there to help or advise, complete breakdown might have been avoided.'*

If there are good grounds for discounting the predictive value of findings derived from short-term studies, what degree of confidence can be placed in the results obtained from longitudinal surveys. One particular survey to which Cobb (1972) attached especial significance was undertaken in Nebraska by Baller, Charles and Miller (1967):

> *'The work of Baller, Charles and Miller is the best example we have of a longitudinal follow-up of a sample of community dwelling persons identified as retarded.'*

The contention that this survey provides convincing empirical support for the proposition that the majority of retarded adults achieve a satisfactory level of community adjustment is not borne out from a close examination of the findings obtained (Jackson, 1977). One particular finding that attracted scant attention is the fact that by the end of the survey nearly one third of the *located* subjects had died (i.e., 46 out of 155). No attempt was made by the authors, or subsequently by commentators, to seek a possible explanation for the high death rate. Yet this finding may be indicative, and may represent the cumulative effect of a number of factors:

(a) a lack of self-care;
(b) unhealthy living conditions;
(c) unsatisfactory diet;
(d) lack of medical attention;
(e) accident-proneness;
(f) a low wage rate limiting a retarded person's ability to purchase adequate food, clothing, housing and medical care.

Uncritical acceptance of the Nebraskan survey's findings has encouraged the view that little would be gained from undertaking further longitudinal research:

> *'The Baller-Charles study and similar investigations carried out of the after careers of institutional defectives makes further purely descriptive studies of little general interest.'* (Tizard, 1965).

Not surprisingly perhaps, this extract was quoted by Baller, Charles and Miller (1967) in support of their view that replications of simple, descriptive, longitudinal studies would probably not be very rewarding. General acceptance of this judgement may have contributed to the dearth of longitudinal surveys in the last two decades.

The historic value of the Nebraskan study lies in the fact that it demonstrated that retarded adults are capable of holding down a job in open employment and are able to function independently in the community. To that extent it corrected certain erroneous ideas as to the potential of the retarded adult. However, we have now reached a point when it is necessary to redress the balance by correcting false ideas that exist at the present time. The unduly pessimistic outlook which characterised thinking in the 20's and 30's would seem to have been replaced by a degree of optimism that is not warranted from a careful examination of available evidence.

Cobb's key assertion that the period of occupational, social and marital instability tends to be confined to the early years is therefore conjectural. In the absence of any extensive or reliable body of evidence, one is forced to speculate. As a proposition it does not seem unreasonable to suggest that as a retarded person becomes older he loses what marketable assets he ever had (e.g., physical strength). In addition, and in contrast to his normal peer, he is less likely over the years either to have acquired specific skills or to have gained valued experience. Thus loss of a job in middle age or later may lead to a protracted or indefinite period of occupational instability. In this context it is relevant to note the findings of a Swedish survey which found that about 30 per cent of all *new retarded* recipients of disability pensions were persons of the age of 35 or over (Sterner, 1976).

It has been argued that one other way of determining whether or not retarded adults make a satisfactory community adjustment is to note if they are in receipt of any special mental retardation service (Gruenberg, 1964). Attention has been drawn to the fact that the rise in the prevalence of mental retardation to a peak in the final school years is followed by a rapid decline. Gruenberg has estimated that the prevalence of retardation among young adults is only half as high as the peak rate reached around the age of 14. Richardson (1978) has commented that these findings pose critical questions for understanding the nature of retardation and for decision making in public policy.

The nature of this problem has been clearly delineated by Gruenberg. Either those individuals, who at school were regarded as retarded, have stopped being retarded in any real sense at all and do not need any special protection, help or services, in which case, one needs a reformulation of what *real retardation* is, or they continue to be handicapped in later life and are unknown because the services they need are unavailable to them. In the latter case, society is failing to do its duty toward them and ought to learn how to find and help them.

Richardson (1978) in a follow-up survey in Scotland sought to determine the level of need for mental retardation services by former pupils from a school for the educable mentally handicapped. Life histories and follow-up data at age 22 were obtained for a total city population of children classified as educable mentally handicapped. Histories were also obtained at age 22 from matched comparisons who at no time had been classified. It was found that two thirds of the retarded sample were not receiving any special MR services and thus, in Richardson's judgment, could no longer be regarded as administratively retarded. However, administrative retardation was narrowly defined in terms of placement in either an adult training centre or a residential institution for the mentally handicapped. In other words, need has been equated with placement. There are problems with this kind of simple equation. First, there is an implicit assumption that the placement is appropriate to the need, that is to say, there has been a careful matching of need to service. It is, however, questionable whether the placement of moderately mentally handicapped young people in facilities specifically designed for *severely* mentally handicapped persons constitutes appropriate placement. Second, some of the placements are likely to have arisen from a breakdown in employment or community adjustment. But there are degrees of need, undetectable by this kind of study, before that critical threshold is reached. In parenthesis, it is worth noting that by

209

Richardson's own criteria *one third* of the sample remained administratively retarded and this in a city - Aberdeen - which over the last decade and due to the discovery of North Sea oil, has been immune from the escalating unemployment rates experienced by nearly every other city in the United Kingdom!

Past research has succeeded in demonstrating the potential of the retarded individual: what it has failed to do, is to discover whether, in the longer term, that potential is realised. The virtual absence of longitudinal surveys over the last two decades means that we possess little useful and up-to-date information about the post-school careers of mentally handicapped young people and adults. This lack of information has had a critical effect. If competently designed and administered longitudinal surveys, of a regional or national nature, had been carried out during the 60's and 70's, and if, as seems likely, a significant proportion of retarded adults had been found to be experiencing serious problems then it is reasonable to suppose that resources, which were then available, would have been deployed to tackle the problems identified. Now, at a time when we know that few retarded school-leavers will enter competitive employment, there exists no framework of supporting community services. The failure to develop these services lies less with government than with those who, on the basis of limited evidence, have repeatedly made unjustifiably ambitious claims as to the extent to which mentally handicapped young people and adults adjust satisfactorily in the community.

IMPLICATIONS FOR EDUCATION

A number of important implications follow from the evidence that post-school failure appears to arise from different causes than school failure:

1) Research workers should perhaps place less emphasis on, or dispense with, conventional and easily accessible educational data (e.g. IQs) as a source of predictive material.

2) There should be a careful review of the present structure and purpose of special education in order to judge its suitability to meet the post-school needs of the retarded.

3) Teachers in special education should question the traditional emphasis on the acquisition by pupils of basic educational skills at the expense of social and vocational skills.

4) Careers staff should attach rather less prognostic value to school records when offering occupational advice and guidance or arranging job placement.

The finding that the proportion of *successes* claimed for the effects of special education appear to be so little different from the proportion *succeeding* without the benefit of special educational treatment should be treated with some care. While Cobb (1972) suggested that this finding may reflect the methodological inadequacy of past research, another reason may be advanced. The apparent failure of special education to achieve more positive results may reside in the nature of special education itself. It is questionable whether much of the special education provided either in the past or at present merits the description *special*. It has been erroneously assumed for some time that low pupil-teacher ratios in special schools necessarily individualise instruction, that the teaching methods and curricula provided have been fully evaluated and found appropriate to the needs and abilities of retarded persons, and that teachers in special schools have received a specialised professional training that has equipped them with the necessary knowledge and skills to teach retarded pupils.

However, the apparently limited impact of special schooling suggested by research should not encourage one to conclude that special schooling is bound to fail. The growing awareness of past deficiencies in organisation, curriculum and teaching methods has led to determined attempts to improve the quality and relevance of special education. Nor should one rush to conclude that the apparent failure of special education to realise many of its aims is sufficient justification to recommend the integration of retarded people into the ordinary school system. On the contrary, integration may set back the advances that have been made by special schools in preparing retarded pupils for their place in employment and society.

The dangers of a too precipitate integration of the retarded into ordinary classes have been clearly noted by MacMillan, Jones and Meyers (1976). While their plea for a more cautious approach to integration is addressed primarily to American special educators, their views are equally pertinent to all those concerned with Special Education. They have argued that if integration is to be successful then a number of formidable obstacles need to be overcome. They stress that a distinction needs to be drawn between the principle and policy of integration and its implementation. Although there is widespread acceptance of the notion that retarded youngsters should wherever possible be integrated within the ordinary school system, it does not follow that the benefits of integration will be achieved simply through belief alone. In order to implement this belief the necessary administrative arrangements need to be available (eg, instructional strategies, curricular materials, specially trained teachers). The authors question whether educators, both ordinary and special, have the sophistication, techniques and materials to implement the policy.

When children are placed in a special class or school they are placed in a system which has a distinct set of goals and objectives which are different from those in the ordinary educational system. The curriculum of the special school tends to be directed to a far greater extent towards vocational competence and social adjustment than in ordinary education. If retarded children are integrated into the ordinary class major changes will have to be made in the programmes provided. Their judgement is that such accommodative changes are unlikely to take place. Further, the success of integration schemes is dependent on the attitudes of teachers and pupils in the ordinary schools. With few exceptions ordinary teachers have little knowledge or experience of retarded pupils, in consequence they will be ill-prepared to deal with them. MacMillan et al. (1976) doubt whether ordinary class teachers in general are enthusiastic over the return of mildly handicapped learners, or are prepared to meet the learning needs of the children, or are willing to make a concerted effort to make integration work. They conclude that even if class teachers can be required to accept the retarded children, they are unlikely to be committed in their efforts and therefore the possibility arises that the success of the programme will be undermined. The attitude of non-retarded pupils will also play an important part in determining the success of integration schemes. MacMillan, Jones and Aloia (1974) suggest that one important reason why retarded children are perceived as different by non-retarded children, and thus rejected or not popular, may arise from the fact that they are seen to receive different treatment. If this hypothesis is valid then retarded children in the ordinary class would seem more likely to be stigmatised, particularly if they are the only children to receive special assistance which may be misperceived as preferential treatment.

IMPLICATIONS FOR REHABILITATION

Cobb (1972) has argued that because most retarded adults appear to achieve satisfactory adjustment, those responsible for offering occupational guidance and arranging job placement should be encouraged to adopt rather less pessimistic expectations for retarded school-leavers. The tendency noted was to assume a poor prognosis until positive evidence appeared. This attitude among those responsible for guidance and placement had the effect of creating its own proof by failing to provide the possibility for the mentally handicapped to attain satisfactory adjustment.

Research evidence also lends strong support to the claim made by Olshansky (1969) that many of the assumptions on which the vocational rehabilitation of mentally handicapped people have been based are false. Namely:

1) Pupils labelled mentally handicapped constitute a homogeneous population.

2) Because of the label we know their capacities and limitations.

3) Measures of intellectual performance are relevant to predicting occupational success.

4) We know the intelligence levels required for the effective performance of a wide range of occupations.

In Olshansky's view the uncritical acceptance of these assumptions has tended to lead those responsible for guidance and placement to direct retarded young people and adults to unskilled and semi-skilled employment irrespective of their individual strengths and weaknesses. This tendency of stereotyping certain jobs for certain handicaps is, Olshansky argues, a continuing professional trait. Thus retarded people are too often placed in jobs characterised by poor pay (often below subsistence level), limited prospects, insecure tenure, uncongenial working conditions and low occupational status. In other words, jobs which by their very nature are more likely to promote occupational instability than encourage adjustment. The occupational stereotype of the retarded worker as unskilled has been reinforced by the tendency of the larger employers to demand more ability and training than a job may require.

Another unsupported assumption to which Olshansky directs our attention is that a slow learner is necessarily a poor learner. Although a retarded person may take two or three times as long to learn a task, it is evident that once a skill is acquired his/her performance can be equal to that of the normal worker. It is also assumed that intelligence is a constant and global quality despite research findings to the contrary (Clarke & Clarke, 1953; Clarke & Clarke, 1954; Clarke, Clarke & Reiman, 1958, Brown, 1972). Some retarded youngsters, who may perform poorly at school, may show some talent at home, work or play. In a sense the retarded person may be more perceptive than the professionals in that they see themselves as *school retarded* and not mentally handicapped.

Two further popular assumptions which are challenged are that retarded workers have a greater tolerance of boredom than the normal person, and that their work performance will be the same whether a task interests them or not.

213

It tends to be concluded that any deficiency in their work performance derives from their mental retardation and not from any lack of interest. Olshansky considers it significant that such factors as interests, values and feelings, attitudes and emotional well-being, which are thought as being relevant in the occupational placement of the normal person, are considered less important as far as the mentally handicapped students are concerned. Olshansky urges professional workers to adopt a more experimental approach to vocational evaluation, training and job placement, to determine more carefully the interests of the mentally handicapped persons, and to provide tasks which would better determine their work potential.

IMPLICATIONS FOR RESEARCH

Although the failure to develop valid prognostic variables has usually been attributed to faulty designs and procedures, there are perhaps more fundamental issues that merit discussion (Edgerton and Bercovici, 1976). First, it is important to recognise the fact that adjustment fluctuates from year to year, month to month and week to week. It is necessary therefore for research workers to provide sufficient continuity in measurement to monitor changes in adaptation. It is certainly misleading to describe the condition of employment adjustment as occupational or employment *success*. Discussion of appropriate terminology is, however, more than a semantic exercise, for the distinction between employment success and adjustment is a real one and has led to misunderstanding. Whereas *success* is usually interpreted as the accomplishment or attainment of an end, thus having a static and absolute value immutable once achieved, adjustment suggests a response to the dynamic processes involved in adaptation, a response which may vary both with time and changing conditions (Jackson, 1968). Second, researchers have tended to predict adjustment by focussing on variables that relate to the persons who are doing the adjustment, and rarely on those environmental variables to which these persons must adjust (e.g., public attitudes, employment opportunities). Third, since both persons and environments change, especially over a period of years, predictive studies must be prepared to tolerate considerable inaccuracy. Finally, few studies have been concerned to obtain an assessment of adjustment status from handicapped people. If adjustment criteria continue to stress competence and independence, when mentally handicapped persons themselves stress personal satisfaction, little progress is likely to be made. Further, if we are to take the principle of normalisation seriously then perhaps we should listen more carefully to what handicapped young

people and adults tells us about their lives. Edgerton and
Bercovici (1976) comment that not only is our knowledge of
the lives of mentally handicapped people in the community
extremely limited, but we know very little about how they
evaluate their own social adaptation.

One further possibility should not be overlooked. We
may never be able to predict with any degree of accuracy or
assurance the adjustment of retarded persons, particularly
specific individuals. No matter how perfect the design and
faultless the procedure we may get no nearer finding valid
predictive measures, or understanding the process of adjustment, or formulating an acceptable theory of vocational
behaviour. The present preoccupation with research methodology and attempts to apply greater scientific rigour to
prognostic studies may simply lead researchers into a
succession of blind alleys. In this context, Windle's
(1962) assessment of the quality of past research is relevant:

> *'Scientific methodology is a tool for performing a*
> *sensitive operation, a dissection of interconnected*
> *relations. Researchers in mental subnormality should*
> *hasten to exchange their current meat axes for*
> *scalpels.'*

Nowhere in Windle's extensive review does he hint at the
possibility that the nature of the material with which we
have to deal may compel us to make do with the meat axe -
blunt and bloody though it is!

The medical allusion in Windle's admonition is
interesting for another reason. It provides a useful
reminder that prognostic studies in the field of mental
retardation are based on a medical model: a condition is
diagnosed, a treatment is prescribed, release is granted
when the condition is wholly or partly remedied and outcome
is predicted on the basis of the patient's response to
treatment. The adoption of this medical model is almost
certainly due to the historical fact that much of the early
research was conducted with more severely mentally
handicapped people whose condition usually did result from
identifiable bio-medical causes which led them to be
hospitalised and thus treated as patients. However, as
Edgerton (1968) has pointed out, mental retardation is not a
unitary disorder in the sense that all persons who are
officially categorised *mentally handicapped* share a common
condition that is produced by a cause that is identifiable.
The handicap experienced by the largest proportion of the
mentally handicapped population (85 per cent) results from a
complex, and as yet undetermined, interaction of a diverse
range of factors. Thus the medical model is a singularly
inappropriate one to apply for the condition is rarely

specific, the nature of the treatment is generally ill-defined, release is usually arbitrary (eg, attainment of statutory school-leaving age) and outcome is dependent on a wide range of external factors, many of which defy quantification and over which neither those offering nor those receiving the treatment have any control (eg, local employment opportunities).

Although the present emphasis on improved methodology will no doubt continue, and more complex research designs and sophisticated procedures be devised, it remains questionable how far these methodological refinements will in themselves further our understanding. As Parmenter (1976) has suggested, more profit may be gained from directing resources away from classical prediction studies, which have not proved very fruitful, to action research involving the personnel directly responsible for training. Acceptance of Parmenter's suggestion should not, however, preclude the conduct of further longitudinal research. The study being currently carried out through the Vocational and Rehabilitation Research Institute in Calgary is an excellent example of the kind of imaginative prospective research that is urgently needed. One important line of advance would be to obtain from mentally handicapped people an evaluation of their own adjustment status. Such studies would perform two useful functions. First, they would throw into sharp relief the aridity of much past research. Second, they would demonstrate that mentally handicapped people can often be as perceptive in their observations as experienced research workers. In that respect the mentally handicapped person may teach us - the professionals - a little humility and diminish our collective conceit that only we have access to the truth.

EMPLOYMENT PROSPECTS

The British Warnock Committee had, as it acknowledged, a unique opportunity to take a comprehensive view of the way in which educational provision for handicapped children and young people, as well as arrangements for their transition from school to adult life, had developed and to make recommendations for the future. This opportunity appears to have been missed. The failure is all the more puzzling given that the economic and industrial trends contributing to the deterioration in employment opportunities for mentally handicapped young people were discernible (Jackson, 1980). What the Committee failed to grasp, and this is evident from a reading of the Warnock Report (Department of Education and Science, 1978), was that Britain was undergoing a profound and irreversible structural change in its economy. We were witnessing the birth pangs of the first post industrial society in the Western world. The far-reaching political, economic, educational and social implications of this historic change have yet to be appreciated. What trends then did the Committee overlook?

High unemployment:
Western European governments seem to have accepted the fact that there is little that can be done by them to reduce the current high levels of unemployment - particularly youth unemployment. Recent European Economic Community and OECD reports have made it clear that a high unemployment rate may be a permanent feature of British economic, social and political life for many years to come. If this analysis is correct then it means that, for the foreseeable future, few mentally handicapped young people will succeed in securing a job in open employment.

Effect of mechanisation and automation:
There has been in Britain over the course of the past five decades a progressive contraction in the demand for unskilled labour. Goldstein (1964) has drawn attention to a similar phenomenon in the USA where the number of jobs usually identified with mentally handicapped workers has decreased and where competition for the jobs remaining has become more intense. It was Goldstein's view that there was nothing on the horizon to suggest any improvement.

It should be said that not all experts are agreed on this analysis. Conley (1973) asserted that the fear that technological change and automation will eliminate many of the relatively unskilled jobs on which mentally handicapped adults are employed is groundless. Technological change, he argued, has two effects. First, it leads to new and improved products. Second, it leads to more efficient methods of production. The second effect is achieved by making labour more specialised. The effect of special-isation and a growing diversity in goods leads to an increase in the number and type of jobs available to the retarded worker. Specialisation of labour breaks down a complex productive operation into specific and uncomplicated tasks, which permit workers to become highly proficient in a limited area and, in addition, enables employers to utilise unskilled labour. According to this analysis it should be possible for handicapped workers to participate in such com-plicated tasks as car assembly, for jobs will become so specialised that human involvement may be simply confined to tightening a few screws.

Conley's argument that the simplification of such complicated operative tasks as car assembly has made them more accessible to mentally handicapped workers warrants closer examination. An increasing number of industries - particularly car manufacturers - have come to question the whole concept of assembly line production. Indeed, the characteristics of the mass production process that Conley has identified as being especially advantageous to the handicapped worker - its simplicity, repetitiveness and unchanging routine - are the same characteristics that have been found to induce boredom, low productivity, poor quality workmanship and labour unrest. In order to counter these adverse effects employers are experimenting with, or adopting, productive processes that place a premium on skill flexibility, adaptability, resourcefulness, initiative and self-discipline in the hope that they will improve productivity, motivation, workmanship, morale and profitability. Changes of this kind are unlikely to work to the advantage of the handicapped worker.

It might be added that if a job can be broken down and refined to the point at which only a screw needs to be tightened, economic logic would seem to dictate that that operation would be more efficiently undertaken by machine rather than man!

Decline in number of small firms and family businesses:

The significance of this decline which has accelerated over the last two decades lies in the fact that many mentally handicapped young people were successfully absorbed in businesses that were able to offer a *sheltered work environment* that was close, caring and protective. Those High Street businesses which have taken their place have tended to be larger-scale, more profit-oriented and remotely administered and much less likely to identify with, or have a sense of obligation to, the particular community in which they are set. This also has implications for rural employment where the trades of small villages may be removed to larger urban centres.

Effect of legislative changes:

Legislation introduced by successive governments has also unwittingly weakened the competitive position of the retarded worker. Prior to 1966 a high percentage of boys leaving special schools for moderately mentally handicapped children were placed by the careers service in the delivery services of dairies, bakeries, breweries, soft drink manufacturers and laundries. With the introduction of Selective Employment Tax in 1966, employers were forced to look for immediate ways to shed surplus labour. The delivery services were particularly affected by this shake-out. Although later this Tax was repealed, its effect was permanent. The implementation of The Health and Safety at Work Act (1974) also appears to deter some employers from engaging handicapped workers for fear they might constitute a health risk or safety hazard and thus be an economic liability!

Contraction in manufacturing sector:

The most far reaching trend that has occurred since the war has been the contraction in the manufacturing sector and the expansion in the service sector. Shanks (1981) has commented that *'it is highly unlikely that the labour shed by manufacturing can be fully absorbed in the expanding parts of the economy until the 1990's - if then. The miracle of the industrial revolution, in short, is unlikely to be fully reproduced in the burgeoning post-manufacturing, knowledge-based society.'*
The service sector expansion is significant for two reasons. In order to gain entry into this sector a person is usually expected to possess certain prescribed qualifications. In an increasingly credentialled and bureaucratic society the unqualified and untrained are going to be at a serious competitive disadvantage (Department of Employment, 1974). Further, the service sector is perhaps the most vulnerable to a wholesale take-over by the microprocessor. One consequence of the office revolution will be a massive displacement of female labour. This will inevitably intensify further competition for those jobs available in open employment.
The inevitable conclusion to be drawn from these trends is that placement in competitive employment is a rapidly diminishing option for most mentally handicapped young people. Acceptance of this assessment has profound and far-reaching implications. There are those who argue that such an assessment is unjustifiably defeatist and pessimistic (Rodgers, 1979). This kind of criticism only has validity if no attempt is made to search ·for alternatives.

CURRICULAR IMPLICATIONS

Confronted with these changes the schools are faced with a difficult dilemma. Do they continue to emphasise in the curriculum the acquisition by pupils of vocational skills in the knowledge that few will obtain jobs in open employment? Or do they pursue their vocational goals less vigorously and thereby deny some pupils the possibility of competing for the rare jobs available? The logic of the situation would seem to warrant a careful re-examination of the aims of special and mainstream education. The traditional emphasis which has been placed on the pursuit of vocational goals can no longer be justified. Indeed one suspects that the time generously devoted to vocational preparation in the final years of special schooling owes more to a lack of knowledge of what else to put in its place. The removal of the school leavers' programme could create a vacuum! One consequence of a reappraisal of the purpose of special education could, and should, be the development of a better balanced and integrated curriculum. Kolstoe (1976) has provided us with a possible curriculum model. Seven core areas of learning are identified:

1. communication skills;
2. arithmetic;
3. social competencies;
4. aesthetics;
5. motor and recreation skills;
6. health and safety;
7. vocational competencies.

There are two important features of this model. First, the same weighting and value is accorded to each core area thus avoiding curricular distortion and imbalance. Second, each curriculum area is structured and sequenced to take account of an individual's development from infancy to early adolescence. Sufficient knowledge and experience has now been gained to indicate what could be incorporated within the new curriculum (Brown & Hughson, 1980; Payne, Polloway, Smith and Payne, 1981; Shackleton-Bailey, 1982; Wehman & McLaughlin, 1980; Wehman & Schleien, 1981; Whelan & Speake, 1981).

The same economic circumstances which are currently forcing a re-examination of the curriculum have also generated pressures to expose the curriculum to public and professional scrutiny. The traditional autonomy enjoyed by the English school, especially the special school, to determine its own curriculum has now been challenged. In his survey of curricular provision for the slow learner Brennan (1979) noted that:

> *'there was no evidence in the project schools*
> *that any LEA had developed any consistent attitude*
> *or policy about the detail of curricula in its*
> *schools, and no evidence of any agreed or centralized*
> *procedure for the recording of curricula or curricular*
> *decisions. Nor did any documents submitted from any*
> *source raise this as a practice or even as a desirable*
> *development. This means that the curriculum in each*
> *school is generated, developed and recorded within the*
> *particular school.'*

Limited resources for education now dictate that schools should be more publicly accountable for what they do.

The claim has frequently been made that in the field of work preparation, special education in Britain has performed a valuable pioneering role. This claim only has substance if it can be demonstrated that the work preparation actually provided is well conceived and executed. A recent study raises doubts and prompts questions (Atkinson, Shone & Rees, 1981). The operation of an industrial training unit in a college of further education was examined. The study revealed that there was:

(a) no assessment of the trainees' abilities, aptitudes and interests;
(b) limited individualised instruction;
(c) no monitoring of trainees' progress; and
(d) no evaluation of individual or overall programmes.

The structureless programme offered encouraged passivity, diminished motivation and reduced skills. The curricular determinants (or constraints) appeared to be the nature of the physical plant and production processes and the exigencies of having to meet contract dead-lines. The most disturbing finding was the complacent attitude of the staff who, without ever questioning what they were doing or why they were doing it, assumed that they were providing a successful programme. An unintended and paradoxical consequence of the way in which the unit operated was that it encouraged dependence rather than independence. The authors concluded that their study exemplified a number of issues which are to be found in many work preparation programmes which are purportedly designed to ease the transition from school to adult life. The innovatory role attributed to special education in this field can have little justification if it can be shown, as in this study, that most programmes are aim-less, extemporary exercises constrained by non-educational factors. The Warnock Committee's (DES, 1978) observations have particular relevance here:

'Wherever the quality of special education is high, we have found that two strands have merged. First, well-defined guidelines for each area of the curriculum have been drawn up, which enable teachers to plan their own work and relate it to that of colleagues and other professionals. Second, programmes have been planned for individual children with clearly defined short-term goals within the general plan. We regard these strands as important criteria of effective special education.'

221

PROFESSIONAL TRAINING

However, it is unrealistic to expect staff to have the ability to define and pursue an effective programme if they have not received an adequate and appropriate professional training (Brennan, 1979; DES, 1978). What seems clear is that the training model adopted for such staff needs to be broader in concept to that of the traditional teacher-training model. Staff need to assume a rehabilitative role and thus require a training that suits them to this new role. A particular value of the rehabilitation training model is that it brings together in the training process, when professional perceptions and attitudes are being formed, people who will be entering different but related services that affect directly the lives of mentally handi-capped young people and their families. The creation of a climate in which the significant professional participants have an opportunity to share the same philosophy and approach to the rehabilitation process must be to the benefit not only of the handicapped person but to each professional worker. Implicit in the rehabilitation training model is a recognition of the fact that the needs of the handicapped person are indivisible. The arbitrary compartmentalisation of needs - vocational, social, educational, recreational, home-living - runs counter not only to the efficient delivery of services but, more critically, to the best interests of the handicapped person.

The first course to be based on a rehabilitation training model was set up in Britain in 1981, with the launching of The Certificate in Further Education and Training of Mentally Handicapped People at Stockport College of Technology (Vickerman and Cronin, 1983). By 1985 it is hoped that four colleges serving different regions will be offering this two year full-time course to staff from educational and social services, health authorities and voluntary organisations.

ROLE OF STATE SECTOR

The critical question that needs to be asked, is, if there are only limited employment opportunities for mentally handicapped young people and adults, what can be done? What are the options? The state could:

    (a)   provide subsidies or tax reliefs to employers to induce them to engage handicapped workers;

    (b)   more vigorously enforce or extend the quota scheme;

    (c)   create more special employment arrangements (e.g., sheltered industrial groups);

(d) designate special occupational areas or posts for handicapped people.

Little enthusiasm has been shown for the idea of introducing tax relief or subsidy schemes. It has been argued that it would be difficult in practice to relate the size of the subsidy to the working capacity of the individual (Department of Employment, 1973). Subsidising handicapped workers in open employment might also lead to the charge of exploitation. It might also be difficult to restrict subsidies to particular categories of handicapped persons and to resist pressures to extend subsidies to other groups with similar employment difficulties. Trade unions are unlikely to look with favour on any arrangement that discriminates unfairly against those who are not handicapped, but who are unemployed.

Proposals that the quota scheme be more strictly enforced have not met with favour. Stricter enforcement, which would entail rigorous inspection, more stringent permit procedures for employers claiming exemption and extensive prosecution of non-compliant employers, would, it is felt, be counter-productive. Whilst the sheltered industrial group (enclave) concept is an imaginative and valuable one, involving as it does groups of handicapped people working under supervision in a normal and undifferentiated work environment, its appeal to host employers is unlikely to be attractive at a time of economic stringency. The designation of particular forms of employment or occupational areas for the handicapped could be interpreted as unfair and discriminatory.

There are good reasons for believing that the state, at best, will adopt a policy of no change, at worst, will be forced through economic pressures to weaken existing provision. The Department of Employment in the United Kingdom, in a number of consultative documents, has made it clear that it would not fight strenuously for the retention of the quota scheme, preferring to rely on periodic public relations exercises designed to effect changes in employers' attitudes (e.g., The Fit to Work campaign).

There are some who feel that the kind of direct and large-scale state intervention to be found in some Eastern European countries should be given some consideration. In Poland, where the state manages most of the economy certain economic activities are totally or partially reserved for handicapped persons working in co-operatives. State authorities believe that they have an obligation to grant exclusivity or priority to the handicapped in selected employment areas (Kucharski, 1978). In practice, this means that no other business, outside the co-operative movement, is permitted to manufacture products or render services that have been specially designated.

223

The likelihood of the Polish model, or a variant of it, being adopted in the Western World is remote. Businessmen would be fearful for their own economic viability if monopolistic rights granted to co-operatives were extended to a broad range of manufacturing activities. Trade unions would be more concerned to safeguard the jobs of their overwhelmingly non-handicapped membership. Conservatively-inclined politicians would resist, as a matter of ideological principle, the introduction of policies that involved state intervention and, by implication, heavy financial support. Resistance might also come from pressure groups, representing different handicap constituencies, on the grounds that such discriminatory action offended the normalisation principle.

No attempt has been made to assess the value of the short-term government measures that have been recently introduced to alleviate the problem of youth unemployment (i.e., Youth Opportunities Programme and its successor the Youth Training Scheme) as there is little evidence that such programmes have much long term relevance for mentally handicapped young people (Grundy & Wagster, 1978).

ROLE OF VOLUNTARY SECTOR

Given the reluctance of the state to sanction significant increases in public expenditure to meet the needs of handicapped adults, the challenge will have to be met increasingly by voluntary organisations. One danger in the present situation is a rapid growth of fringe enterprises which purport to offer workshop or training provision, but which in reality are no more than crude commercial exploitative undertakings. A proliferation of workshop and residential communities of this kind without some form of control and regular monitoring would be no solution. Although the notion of establishing an agency responsible for the oversight of such developments might appear to challenge one of the fundamental principles on which the voluntary sector is based - namely its independence - such a proposal can be justified by pointing to the depressing frequency with which handicapped children and adults continue to be exploited and mistreated. Maintenance of some kind of oversight could be achieved through a licensing (or accreditation) system whereby organisations proposing to establish a workshop or centre have to demonstrate that they have the resources (i.e., personnel, plant, equipment, etc.) to fulfil their goals. A monitoring capability would need to be built into the system so that periodic inspections could be made to ensure that the workshop and communities were operating effectively and efficiently. While such a system might not eliminate abuse, it could help to reduce it.

The forecast has been made that in any energy-short society mobility will be a high cost factor (Adelson, 1980). One result of this may be the development of more community-based activities. Such arrangements may have a number of benefits. There is likely to be a higher level of interaction between people who live close together. This may generate greater community feeling, understanding and mutual supportiveness and a greater tolerance for those whose economic productivity is limited. The growth of local workshops as important places of employment could involve mentally handicapped adults not only in productive processes but in support services. Where mentally handicapped people have aptitudes, abilities and interests in particular areas these strengths could be tapped and developed. Involvement by handicapped workers in some *neighbourhood industry* on the same basis as other members of the community would create real and not synthetic integration in which the psychological and social benefits would be high.

Enterprises of this kind require a measure of modest capital support whether from local lending institutions or national or local government departments. In order to secure that support it would be necessary to develop and publicise a number of successful programmes that demonstrated that mentally handicapped people can contribute to their communities in ways that others can note and appreciate. At the same time it would be necessary to show the economic benefits available through involvement in such programmes. The urgency of the situation derives from the fact that there is a risk that time may run out on people's willingness to support mentally handicapped people. As Adelson (1980) warns: *'...the bottom line of this argument is that there may not be all the time in the world left to deal effectively and humanely with mental retardation'*.

ROLE OF HORTICULTURE

The success of the Melwood Horticultural Training and Work Coop Project is one of the best documented examples of a cooperative enterprise involving mentally handicapped workers (Copus, 1980). Its success possibly stems from the natural and intrinsic values found in the horticultural environment:

Societal value: as society tends to place a value on the beauty of plants and well landscaped grounds, those working with plants often have a value placed upon them that would not be as readily bestowed if they worked in the less favourable environment of a factory.

People-plant value: horticultural activity provides an opportunity for a reversal in the caregiving role. The plant is dependent for its survival on the care given by the handicapped person. This experience may facilitate personal growth, engender competence and enhance self-esteem.

Programme option value: the horticultural setting as a training and work co-op activity, offers certain unique opportunities, a wide range of tasks of varying complexity; practical opportunities for problem solving, communication, decision making; opportunities for exercising responsibility, initiative and self-criticism.

Community integration value: horticulture provides numerous opportunities for persons to integrate in the community (e.g., plant/produce sales; grounds maintenance projects) and the chance for the handicapped person to see that the community places a value on his efforts.

The advantages and disadvantages in establishing a horticultural programme as a business are clearly identified in *The Melwood Manual* (Copus, 1980). The outstanding advantage is the impact on the handicapped person of being in the real world of work. There can be no greater motivational stimulus than deadlines, quotas and the weekly pay-check. A further crucial advantage is the opportunity to generate income. At a time of increasing uncertainty as to the ability of the state to maintain its existing level of support for services for the handicapped, it is important to encourage government to invest by way of modest initial grants or small subsidies in programmes that have the potential for being cost-effective. However the horticultural business, whether operated as a full or semi-commercial undertaking, is not immune from the pitfalls of the competitive world. There is no certainty of success. In other words, the commercial disciplines operative in a normal business must be applied. Inevitably, any work co-op and training centre must operate at less than 100 per cent efficiency. The delicate balance that has to be achieved is maintaining high levels of training *and* productivity, but in such a way that neither is emphasised at the expense of the other.

Recognition of the important role that horticulture can play in the rehabilitation of the handicapped has led to two important developments in Britain, both initiated by voluntary organisations. In 1969 the National Society for Mentally Handicapped Children (now the Royal Society for Mentally Handicapped Children and Adults) opened Lufton Manor Rural Training Unit and offered two-year residential courses for mentally handicapped people who showed an aptitude and enthusiasm for rural pursuits. Building on the experience gained from Lufton Manor a Rural Advisory Service was established (Carter and Carter, 1982). The RAS, in conjunction with other bodies, has been responsible for promoting a number of innovative projects:

(a) a rural adult training centre in Buckinghamshire which uses agriculture/horticulture as the only media for training;

(b) a mobile rural Adult Training Centre to serve a sparsely populated region of North Yorkshire;

(c) a research project with the University of Bath to identify crops which require labour intensive methods of husbandry, produce high value commodities and are suitable for growing by mentally handicapped people working under skilled supervision; and,

(d) after long discussion with the Sheltered Employment Branch of the Manpower Services Commission, agreement to the principle of establishing horticultural sheltered workshops for mentally handicapped workers only.

The second significant development was the setting up in 1978 of The Society for Horticultural Therapy and Rural Training. Horticultural Therapy (HT) has developed a range of practical services to offer people with different handicaps and those who work with them. For anyone planning to establish a sheltered employment project HT can help by providing a feasibility study, an evaluation or review, cropping suggestions and planning help. A landscape architect can assist by identifying the potential within a site and help realise that potential by providing advice on site planning, design, construction and maintenance. Practical assistance to a project for up to a period of one year can be provided by land use volunteers (LUVs) who are qualified or experienced young horticulturalists. That assistance is given in return for board, lodging and pocket money. Finally, the Horticultural Therapy Training Centre, which is based at Warwickshire College of Agriculture, seeks to meet the training needs of those who work with handicapped people.

Chigier (1978) is in no doubt that by drawing on the resources of experts from different fields *'dynamic, progressive, challenging and exciting programmes in the rehabilitation of retarded persons in agriculture and related activities can be drawn up and established in any country of the world, without major investment in capital, machinery or manpower'.*

DEPARTMENT OF REHABILITATION

It is important not to view the problems of mentally handicapped young people in isolation. Provision is required for
other groups which are as deserving and are as equally
neglected by the state (e.g., physically handicapped, blind,
partially sighted, etc.). The fact that these apparently
disparate groups share many problems in common suggests the
need to establish a single government department with
overall responsibility for all forms of rehabilitation.
Such a department would take over from existing departments
those areas relating to rehabilitation which have tended in
the past, and at present, to be regarded as being of only
peripheral interest. While there are some risks in creating
a centralised department, it is preferable to a situation
where the provision of rehabilitation services is so
fragmented, complex and disorganised that both national and
local government can and do evade their statutory responsibilities. A comprehensive and effective rehabilitation
service cannot be created as long as the responsibility for
its provision rests with different and often competing
government departments, which tend to see this area - in the
context of their other commitments - as being of only minor
importance. The value of a Department of Rehabilitation
would rest not simply on its ability to coordinate, integrate and direct effort more effectively. Its creation
would help to create an awareness - a public consciousness -
that this is an area of crucial national concern.

SUMMARY

1. The first part of the chapter seeks to describe some of
   the main findings of past research and to discuss some
   of the philosophical and practical implications which
   arise from these findings.
2. The possibility is explored that certain critical
   factors have been overlooked by past research which may
   later adversely affect the community adjustment of
   mentally handicapped adults.
3. The point is made that the unduly pessimistic outlook
   which characterised thinking in the 20's and 30's
   about the employment potential of mentally handicapped
   adults has been replaced by a degree of optimism that
   is not warranted from a careful examination of
   available evidence.
4. Some of the economic and industrial trends which have
   contributed to the significant decline in employment
   opportunities for mentally handicapped young people and
   adults are identified and discussed.

5. The cumulative effect of these trends is that placement in competitive employment is no longer a realistic possibility for most mentally handicapped young people in Britain.
6. The logic of this new situation requires an urgent reappraisal of educational philosophy and practice, in particular, the development of a better balanced and integrated curriculum.
7. Radical changes in philosophy and practice, however, require staff who have received an appropriate professional training that will equip them to assume a new role. It is proposed that a habilitation training model, which lays stress on a broader integrated approach, be adopted in preference to the traditional teacher training model.
8. A brief examination is undertaken of some of the measures that could be taken by the state to enable the handicapped to remain in open employment. The reasons why such measures are unlikely to be adopted are given.
9. In the absence of significant state intervention the onus for the development of services for the handicapped will rest increasingly on the voluntary sector. The risk of uncontrolled proliferation of workshops and residential communities prompts consideration of a licensing (or accreditation) system to monitor developments and restrict exploitation.
10. The increasing cost of mobility in energy short societies may lead to the development of more community-based activities (e.g., co-ops), within which mentally handicapped people can be successfully integrated.
11. The particular value of the horticultural environment as a setting for work co-ops and the advantages and disadvantages of running a horticultural work co-op as a business are examined.
12. Finally, the proposal is advanced that a Department of Rehabilitation be established which (a) could develop an identifiable and coherent rehabilitation policy, and (b) could rationalise the provision of rehabilitation services.

REFERENCES

Adelson, M. (1980) 'Mental Retardation: Toward a Different Kind of Future', In S.C. Plog and M.B. Santamour (eds.), *The Year 2000 and Mental Retardation*, Plenum, New York.

Atkinson, P., Shone, D. and Rees, T. (1981) 'Labouring to
    Learn? Industrial Training for Slow Learners', in L.
    Barton and S. Tomlinson (eds.), *Special Education:*
    Policy, Practices and Social Issues. Harper and Row,
    London.
Baller, W. R. (1936) 'A Study of the Present Social Status
    of a Group of Adults, Who, When They Were in Elementary
    School, Were Classified as Mentally Deficient',
    Genetic Psychological Monograph, 18, 165-244.
Baller, W. R., Charles, D. C. and Miller, E. L. (1967)
    'Mid-Life Attainment of the Mentally Retarded: A
    Longitudinal Study', *Genetic Psychological Monograph,*
    75, 235-329.
Bayer, M. B. and Brown, R. I. (1982) *Benefits and Costs of*
    Rehabilitation at the Vocational and Rehabilitation
    Research Institute, V.R.R.I., Calgary, Alberta.
Brennan, W. K. (1979) *Curricular Needs of Slow Learners,*
    Schools Council Working Paper 63, Evans/Methuen
    Educational, London.
Brown, R. I. (1972) 'Cognitive Changes in Adolescent Slow
    Learners', *Journal of Child Psychology and Psychiatry,*
    13, 183-193.
Brown, R. I. and Hughson, E. A. (1980) *Training of the*
    Developmentally Handicapped Adult, Charles C. Thomas,
    Springfield.
Carter, D. and Carter, A. (1982) 'The Development of New
    Services for Mentally Handicapped People in
    Horticulture and Agriculture', *Wessex Studies in*
    Special Education, 2, 1-12.
Charles, D. C. (1953) 'Ability and Accomplishment of
    Persons Earlier Judged Mentally Deficient', *Genetic*
    Psychological Monograph, 47, 3-71.
Chigier, E. (1978) 'Training and Employment of the Mentally
    Retarded in Agriculture', in International Labour
    Office, *Vocational Rehabilitation of the Mentally*
    Retarded, ILO, Geneva.
Clarke, A. D. B. and Clarke, A. M. (1953) 'How Constant is
    the IQ?' *Lancet, 2,* 877-880.
Clarke, A. D. B. and Clarke, A. M. (1954) 'Cognitive
    Changes in the Feeble-Minded', *British Journal of*
    Psychology, 45, 173-179.
Clarke, A. D. B., Clarke, A. M. and Reiman, S. (1958)
    'Cognitive and Social Changes in the Feebleminded -
    Three Further Studies', *British Journal of Psychology,*
    49, 144-157.
Cobb, H. V. (1972) *The Forecast of Fulfillment: A Review*
    of Research on Predictive Assessment of the Adult
    Retarded for Social and Vocational Adjustment,
    Teacher's College Press, New York.
Conley, R. W. (1973) *The Economics of Mental Retardation,*
    John Hopkins University Press, Baltimore.

Copus, E. (1980) *The Melwood Manual: A Planning and Operations Manual for Horticultural Training and Work Coop Programs*, Melwood Horticultural TC, Inc., Upper Marlboro.

Department of Education and Science. (1978) *Special Educational Needs*, (Warnock Report), HMSO, London.

Department of Employment. (1972) *Resettlement Policy and Services for Disabled People*, Department of Employment discussion paper for the National Advisory Council for the Employment of the Disabled.

Department of Employment. (1973) *The Quota Scheme for Disabled People: A Consultative Document*, HMSO, London.

Department of Employment. (1974) *Unqualified, Untrained and Unemployed*, HMSO, London.

Edgerton, R. (1968) 'Anthropology and Mental Retardation: A Plea for the Comparative Study of Incompetence', in H. J. Prehm, L. A. Hamerlynck, and J. E. Crosson (eds.), *Behavioural Research in Mental Retardation*, University of Oregon, Eugene.

Edgerton, R. B. and Bercovici, S. M. (1976) 'The Cloak of Competence: Years later', *American Journal of Mental Deficiency, 80*, 485-497.

Farber, B. (1968) *Mental Retardation: Its Social Context and Social Consequences*, Houghton Mifflin, Boston.

Fisher, H. L. and Krajicek, M. J. (1974) 'Sexual Development of the Moderately Retarded: Level of Information and Parental Attitudes', *Mental Retardation, 12*, 28-30.

Floor, L., Baxter, D., Rosen, M. and Zisfein, L. (1975) 'A Survey of Marriages Among Previously Institutionalized Retardates', *Mental Retardation, 13*, 33-37.

Goldstein, H. (1964) 'Social and Occupational Adjustment', in H. A. Stevens, and R. Heber (eds.), *Mental Retardation*, University of Chicago Press, Chicago.

Gruenberg, E. M. (1964) 'Epidemiology', in H. A. Stevens and R. Heber (eds.), *Mental Retardation*, University of Chicago Press, Chicago.

Grundy, S. and Wagster, J. (1978) 'The Value of Past and Present Employment Schemes: With Particular Reference to Educationally Handicapped Youngsters', *Rathbone News*, 20-24.

Jackson, R. (1966) 'How Reliable are the Follow-Ups?' *Special Education, 55*, 4-6.

Jackson, R. N. (1968) 'Employment Adjustment of Educable Mentally Handicapped Ex-Pupils in Scotland', *American Journal of Mental Deficiency, 72*, 924-930.

Jackson, R. (1977) 'Post School Adjustment of the Mentally Retarded: A Critical Note on the Nebraskan Longitudinal Survey of Baller, Charles and Miller', *Journal of Mental Deficiency Research, 21*, 273-281.

Jackson, R. (1980) 'Employment Prospects for the Mentally
    Retarded in a Post Industrial Society', *Journal of
    Practical Approaches to Developmental Handicap*, *3*, 4-9.
Kolstoe, O. P. (1976) *Teaching Educable Mentally Retarded
    Children* (2nd Ed.), Holt, Rinehart and Winston, New
    York.
Kucharski, R. (1978) 'State Assistance for Invalids'
    Cooperatives', in International Labour Office,
    *Co-operatives for the Disabled: Organization and
    Development*, ILO, Geneva.
MacMillan, D. L., Jones, R. L. and Aloia, G. F. (1974) 'The
    Mentally Retarded Label: A Review of Research and
    Theoretical Analysis', *American Journal of Mental
    Deficiency*, *79*, 241-261.
MacMillan, D. L., Jones, R. L. and Meyers, C. E. (1976)
    'Main-Streaming the Mildly Retarded', *Mental
    Retardation*, *14*, 3-10.
Matthew, G. C. (1964) *Post School Adaptation of ESN School
    Leavers*, unpublished master's thesis, University of
    Manchester, England.
Meyerowitz, J. H. and Farber, B. (1966) 'Family Background
    of Educable Mentally Retarded Children', in B. Farber,
    (ed.), *Kinship and Family Organization*, Wiley, New
    York.
Olshansky, S. (1969) 'An Examination of Some Assumptions in
    the Vocational Rehabilitation of the Mentally
    Retarded', *Mental Retardation*, *7*, 51-53.
Parmenter, T. R. (1976) 'The Vocational Development of the
    Learning Disabled: Implications for Life-Long
    Learning', *Australian Journal of Mental Retardation*,
    4, 8-14.
Payne, J. S., Polloway, E. A., Smith, J. E. and Payne, R. A.
    (1981) *Strategies for Teaching the Mentally Retarded*,
    (2nd Ed.), Merrill, Columbus.
Richardson, S. A. (1978) 'Careers of Mentally Retarded
    Young Persons: Services, Jobs and Interpersonal
    Relations', *American Journal of Mental Deficiency*, *82*,
    349-358.
Rodgers, B. (1979) 'The Prospects for ESN(M) Leavers',
    Special Education: Forward Trends, *6*, 8-9.
Shackleton-Bailey, M. (1982) 'HANC: Hampshire New
    Curriculum', *Wessex Studies in Special Education*, *2*,
    13-26.
Shanks, M. (1981) 'This Unemployment Crisis is Never Going
    to Go Away', *The Guardian*, *17*, May 1981.
Stein, Z. and Susser, M. (1960) 'The Families of Dull
    Children: A Classification for Predicting Careers',
    British Journal of Preventative Social Medicine, *14*,
    83-88.

Sterner, R. (1976) *Social and Economic Conditions of the Mentally Retarded*, Division of Social Affairs, United Nations Office, Geneva.

Tizard, J. (1965) 'Longitudinal and Follow-Up Studies', in A. M. Clarke, and A. D. B. Clarke (eds.), *Mental Deficiency: The Changing Outlook*, Methuen, London.

Vickerman, B. and Cronin, J. (1983) 'The Old and the New - A Radical View: The Certificate in the Further Education and Training of Mentally Handicapped People', *Wessex Studies in Special Education, 3*, 165-174.

Wehman, P. and McLaughlin, P. (1980) *Vocational Curriculum for Developmentally Disabled Persons*, University Park Press, Baltimore.

Wehman, P. and Schleien, S. (1981) *Leisure Programs for Handicapped Persons*, University Park Press, Balitmore.

Whelan, E. and Speake, B. (1981) *Getting to Work*, Souvenir Press, London.

Windle, C. (1962) 'Prognosis of Mental Subnormals: A Critical Review of Research', *Monograph Supplement for American Journal of Mental Deficiency, 66*, 1-180.

Wolfensberger, W. (1967) 'Vocational Preparation and Occupation', in A. A. Baumeister (ed.), *Mental Retardation: Appraisal, Education and Rehabilitation*, Aldine Publishing Co., Chicago.

Wolfensberger, W. (1970) 'Models of Mental Retardation', *New Society, 15*, 51-3, January.

Chapter Nine

REHABILITATION EDUCATION - SOME FUTURE DIRECTIONS

Roy I. Brown

INTRODUCTION

In the preceeding chapters it is argued that some major
changes are required in the field of rehabilitation. Such
changes are not argued simply on the basis of rehabilitation
knowledge, but on the implications of political, economic
and social conditions and attitudes. This chapter is
concerned with two major themes:

a) quality of lifestyle for handicapped persons within
   the community and within their training agencies
   and,
b) quality in the education of personnel within the
   field of rehabilitation.

It is argued that these two factors are inextricably
intertwined, for without quality education for staff there
can be no quality rehabilitation. The latter means that
have received inadequate training and, further, will be
faced with inappropriate community services for their
support and guidance. In turn, this discredits the normalisation movement and encourages political and social
arguments for the redevelopment of forms of institutionalisation.
    Considerable emphasis has been placed on the concept of
normalisation. Yet it can be argued that normalisation is a
philosophy without an adequate technology. As a philosophy
it encourages the growth and community integration of
handicapped individuals, and demands that they should
receive as normal a lifestyle as possible including living
space and normal daily rhythm of life (Marlett, 1978). Yet
in most countries there is little evidence of a comprehensive network of informed personnel who can carry out this
philosophy in terms of designing practical, integrated and

long-range programmes. It may now be possible to place a wide range of handicapped persons within the community, yet there is little guarantee that once placed there will be continuing links with their training agency or there will be resources which relate to the changing needs of individuals as they grow and as society places new demands upon them.

Rehabilitation Over Time

Rehabilitation is seen as a process with an end goal rather than a continuing system of training and support, which encourages the continuous involvement of each individual with society. We live at a time when there are major changes in our society, including advances in technology. This, together with changes in the economic situation and new social opportunities, places exceptional demands on handicapped persons. In order to survive effectively in the community one must be aware of these changes and also have knowledge, or access to expertise, in order to make adjustments in one's lifestyle. Unless we are prepared to mount more detailed observation, monitoring and assessment procedures, in terms of the long-term adaption of rehabilitated individuals within the community, and from that knowledge build services directed to the full life span, it seems likely that there will be considerable breakdown in rehabilitation efficiency.

Reinstitutionalisation

McKerracher argues that some forms of institutionalisation may not be inappropriate, particularly for the more severely handicapped individual. But it is also argued that the nature of institutionalisation must change to provide a quality lifestyle. Whether or not this is done will probably depend not so much on our knowledge of rehabilitation as on the social, political and economic pressures. Reinstitutionalisation may be occasioned by the desperation of parents and handicapped people, themselves living in inappropriate circumstances. To date we have shown little ability to ensure that any form of institutionalisation is adequately and carefully monitored to ensure that it does not become dated through out-moded practices. It must be accessible to changes that are occurring in the outside society. It is argued that the development of advocacy systems and the recognition of an individual's rights, the formation of ethics committees and monitoring groups can do much to overcome such difficulties. Unfortunately, in different guises, they have been seen before, and it will take considerable ability on the part of organisations to ensure that poor conditions, or limiting conditions, do not arise again. Institutions, when built, provide a positive alternative to poor community conditions. Because they do not change over time, they are eventually seen as out-moded and as encouraging constricted lifestyles, that is, they provide a deteriorating lifestyle in relation to knowledge and community development.

Demonstration Centres

It has also been argued that there should be the development of demonstration centres. The idea of research centres of a multidisciplinary nature within major geographical regions, which devise and develop innovative services, is an attractive one. Such centres should be associated with universities and community colleges. They can provide education and training for handicapped people but also ensure that the most recent advances and technology are taught to rehabilitation students. Much of the training in the rehabilitation field is seen as technology. We teach how to apply practical skills without providing an indepth theoretical knowledge of the process of rehabilitation. Unfortunately rehabilitation is not seen as an academic area of study, but merely as one technical facet of the practice of practitioners, including educators, psychologists, nurses and social workers.

Programme Evaluation

The measures of success and failure employed in studies of handicapped people are essentially simplistic, and, as indicated in Jackson's chapter, merely report whether or not individuals obtain and retain employment. Few investigations relate to the quality of life that individuals enjoy once they are integrated or placed within the community. Furthermore, few of the agencies that advocate training strategies are themselves the subject of evaluation, either in terms of their philosophy or the quality of lifestyle within the agency. Many agencies do not have a coherent and formal philosophy which is shared by staff and boards of management. There must be a concerted effort to ensure a normalisation philosophy espoused by both management and staff. This, in turn is reflected in the development of appropriate staff attitudes and skills, as well as changes in the physical environments during and after training. It includes access to enlightened and comprehensive programmes. Unless programme evaluation occurs we shall precipitate a re-cycling of rehabilitation concepts with consequent institutionalisation of handicapped individuals.

Programme Effectiveness

Worse, many training agencies do not separate training from sheltered workshop functions. Some vocational workshops have a detailed manual of training procedures. Others develop detailed administrative and management procedures. There is little knowledge about the relationship of these procedures to effectiveness in terms of programme success of clients. Procedures to investigate this are required. Quality of life should be defined clearly in terms of agency and life experiences in the community. Economic indicators relating to the specific geographic areas are relevant. Although the principles of rehabilitation may be the same in various agencies, the specifics in terms of content and level may vary.

If we accept a developmental process of historical cycling within rehabilitation, we shall not, for example, be surprised to see the development of horticultural models. They will develop on a different basis from before, not only making use of modern technology, but can also be used as a means for creating a higher quality of life for individuals, both from a training and community perspective. Such models may be appropriate in developing countries and in under-populated areas of developed countries.

Horticultural ventures may be more relevant to some areas than industrial projects. The question is not, as is often supposed, whether industrial projects are better suited to the needs of handicapped persons than horti-cultural ones. The question must be posed and answered in relation to community needs, and opportunities which relate to geographic and social factors in the local neighbourhood. Normalisation must relate to the processes developing in the local community.

Follow-Up Studies and Quality of Life

Follow-up studies consider employment characteristics. The type and amount of goods that an individual owns are a positive measure of quality of life together with the interactions and support that are gained from other family members. Incidence of crime, marriage, divorce and the like are also important aspects of lifestyle but involvement in leisure and social activity must be taken into account. Thus availability of leisure resources, as well as the use of leisure resources, has to be monitored. Even superficial examination of these processes shows that many individuals who attend local agencies do not, in terms of leisure time, make use of local amenities. Quality of life basically involves a process whereby the individual becomes increasingly in control of his environment regardless of baseline.

It must be recognised that social conditions are changing and differ in different communities. Thus we must continue to carry out follow-up studies where long-term monitoring of success and failure are recorded. In one sense the label of follow-up is now a misnomer since rehabilitation should continue throughout the life of the individual.

As a work-oriented community we tend to argue for rehabilitation which provides work. But as the economic situation indicates, many individuals, not just handicapped persons, are lacking employment. The lack of employment opportunity means that training positions within rehabilitation agencies become permanently filled. Unless we can find other modes of rehabilitation through community living, and social contributions within the home and local community, including the pursuit of active leisure time enjoyment, the rehabilitation model will break down.

Many research workers (e.g. Brown and Bayer, 1980), have worked with a wide range of parents who decline to take their handicapped youngsters into the community because of adverse behaviour patterns. For example, a father will not eat in a restaurant with a handicapped youngster because of inappropriate manners and eating habits, or a handicapped youngster may not be allowed to travel across a city because parents are concerned that she is unable, despite teaching, to use the transit system appropriately. Once a worker deals with the family directly, rather than just the handicapped individual in his agency, more fundamental changes in attitude, and therefore learning, can come about. For example, a young man suffering from a cerebral accident was encouraged by staff who had seen him in his home environment to build a patio at his house even though he had no comprehensible encoding language skills. The success of this operation illustrated to his wife and to other practitioners that much residual ability remained. The success of this venture made very considerable difference to the self image and motivation of the individual concerned. If this had been attempted in a traditional setting, the gains would have been more hard come by, and the individual would also have had great difficulty in demonstrating his powers to others who had thought him incompetent. He could not have built his patio in the local workshop!

In a current study into quality of life, Brown, Bayer and MacFarlane (1984) observe that some parents, who are asked to define quality of life and describe the lifestyle of their youngsters, indicate they have not thought about this. Merely posing questions on quality of life has caused parents, in some cases, to visit the agency their youngster is attending, to ask new questions about rehabilitation. It is essential that there be a dialogue between clients, parents, and professionals about the details of lifestyle.

It was also noted that many professionals, who have intended to bring about improved lifestyles, for example by attempting to build leisure time programmes, have found that it becomes very difficult, when using an agency or institute base, to transfer the individual into the community in such a manner that he or she can make use of local facilities. The examples point to the need to use a community base, but they also underline the importance of having community workers who have a broad knowledge of rehabilitation processes within the local community.

Rehabilitation Personnel

This need for change in rehabilitation argues for change in terms of staff attitudes and knowledge. It demands a more diversified and complex education than is presently offered to rehabilitation personnel in most countries. It requires the development of new relations between parents, clients and trainers that permits and encourages access to the home and the local community.

Parents must be given more resources, not only to train, but also to receive advice and support from experienced workers. Not all parents will accept this nor will they argue for it. But the experience of many parents is not of enabling, supporting and understanding staff with a broad base of knowledge. Most personnel are agency-bound. The concept of moving into the home environment is foreign to most personnel. Many students who are learning how to function in this area are at first inhibited and find it difficult to perform, because they have to adapt their style and knowledge to new and unfamiliar situations.

The model argues for staff who have considerably more knowledge than at present and are able to call on a cadre of consultants. Personnel are in a position to make decisions on their own which demands a wide knowledge and experience base. Although this is rarely stated, one of the major reasons for the development and maintenance of any institution appears to be that a hierarchial personnel model can be built - staff report to others from whom they receive instructions. It is believed that many people cannot function without such a model, yet it is argued here that community diversification of a service requires personnel to act in the physical absence of a senior staff member.

Training and Independence

This same model is reflected in the changes developing within the lifestyle of disabled persons. In their case, there is also a demand for increasing freedom to make choices, and speak on one's behalf, either with or without the help of an advocate. But rights are not necessarily given, they are earned. Unless handicapped people can move along structured and integrated programme continua with graduated support, choice becomes only a hollow opportunity to respond to immediate wishes and concerns, without bearing in mind that choice has effects over time and is relevant to later opportunities and decisions.

Throughout this book integrated programming has been proposed. It is only when we deliver a service which ensures all facets of living are dealt with that an individual can hope to survive effectively within the community. Some individuals are more advanced than others in certain structures of learning, but quite frequently it is the social, home-living and leisure time aspects of life which appear to be the downfall of many individuals once placed in employment. McKerracher points out the need to identify those who may succeed without support, but it is necessary to go further than this. The advantage of training is that it can enable handicapped people to live a quality life where choice and decision are made in relation to personal needs and preferences. But we are unclear how to do this. First we must describe the qualities of this life in terms of both environmental and training facilities. What are they? Even within many training agencies, availability of space, basic vocational safety measures employed in industry, the presence of adequate observation and training areas are wanting or poorly designed.

Frequently, criteria for defining when an individual should move along the training continua are missing. We find individuals who are still kept on a job because they are good at it; they are needed for production purposes. By now such practices should have ceased and only be observed within environments which are dedicated to sheltered work and employment.

There are dangers in the processes outlined. For in attempting to reproduce programme continua we may start to teach a very wide range of specific skills. Time for training is limited in terms of the wide range of skills that are necessary to function in an everchanging community environment. The need for effective transfer training strategies is apparent, together with improvement of incidental learning, and the development of problem-solving strategies such as those advocated by Feuerstein (1979). Many of the principles discussed are relevant to other areas of rehabilitation. Many of the issues raised in relation to adults are issues which should also be directed towards the training of young handicapped children within the home and school.

Part of this book has dwelt on the importance of self-assertion and personality development. Some of the

major behavioural difficulties in terms of emotional
operation are at last being looked at in the context of
community programming, and specialised resources are being
made available as a result of the "hands on experience" of
consulting staff providing services within homes as well as
community, residential and training settings. In this
context Johnson's view that handicapped people need to be
taught to be dispensers of rewards is important. Further we
must recognise that we receive as well as give service.
Handicapped people can become contributing members to our
society, but should also experience the positive effects of
dispensing reinforcement. In recognising this, a fundamental change occurs in our own behaviour. Unless we can
recognise that persons with handicaps are able to provide
society and specific individuals with reward within a non-
handicapped community, there cannot be an acceptable concept
of equality in the partnership of rehabilitation.

Hostility and aggression are aspects of behaviour that
are not easily accepted from physically or mentally handicapped persons. On a broader plane, it is of interest that
aggression amongst women is found to be largely unacceptable, and depression is often seen as the behavioural
outcome. In the field of rehabilitation we applaud and
reinforce behaviour which depresses performance. It is of
interest that McKerracher reported that some trainees who
showed so-called negative emotional behaviour appeared to do
rather better than individuals with more acceptable
characteristics. Mild aggression leads to assertiveness and
control of the environment. Ryba and Brown (1979) noted
that personnel tend to record obedient clients as assertive!
Control of a situation by individuals who are handicapped
improves their environment, for with environmental control
as an aid to learning, individuals can make error with
little fear of punishment. Without error, learning is
likely to be minimal, yet the right to make an error is
often denied handicapped persons.

Rural Programmes

The above concerns have direct relevance to the rehabilitation of handicapped individuals within rural areas. Elsewhere (Brown, Hughson and Nemeth, 1981) it has been pointed
out that individuals often move from rural communities to
industrialised cities in order to obtain services, including
vocational training for handicapped people. Such handicapped young adults often migrate back to their rural areas
after training. Yet the training received relates to an
urban community. Training has to relate to one's previous
experience, and one's future opportunities, thus it would

seem wise to deliver such services within the rural community itself.

There has to be a programme which enables the individual to function in his own society. In highly industrialised areas the problems of transportation tend to be less severe than in vast rural communities, such as Canada and parts of Australia, where populations may be scattered and services only centralised at particular points. The idea of busing people great distances to attend rehabilitation workshops would seem an inappropriate way of going about service delivery.

If we are to overcome the geographical and social problems in rural areas it may be necessary to review the role and skills of the rural community worker, including the need to break away from the traditional hierarchial model of service. An eclectic professional who combines the resources of many professions, has an overall concept of services and understands both short and long term goals of the individual clients is critical. This type of service might also resolve some of the major problems that we have in industrial communities, where it is assumed that by massing handicapped individuals together, or by distributing them in small but organised groups within the community, we can solve the problems of handicapping conditions.

Rehabilitation in Developing Countries

It is becoming recognised that there is an urgent need to apply rehabilitation techniques to needs within developing countries. Existing models cannot be simply transferred for there are different requirements in such countries. We have learned that local social mores are critical in the field of rehabilitation as in other areas. For example, in applying techniques of assessing behaviour, a basic knowledge of behavioural habits within the local community is necessary. The ability to make a bed may be replaced by ability to roll up and put away a sleeping mat, or ability to use a knife and fork may be replaced by ability to use one's hands effectively in eating.

Individuals who are learning to build rehabilitation programmes in their own countries must be in charge of their own development; that is, it is inappropriate that we apply our knowledge to their programmes unless we do so as advisors. The final decisions must be made by local personnel. This, too, is a break from the hierarchial model. Once knowledge is imparted as principles, it must be applied, using local examples, by people with life experience and field knowledge in the local community.

In developing countries it is beginning to be recognised that academic education must blend with field

experience. In many developing countries formal knowledge
in college and university is academic, and does not enable
the individual to apply his skills in practical situations.
This has relevance to the training of rehabilitation
personnel. Even in developed countries there is a tendency
to ensure that the behavioural and social sciences provide
academic knowledge rather than practical knowledge from the
field. In this context it is perhaps worth noting the
recommendation by Jackson that a department of rehabilitation should be formed within government ministries. It
must, for once and all, be recognised that rehabilitation is
a multidisciplinary area based on formal principles, derived
from a rehabilitation knowledge base, which directs and
regulates practice, but this is no substitute for practical
experience.

The Future

The components of rehabilitation will expand dramatically in
the coming years as we learn to overcome some of the
physical, psychological and social aspects of deterioration
and damage. Unless we have in place a comprehensive multidisciplinary department of rehabilitation we will again be
dwelling on the knowledge of specific fields, rather than
integrating our knowledge by crossing disciplinary boundaries. It must be stressed that this applies not just to
mental handicap, although this book takes this as a major
theme. But the principles, causative processes, and
training paradigms apply to the broad field of rehabilitation. Yet these general principles are not yet accepted or
applied within any one area. In order to overcome this
problem it is important to involve personnel from various
agencies, as Whelan, Speake and Strickland suggest, in
devising research programmes and subsequent practical
application of knowledge. The concept is again one of
demonstration research. Research is no longer the preserve
of academics, but should be recognised in the development of
pilot and progressive programmes in the broad field of
rehabilitation.
     Many handicapped people appear to have considerable and
ongoing support from their parents. Such support may have
differing effects. Sometimes growth is promoted and at
other times support controls, and limits the individual's
growth and lifestyle. We have yet to develop satisfactory
measures of these processes. Further, until rehabilitation
can enter into the environment where these processes occur,
it is unlikely that the majority of handicapped people are
going to show major improvement in terms of life quality.
     Other contributors have referred to highly successful
rehabilitation rates in certain areas of performance,

although the point has been made that success with training is sometimes no different from success without training. The argument should surely be around the difference of quality of life produced by training, rather than simply whether an individual stays in a job for a particular period of time.

The issues relating to integration are often seen as immediate rather than longitudinal processes. Integration implies that individuals who are handicapped will face changes in the community over time, including their own aging. Many disabled persons live alone or have poor support systems. Further, those who do have support systems often receive them from aging parents. The issues of death and dying, including the process of one's own and inevitable death, are not issues which have been studied comprehensively within the field of handicap. These are important issues for handicapped persons, yet for those who are mentally handicapped in particular, the issues are rarely faced (Bihm and Elliott, 1982). Once again, this does not represent an inability on the part of the handicapped person, but our inability to recognise the need, the language or the experience which is necessary if we are to experience growth, and reach a modus vivendi with ourselves in a common and acceptable environment.

REFERENCES

Bihm, E. M. and Elliott, L. S. (1982) 'Concepts of Death in Mentally Retarded Persons, *The Journal of Psychology, 111,* 205-210.

Brown, R. I. and Bayer, M. B. (1980) *Benefits and Costs of Rehabilitation at the Vocational and Rehabilitation Research Institute,* Health and Welfare Project #4558-29-2, Calgary.

Brown, R. I., Bayer, M. B. and MacFarlane, C. (1984) *Rehabilitation Programs Study,* Health and Welfare Project #4558-29-4, Calgary (In progress).

Brown, R. I., Hughson, E. A. and Nemeth, S. (1981) *The Total Life Program,* Health and Welfare Project #4558-1-29, Calgary.

Feuerstein, R. (1979) *The Dynamic Assessment of Retarded Performers,* University Park Press, Baltimore.

Marlett, N. (1978) 'Normalization, Integration, and Socialization', in J. P. Das and D. Baine (eds.), *Mental Retardation for Special Educators,* Charles C. Thomas, Springfield, Illinois.

Ryba, K. and Brown, R. I. (1979) 'An Evaluation of Personal Adjustment Training with Mentally Retarded Adults', *British Journal of Mental Subnormality, 5,* 55-66.

long-term adaption 47, 204, 235
love 163-170, 164-165

mainstreaming 32
maladjustment 24, 32, 40, 165
management 109, 114
  consultancy group 21, 101, 102, 104
  systems 111
manager 121, 126
manual dexterity 45, 203
manufacturing 219
marriage 204, 205, 237
  counselling 189
maturation and growth 39
medical attention 126, 208, 215
  model, 5, 158, 215
medicine 1, 3, 5, 151
memory deficits 174
mental deficiency nursing 5
  illness 14
  retardation centres 87
model-based service 117-131
modelling, 120, 124
money management 43, 96, 123, 128
monitoring, 221, 235
motivation 2, 6, 8, 73, 145
motor skills 4, 24, 44, 68, 73, 220
  performances 24, 44
multidisciplinary 1
multiple handicaps 25, 115

needs hierarchy 168-169
neurotic disorders 147
New Zealand 18, 29, 32, 45
normal daily rhythm 234
norm-referenced testing 36
normalisation 15, 26, 83, 107, 108, 109-110, 112, 114, 131, 144, 145, 214
North America 15, 19
numeracy 43, 73, 74, 96
nursing 88, 126, 236

occupational therapy 1, 3

O'Connor Manual Dexterity test 44
operant 112
organic brain disorders 145
Outreach Team 149, 150, 151, 152, 153, 159

paraprofessionals 114, 121, 126, 128
parents 6, 15, 32, 64, 70, 71, 110, 111, 114, 118, 119, 120, 170, 179, 182-187, 190, 204, 235, 239
peer feedback 124
  friendships 165
  interaction 124
peers 124, 172, 185, 187, 189
People First 15
penology 201
perceptual motor skills 64, 73
personal adjustment 31, 146
  and social skills 64, 123
  record system 103
personality 42, 43, 145, 240
  disorders 33, 147
  questionnaires 45
personnel 3, 16, 17, 110, 234
physical 24, 126
  environment 107
  factors 117
  handicap 25, 32, 115, 126, 130, 146
  health 127
  performance 44
physio-therapy 1. 3
placement 17, 26, 65
Poland 223, 224
political considerations 6, 14, 23, 234, 235
pornography 173, 195
prediction 5, 23, 24, 25, 30, 35, 39, 41, 42, 47, 48, 49, 145, 201, 202, 203, 215, 216

Doyle, D. A. 108, 139
Duerdoth, P. 68, 80
Durojaiye, M. O. A. 33, 53

Eagle, E. 30, 53
Earnhart, T. 75, 81
Ebbinghaus, H. 9, 22
Edgerton, R. B. 71, 80, 214, 215, 231
Edwards, J. P. 185, 197
Egnatios, E. 121, 134
Elliott, L. S. 244
Engman, J. M. 12, 22
Epple, W. 118, 135
Evans, C. 166, 197
Evans, I. M. 112, 142
Ewell, M. D. 128, 139
Eyman, R. K. 112, 118, 135
Eysenck, S. B. G. 45, 49, 53
Eysenck, H. J. 49, 53

Farber, B. 205, 206, 231
Farnsworth, D. 67, 80
Fearing, F. M. 27, 51
Felsenthal, D. 122, 135
Ferguson, T. 42, 53
Ferster, C. B. 177, 197
Feuerstein, R. 8, 22, 240
Findykian, N. 127, 135
Fielding, L. 129, 135
Fiorelli, J. S. 113, 135
Fischer, H. L. 161, 197
Fisher, H. L. 205, 231
Fitts 167
Floor, L. 205, 231
Foale, M. 42, 53
Foden, S. 185, 187, 197
Foley, G. M. 112, 127, 135
Ford, V. B. 12, 22
Forehand, R. 119, 136
Foshee, T. J. 128, 137
Foss, G. 71, 81
Foster, V. H. 28, 53
Fox, R. 29, 55
Foxx, R. M. 129, 136
Francis, R. J. 44, 58
Frankosky, R. J. 124, 136
Frey, R. M. 44, 55
Fristoe, M. 67, 80
Fry, L. M. 42, 53

Fulton, R. W. 25, 30, 53

Gambill, E. D. 118, 142
Garber, S. 119, 132
Garvey, B. 127, 138
Gibson 33
Gilbert, K. A. 113, 136
Gladstone, B. W. 128, 136
Gladwin, T. 25, 32, 58, 145, 160
Glaser, R. 35, 36, 53
Glenn, L. 109, 143
Gold, M. W. 6, 22, 73, 145, 160
Goldman, M. 40, 42, 53
Goldman, R. 67, 80
Goldstein, H. 25, 31, 34, 53, 202, 217, 231
Gordon, N. 121, 137
Gorelick, M. C. 44, 54
Grabowski, J. G. 128, 133
Graham, P. E. 27, 54
Grant, D. 192, 198
Gray, J. A. 49, 54
Greene, C. L. 40, 42, 54
Gregory, A. 78, 81
Griffiths, R. 129, 133
Groner, N. E. 125, 136
Gruenberg, E. M. 209, 231
Grundy, S. 224, 231
Guralnick, D. 41, 54
Gullion, M. E. 119, 140
Gunzburg, A. L. 145, 160
Gunzburg, H. C. 7, 11, 22, 35, 54, 110, 122, 136, 145, 160, 176, 197

Hall, J. 86, 106
Hall, M. 32, 55
Halpern, A. D. 25, 44, 54
Hammill, D. 67, 80
Hand, R. J. 127, 142
Haney, J. I. 112, 136
Harbough, J. H. 167, 199
Hardy, R. E. 44, 54
Haring, N. G. 36, 54
Harper, R. S. 124, 141
Harris, S. L. 119, 136
Harris, J. M. 130, 136
Hartzler, E. 38, 54
Hauber, F. A. 123, 133

Heber, R. E. 25, 32, 54
Hemming, H. 113, 136
Hermelin, B. 10, 22
Hersen, M. 119, 142
Hetherington, E. M. 183, 197
Hill, B. K. 115, 136
Hilliard, L. I. 42, 54
Hinshaw, S. P. 183, 196
Hirst, W. 44, 54
Hitzing, W. 121, 136
Hoekstra, R. R. 183, 198
Hornell, H. 28, 31, 60
Houts, P. S. 127, 137
Huff, T. M. 127, 135
Hughson, E. A. 7, 22, 26, 27, 52, 145, 160, 167, 178, 196, 220, 230, 241, 244

Insel, P. M. 112, 137
Intagliata, J. 118, 123, 137
Irvin, L. K. 44, 54
Ittelson, W. H. 112, 137
Iwata, B. A. 124, 128, 137, 139

Jackson, R. 31, 55, 203, 216, 231, 232, 236, 243
Jacobson, J. W. 108, 110, 115, 121, 126, 137
Janicki, M. P. 115, 108, 110, 121, 125, 126, 137
Jaslow, R. I. 122, 137
Jerrold, M. A. 42, 55
Jesness, C. F. 45, 55
James, N. J. 127, 141
Johnson, H. A. 28, 55
Johnson, M. R. 124, 129, 138
Johnson, M. S. 112, 119, 138
Johnson, P. R. 161, 167, 172, 176, 178, 183, 185, 187, 189, 192, 197, 198, 241
Johnson, S. W. 25, 55
Johnson, V. E. 174, 198
Johnson-Silver, E. 115, 138
Jones, R. L. 211, 232

Jones, R. T. 112, 136
Jerrold, M. A. 29, 55
Judd, L. C. 128, 139

Kaplan, H. S. 174, 198
Kaprowy, E. A. 112, 114, 138
Kaufman, H. I. 38, 44, 55
Kazdin, A. E. 109, 112, 113, 138
Kehle, T. J. 75, 80
Kellogg, R. M. 28, 55
Kelly, B. R. 108, 133
Kennedy, R. J. 30, 32, 55, 206
Kempton, W. 161, 187, 194, 198
Kerr, B. A. 42, 44, 55
Keys, M. 28, 55
Koegel, R. L. 113, 141
Kokaska, C. J. 27, 39, 58
Kolstoe, O. P. 29, 30, 38, 39, 40, 42, 44, 55, 220, 232
Konarski, E. A. 112, 119, 138
Koppitz, E. 67, 80
Kirman, B. H. 42, 54
Kivitz, M. S. 145, 146, 160
Klaber, M. M. 88, 106
Krajicek, M. J. 161, 197, 205, 231
Kraus, S. 123, 137
Krishef, C. 32, 55
Kucharski, R. 223, 232
Kudla, M. J. 123, 133

Landesman-Dwyer, S. 108, 113, 133, 138
Landino, J. E. 8, 22
Lankford, C. W. 127, 142
Large, P. 31, 56
Lavigneur, H. 114, 119, 138
Lei, T. 112, 135
Lerner, J. W. 25, 56
Leung, P. 167, 198
Levin, B. M. 125, 136
Levy, E. 130, 138
Lewis, M. 34, 57
Lovitt, T. 36, 56
Lindsley, O. R. 109, 138